BEREAVEMENT GROUPS AND THE ROLE OF SOCIAL SUPPORT

All too frequently, clinical practice consists of repeating year after year the methods learned in graduate training, occasionally seasoned by a technique learned in a continuing-education workshop. *Bereavement Groups and the Role of Social Support* gives clinicians what they've been missing in other volumes: practical techniques that have a solid contemporary empirical basis. Deftly weaving together theory, research, and practice, this volume is a compendium of the latest practical thinking about bereavement support groups. Readers will learn when well-loved practices make sense and are supported by sound evidence, as well as which practices should possibly be discontinued. The book also contains the results of a qualitative study bringing together the best practices of experienced bereavement group leaders from around the world.

William G. Hoy, DMin, FT, is clinical professor of medical humanities at Baylor University. For sixteen years, he directed the bereavement counseling program for Pathways Volunteer Hospice in Long Beach, California. In that role, he led hundreds of bereavement support group sessions, trained volunteer and clinical group leaders, and provided clinical oversight to a program serving as many as 500 bereaved adults, children, and teens each year.

BEREAVEMENT GROUPS AND THE ROLE OF SOCIAL SUPPORT

Integrating Theory, Research, and Practice

William G. Hoy

Routledge
Taylor & Francis Group
NEW YORK AND LONDON

First published 2016
by Routledge
711 Third Avenue, New York, NY 10017

and by Routledge
2 Park Square, Milton Park, Abingdon, Oxon, OX14 4RN

Routledge is an imprint of the Taylor & Francis Group, an informa business

Library of Congress Cataloging-in-Publication Data
Names: Hoy, William G., author.
Title: Bereavement groups and the role of social support : integrating theory, research, and practice / William G. Hoy.
Description: New York, NY : Routledge, 2016. | Includes bibliographical references and index.
Identifiers: LCCN 2015035847 | ISBN 9781138916883 (hardback : alk. paper) | ISBN 9781138916890 (pbk. : alk. paper) | ISBN 9781315686844 (ebook)
Subjects: LCSH: Grief therapy. | Self-help groups. | Bereavement—Psychological aspects.
Classification: LCC RC455.4.L67 H69 2016 | DDC 155.9/3708—dc23
LC record available at http://lccn.loc.gov/2015035847

ISBN: 978-1-138-91688-3 (hbk)
ISBN: 978-1-138-91689-0 (pbk)
ISBN: 978-1-315-68684-4 (ebk)

Typeset in Sabon
by Apex CoVantage, LLC

For Debbie, the one with whom I am
so grateful to share love, learning, and life

CONTENTS

PREFACE

Though I no longer remember the specifics, my first opportunity to lead a bereavement support group, of all places, came with a call from the Recreation Department in the City of Seal Beach, California. In the early months of leading a congregation in that community, my interest in bereavement had surfaced on "the radar" of the small city, whose population was 40% over the age of 55. Eight people came that first night at the Marina Community Center, and they faced a variety of losses. Several were widowed, one woman was a bereaved mother, two were going through nasty divorces, and one had been "downsized" from his job after a 20-plus year career at a large industrial employer. To call the group a "menagerie" would be an understatement of epic proportions.

For the most part, they bonded with each other in spite of their varied life stories and life losses. A momentary "glitch" occurred on about week three when the discussion turned tense. The newly unemployed man was sitting between one recent widow and a divorced woman. In a context still unclear to me all these years later, the widow leaned around the unemployed man to pointedly announce to the divorcee in a voice all could hear, "At least you got a choice in the ending of your marriage; you *could* get him back. When your husband dies, there's just *nothing* you can do to get him back." Without even a pause, the divorced woman retorted, "Well at least you got to bury your husband; I only wish I could have buried mine!" That collection of people was the first and last time I welcomed all individuals to the same grief support group, regardless of the loss they were facing.

I would imagine every reader who has led a bereavement group has had a similarly harrowing experience. Undoubtedly, my story of a few tense moments experienced that night so long ago would pale in comparison to the tales of some of my colleagues, who proudly wear the "battle scars" of leading bereavement support groups made up of individuals who were hurting deeply and lashed out at any person in their pathway. Like many who share this work with me, our desire to care has often transcended the evidence to support our efforts. Nevertheless, we have ploughed ahead, confident that we could be part of helping groups of grieving individuals become caring communities. Hard as it is to believe, more often than not, we have sat in "front row seats" at the utter transformation of hurting, self-focused individuals into collaborative communities of compassion and discovery. "Amazing" is the only word I have ever found to describe what can happen in a bereavement support group.

This book is about some of what makes that happen. It is a compendium of what I have learned over way more than a quarter century of learning from bereaved people as they patiently taught me what they needed done and what I needed to do to help them find their way in grief. I will always be grateful for the opportunities they have so generously afforded me as we have discovered what it means to walk together in a collaborative process that is so often characterized by utter aloneness. There are parts of this book that are necessarily brief—either because information is lacking or my own education and experience is deficient. I trust that readers will patiently tell me of the parts I overlooked completely or to which I paid woefully little attention.

The subtitle of this volume explains my vision. My hope is that this book integrates three ways of thinking about grief that too often exist in their own silos: theory, research, and practice. Practice is an unstable force blown about in the gale-force winds of change if it is not firmly anchored by theory and research. Theory is the collection of musings with no verified basis in fact and no practical usefulness without research and practice. Research is a dry reckoning of numbers and stories through which we learn more and more about less and less unless it is informed by good theory and applied to practice. As a clinical scholar, I get the unique opportunity to live in the unique melding of those frequently disparate cultures. May these words be the impetus for better care for bereaved individuals and families around the globe.

William G. Hoy
Waco, Texas

ACKNOWLEDGMENTS

I am indebted to the efforts, advice, and support of many people in bringing this book to the point of publication. As I have said in introducing him before, I have participated in "hero worship" almost from the day 35 years ago I discovered the first edition of J. William Worden's *Grief Counseling and Grief Therapy: A Handbook for the Mental Health Practitioner* on the "new books" shelf of the Louisiana State University Library when I was an undergraduate there. A few times in every professional's life, those heroes become personal mentors. More rarely, they become colleagues with whom one shares cases, quotes, and references in one another's books. Almost never, however, do they become friends with whom one shares the privilege of relaxed dinners, the anxieties of moving cross-country and "starting over" as a college professor, and the joys and sadness of life. Bill Worden, for me, fits all of those categories, and I consider it a unique blessing to know such a man of clinical excellence, research acumen, and gentlemanly grace.

Louis Gamino and I became friends after I made the "pilgrimage" from California to Texas, though I had known of and read his famous research reports from the Scott & White Bereavement Study for years as a clinical practitioner in the field. When Louis and I first met, he and Hal Ritter were putting the finishing touches on their phenomenal work *Ethical Practice in Grief Counseling*, a work that has been formative in my thinking about ethics in group work and in the perspectives I explore throughout this volume. Practicing just "down the road" in Temple, Texas, he has challenged me to think more scientifically about the bereavement process than I ever could have imagined. His mentorship, collegiality, and friendship are a constant source of refreshment for me. When we were simultaneously teaching our 16-year-old daughters to drive, we even earned a few gray hairs together.

Jane Bissler, Janet McCord, Jon Reid, and Chris Hall co-led the Association for Death Education & Counseling (ADEC) along with me during the year this book was coming together. They tolerated forgetfulness to follow through on projects, scattered thoughts during meetings, and a hundred other "slackened" details while my mind was on this topic. For their friendship and their grace, I will be forever grateful.

Helen Harris is my best friend and colleague in the "grief tribe" at Baylor. As readers of this volume understand all-too-well, those outside the "fold" often poorly understand our work. We do not need too many people who "get it," but we all need at least one. As a researcher and clinician par excellence, Helen has been that for me. She has likely forgotten more about bereavement support groups than I will ever know, but I am so grateful for her friendship in these years we have been together at the same institution, even though not in the same building (or even the same side of Interstate 35).

My Baylor colleagues in equipping the next generation of physicians and other healthcare professionals—Bill Neilson, Lisa Baker, Troy Abell, Lauren Barron, and Dan Samples—are more than colleagues; they are also friends who inspire my own work. Long before we were academic colleagues, we all labored in clinic, hospice, and hospital, unknown to one another, taking care of the ill and dying. As readers of this volume understand well, that kind of shared experience in people's past has a unique way of uniting them in the present. These unique sounding boards encourage me to think deeply, act courageously, share unselfishly, and teach practically.

Harold Ivan Smith is a constant inspiration in the process of authoring books. With humor and grace, he has encouraged me to "stay at it" even when I was sorely tempted to give up. Rarely does a week pass when an envelope does not arrive in the mail with a handful of newspaper clippings and photocopies he has cobbled together, knowing with great intuition how much they would interest me. Everywhere I go, I meet people who have been influenced by his writings, his friendship, and even similarly by those welcome "packages" in the mail. With all the reading, clipping, photocopying, and mailing he does, it makes me wonder how he has ever found the time to author more than 40 books, but millions have benefitted from his practical care and wisdom. I am one of those millions whose life has been touched, and our friendship over more than two decades means more to me than I can ever say.

Carolyn and Greg smiled (and occasionally grimaced) through many vacation stops at cemeteries, an uncounted risk of high prevalence when one is born into a home with a dad who does death for a living. Even on our long-awaited trip to Hawaii when they were in elementary school, they patiently endured tromping around Punchbowl National Cemetery and the USS Arizona memorial—before we set out for the beaches of Waikiki and Lihue. Greg will make a fine physician and I trust will appreciate the role of death and grief in his practice more than most. Perhaps the memorial visits made a lasting impression; when Carolyn honeymooned in Hawaii with her husband, Matthew, they visited some of those same "memorial" places. Periodically, she tells me how, in her own career in customer service, she has practiced her "grief counseling skills."

Debbie, the woman to whom I have been married for more than 27 years, is a constant cheerleader and encourager. We started dating as my career was beginning, and she has listened to more talk about death and grief than any human should have to endure. She has patiently slogged through many manuscripts over my career, painstakingly correcting grammar and offering style suggestions, always careful to not step on my fragile ego. Now in the "empty nest" phase of our lives, we have often sat together editing while watching the Houston Astros play baseball or basking in Waco's newfound celebrity status as we watched Chip and Joanna Gaines renovate homes—even for people we know—on HGTV's *Fixer Upper*. This book should really bear Deb's name on the cover also.

There is an exhaustive list of program and group leaders who consented to be interviewed as part of the Bereavement Leader Experiences, Attitudes and Perspectives (LEAP) study, the results of which enliven this text. In compliance with consent overseen by Baylor's Institutional Review Board, they must remain anonymous, protecting their trust and the integrity of the research process. Nevertheless, their candor, thoughtfulness, experiences, successes, and failures with bereavement support groups have made this book far more than a theoretical academic work.

The greatest debt of gratitude owed in this volume is to the countless men, women, adolescents, and children who have shaped this work by their own stories and experiences shared in bereavement groups I have led. Their number is legion, and their names fade in my memory with the passage of time. What I cannot ever forget, however, is the shaping influence they have had on this work. Few of them will ever read this volume. Most will not even remember the name of that counselor who facilitated a group or met them in the consultation room, but they have given me far more than I could ever repay.

To all of you and the countless ones whose names I did not record, thank you. This book would not have been possible without your encouragement, input, teaching, mentoring, and support.

INTRODUCTION

Bereavement support groups have arisen across the Western landscape with hospices, funeral homes, and faith communities all participating in sponsoring such endeavors. The Compassionate Friends, Bereaved Families of Ontario, and Bereaved Parents USA are a few notable examples of networks, sometimes international in scope, that began as loosely connected collections of local support groups knitted together by the commonality of loss. Questions remain, however, about the efficacy of these groups. Does participation in them make a significant difference in the outcomes of the bereaved people who participate? If groups are effective, what makes them so?

While it may be theoretically possible for an individual to navigate the experience of bereavement alone, a central premise of grief support—at least as it is practiced in the English-speaking world—is that grieving people benefit from strong social support. I must confess my bias: I think that bereavement is rarely managed well when one tries to navigate this process alone.

As this book developed, it did so with three audiences in mind. Though I now teach full-time, my years as a clinical counselor working in a hospice setting involved day-to-day interaction with dying and grieving individuals. *Bereavement Groups and the Role of Social Support,* therefore, provides practical, "applied" guidance for the leadership of bereavement support groups. The techniques utilized in bereavement groups grow out of one or more theoretical constructs, even though practitioners might sometimes be unaware of those implicit theories. For example, the choice to gather a group of people together grows out of the practitioner's "theory" that group support is better than solitary attempts at managing one's grief. Suggesting that a potential participant wait a prescribed length of time after the loss before joining a group is based on a theory that early (acute) grief is too unstable for a bereaved person to meaningfully participate. Just because a theory or assumption undergirds a practice, however, does not mean that the theory or assumption is correct.

In a recent study, Ober, Granello, and Wheaton (2012) found that approximately 40% of practicing counselors reported no familiarity with the then-dominant theories in bereavement. More than half of respondents reported no specific coursework about bereavement in their clinical training, though nearly 70% indicated they had completed some professional development hours on the topic. Their study also pointed out the lack of empirically based standards for training the people who counsel and support bereaved individuals.

This reality accounts for the growing call for evidence-based practices throughout the behavioral health fields. The perspective of this volume is that our desire to be practical must always be grounded in the existing research evidence for group effectiveness and the best theoretical constructs of how these pieces fit together to best support bereaved individuals, families, and communities. While the evidence for how and why bereavement support groups provide help to grieving people is focused on a handful of studies, those studies demonstrate a common theme of generally positive help for participants. Furthermore, while we can increasingly make a case for group support for bereaved individuals specifically and grief counseling more generally, this all must make sense in light of our best understandings of how humans find belonging in the context of social groups.

Those caregiving professionals and volunteers who desire practical guidance for starting and leading groups are not the only audience. As I wrote, I envisioned the legions of students—my own and those of colleagues—who in these foundational years of training need to enhance their understanding of what works in grief and why we think it works. In light of the Ober et al. (2012) study referenced above and the common wisdom that bereavement is a significant life-altering issue in many clinical encounters, my hope is that students in training receive significant practical, evidence-based information about the role of counsel and support for bereaved individuals. The questions for reflection and discussion that follow each chapter will hopefully assist in that reflective learning process, whether we are engaged formally as students now or simply as lifelong learners.

As in any young field, our theoretical foundations for why bereavement groups may help bereaved people far outstrip the scientific evidence that people are helped. That is true in most fields of inquiry, but in the absence of evidence of harm (which I and many others are convinced we do not have), we cannot afford to stand idly by refusing to help until we learn all there is to learn about efficacy. In the words of Irvin Yalom (1995), one of the masters of group psychotherapy, "front-line therapists faced with suffering patients obviously cannot wait for science" (p. xiv).

As is the case when books are under consideration by academic publishing houses such as Routledge, when this book was still just a concept, the publisher sent the proposed outline to a group of peer reviewers, colleagues with deep understanding of the bereavement process, the current literature, and the role of support. One of the reviewers helpfully questioned how the author planned to "ground" the volume in the research when there is such a dearth of good published research on the efficacy of bereavement groups. It is a point well-taken, and the candor of this reviewer, I believe, has greatly strengthened the content of this volume.

The empirical quantitative literature on the function and helpfulness of bereavement groups is far less substantial than in many other fields of inquiry. While the assessment and treatment ideas discussed in Chapter Seven on complicated grief are now well documented (if not universally accepted by clinicians), the literature on the helpfulness of bereavement support groups is far less well established. For clinical readers who are most interested in "practical matters," perhaps some overview of research protocols and terminology is in order.

Much of the research done thus far on the effectiveness of bereavement support groups is of a qualitative type. For readers unacquainted with research principles and methods, it is helpful to know this data depends on interviews and observational studies about how bereaved people seem to be faring during and after participation in a group. While some research "purists" discount qualitative methods of inquiry, these methods are unequaled in their ability to plumb depths of experience not yet adequately labeled and described. Qualitative research typically helps provide the framework of nuanced experiences and phenomenon, which it turn, informs the development of questionnaires typically used in quantitative psychological studies (Peters, 2010; Rubin & Shechory-Stahl, 2012–13). In commenting on the need for a qualitative approach in understanding the bereavement experiences of mothers whose infants had died from Sudden Infant Death Syndrome (SIDS), Rubin (1999) noted, "Statistical findings, however, cannot easily convey the power of the loss and what the interview and direct contact with the bereaved conveyed" (p. 689). In analyzing content from another mixed-method (quantitative and qualitative) study, Rubin and Shechory-Stahl (2012–13) explained,

"This (interview/narrative) methodology is particularly suited to deepening our understanding of the experience of loss across time and with the added ability to classify the respondents' responses on objective measures sorting them into improved or not-improved" (p. 368).

Semi-structured interviews, for example, allow the researcher to follow ideas described by the interview participants rather than simply administering a questionnaire of predetermined items in the hope that the researcher's original hypotheses really does yield the best questions to explore. My own research study of bereavement group leaders (LEAP Study), on whose results I have drawn in this volume, is an example of this qualitative type of investigation. As in the LEAP study, literature review and clinical experience provide the framework of topics to discuss in interviews. However, the respondents' own narrative becomes the "evidence" analyzed to discover what the important nuances of the topic really are. One hoped-for characteristic of research is that the results can be generalized to a wider audience; what is observed in population A can be assumed to be evident in population B. Strictly speaking, the goal of qualitative inquiry is not generalizability but, rather, "transferability" (Ghesquiere, 2013; Seale, 1999). In other words, qualitative studies invite research consumers to make application of the results discovered, considering the research user's own context.

Quantitative studies, on the other hand, attempt to provide a numerical prevalence of phenomena, classifying the studied phenomena into distinct categories on this basis. One colleague differentiated qualitative and quantitative analyses this way: "If you count it, it's quantitative. If there aren't numbers, it's qualitative" (Lisa Baker, personal communication, 21 June 2015). Based on a long and proud history in the philosophical school known as empiricism, quantitative studies categorize individuals, attempting to define the prevalence of a particular condition among a group of people. Administering quality assurance surveys to participants after a group concludes is a type of quantitative study. Though vital for assessing "customer satisfaction," what these surveys lack is the presence of a "control group." In other words, participants might rate their experiences in a group very highly, even saying they feel they are better off after eight weeks or three months of participation in a group. Without a group of "matched control" individuals who experienced similar losses and who did not participate in the support group, it becomes difficult to scientifically measure the group's effectiveness; what a quality assurance survey cannot tell us is how the same individuals would have been doing if they had not participated in a group. Is it possible that the intense focus on the loss story engendered by many support groups might actually *increase* the prevalence of unhealthy rumination, thereby rendering the participants worse off at the end of the group than they would have been if they had not participated at all?

One way to conduct a quantitative study among bereaved people in groups, for example, would be to administer a well-regarded instrument (such as the Grief Experience Inventory, the Texas Revised Inventory of Grief, or the Beck Depression Inventory) to people before and after participation in a group session. Then, at least theoretically, researchers could "measure" the effectiveness of the group over a period of time? Of course, what such a "longitudinal" study would not demonstrate is whether the improvement (or worsening) of the bereavement experience is due to involvement in the group, the simple passage of time, some previously undetermined factor(s), or, most likely, some combination of these factors. To attempt to control these variables, quantitative researchers long ago developed ways to test for the hypothetical impact one variable has on another, developing analysis of variance (ANOVA) and multivariate analysis of variance (MANOVA), terms that appear throughout the "results" sections of quantitative research reports in scholarly journals (Jarman, 2015; Zedeck, 2014).

Long considered the gold standard in the research field is the randomized control trial (RCT) and its several derivations. When a new pharmaceutical compound is developed, for example, manufacturers engage in a series of studies to assure that the medication does what it promises within the context of acceptable side effects. In the RCT, researchers assemble a cohort of people with a given medical condition and administer to them the proposed medication. They match these people with another group of individuals who also have the medical condition and who are similar in age and demographics to the "intervention/treatment group" but do not offer them the medication. Often the participants are unaware in which group they fall, whether the compound they are receiving is the compound being tested or is a placebo; this is a *blind randomized control trial.* Sometimes, even the researchers themselves are kept "in the dark" about which people are in which group (a *double blind randomized control trial*).

While quantitative studies are vital in testing the efficacy and side-effects of new medications, the use of such strategies becomes more problematic in the psychosocial research field. In reviewing manuscripts for their fine book, *Continuing Bonds*, Silverman and Klass (1996) noted, "it seems to us that the quantitative method, with its roots so deep in the logical positivism of modernity, is based on the same inadequate assumptions underlying the model of grief that this book sets out to correct" (p. 4). Later in the volume, the authors offer an alternative method for conducting research in bereavement. In their analysis of 1,554 articles published in two leading thanatology journals from 1991 to 2010, Wittkowski, Doka, Neimeyer, and Vallerga (2015) observed that the increase in quantitative studies published from 1991 and 2005 was followed by a significant decline in the next five years, while the number of qualitative empirical studies published increased significantly during the first decade of the 21st century. They concluded,

> thanatology has progressed as have other disciplines in the social sciences, namely by empirical research strategies. The upsurge during the last decade of studies using qualitative methods provides a possible refinement in a predominantly quantitative paradigm, arguably providing a more textured analysis of the general patterns of human reactions to dying and loss reliably identified by the latter studies. (Wittkowski et al., 2015, p. 260)

To critics who accuse bereavement in general and support group methodology in particular to be predicated on shaky science, my response is that this is not the only field of endeavor to struggle with such problems. A urological cancer biology researcher at Johns Hopkins University Medical Center has been at the center of a firestorm over whether some discoveries touted as scientific "breakthroughs" are really scientific at all. Robert Getzenberg and his colleagues have retracted at least seven papers, reporting the results of their research had flaws preventing "reproducibility," a cardinal rule in research. Amid accusations by other researchers of "fraud" and "incompetence," Getzenberg has now departed Johns Hopkins (Hughes, 2009; Oransky, 2014). Apparently, Getzenberg's problems are the "tip" of the proverbial "iceberg." Biotechnology and pharmaceutical companies have had repeated problems reproducing results reported in leading scientific journals, with Amgen reporting its lab scientists could reproduce the results in only six of 53 papers it tested and Bayer reporting its scientists could reproduce only 14 out of 67 (Kaiser, 2015).

Many research studies attempt to utilize the best elements of the perceived objectivity of quantitative methods and the breadth of nuance available in ethnographic or interview-based qualitative methodology. These so-called mixed method research studies allow researchers to look at a population through multiple lenses. Finding appropriate ways to effectively and objectively evaluate these varied kinds of research studies, however, has proven to be a greater challenge (Pluye, Gagnon, Griffiths, & Johnson-Lafleur, 2009). Through history-taking and hearing the story of patient perceptions of illness, health care professionals have traditionally dealt with a complex web of social, spiritual, and emotional issues in addition to the biomedical/physical aspects of patient care. Quantitative measures alone, regardless of how good they are, are simply not enough. Such realization has led the U.S. Food and Drug Administration (FDA), European Medicines Agency, and British National Health Service (NHS) to increasingly approve the use of *patient reported outcome measures* (PROMs) in pharmaceutical clinical trials to evaluate subjective "quality of life" improvements because of their potential to advance "patient-centered care" (McClimans & Browne, 2011; Weldring & Smith, 2013).

Therefore, Andrew and Halcomb (2011) suggest, "the complexity of health problems and health teams aptly support the need for multiple data sources when researching health issues. It is not surprising, therefore, that mixed methods is an increasing method of choice for research in health disciplines" (p. 139). A single methodological protocol leaves the researcher at grave risk of missing the most important aspects of the participants' lived experience. In spite of the quest for evidence-based practices, such oversights leave clinicians grappling for best interventions and, in the end, potentially create more distress for bereaved individuals.

This book is the culmination of just this sort of mixed-method study. I have reviewed the literature including the various quantitative studies, qualitative assessments, and mixed-methods studies published in the last couple of decades. However, I have tried to assess those studies in the light of the manifold clinical experiences of colleagues around the world who have been engaged thoughtfully and effectively in the support of bereaved people. In my mind's ear, I often hear the echoes of a truism I first heard quoted by a professor in one of my own undergraduate sociology courses:

> It would be nice if all of the data which sociologists require could be enumerated because then we could run them through IBM machines and draw charts as the economists do. However, *not everything that can be counted counts, and not everything that counts can be counted.* (Cameron, 1963, p. 13, emphasis added)

Controlling variables and reducing researcher bias are clearly valuable goals often missing from bereavement research. In many ways, the work of bereavement support groups has been a "wild, wild West," where instinct and personal experience have ruled the day. A plethora of bereavement support groups has arisen, often led by people who not so long ago were struggling mightily with their own loss experiences. Sometimes, the groups they created were predicated on their own experiences with loss, encompassing interventions and perspectives they personally found helpful while dismissing those of which they were either unaware or had simply found unhelpful in their own personal experiences. Making matters worse, the so-called experts on whom these individuals depended for advice have often had no real expertise in bereavement and dispense perspectives that are dated or out of step with contemporary thinking of those who specialize in bereavement.

Across the three decades of my career, I have led hundreds of bereavement group sessions and attended many more led by trainees and others. Some group facilitators and a few group participants have described their own unique experiences with grief as if they were the single way (or at least the most effective way) to experience loss. What we know as a community of clinical scholars in bereavement is that human grieving processes include a far more rich and nuanced texturing of experiences than the "one right way to grieve" approach that I have heard popularized in grief groups far too often (Hall, 2014).

Throughout the following chapters, my goal has been to address what seem to be vitally important areas in the creation and development of bereavement support groups. Where the research evidence is clear, I will explain how I see those findings informing the practice of group leadership. Where the ideas presented are simply extrapolated or inferred from other fields of study (such as the sociology of groups), I have tried to honestly declare those inferential connections.

There are, however, other ideas in this book that have no evidence basis or even a clear inferential basis from another field. In these cases, I have attempted to offer the sage wisdom of the community of professionals who have been at the task of shepherding people through grief for many years. In this volume, these common practices are the ideas gleaned from the LEAP (Leader Experiences, Attitudes, & Perceptions) study described later in this introduction. I have tried to make clear the differences between what is evidence-based and what is common practice based on clinical wisdom. Most certainly, clinical wisdom is sometimes wrong, but, on the whole, there seems little reason to discount practices in the latter category.

The World Health Organization (2015) estimates 56 million people died in the most recent year for which statistics are available, a figure similar to previous years. If each of these deaths significantly affected four family members and/or friends, the number of newly bereaved people in the world exceeds 200 million annually. At least in mobile, frequently individualistic societies such as North America and Western Europe, many of these individuals will lack social support they deem as helpful. One small Swedish study found about one-third of bereaved people articulated needing social support outside of their natural networks of family and friends in the months following the death (Benkel, Wijk, & Molander, 2009) and my own clinical experience indicates the numbers in the southern California community where I practiced were at least as high.

The nearly incontrovertible evidence is mounting that complicated grief potentially reduces life expectancy and diminishes quality of life (Guldin, O'Connor, Sokolowsi, Jensen, & Vedsted, 2011; Shear et al., 2011, 2014). With such massive numbers of newly bereaved individuals every year, many of whom desperately need more support than they currently have, clinical support professionals must be prepared to act on the basis of solid theoretical constructs about how bereavement works and how social support helps, even in advance of a clear research-proven protocol. Following the best clinical wisdom at our disposal, sometimes we must not wait until the case is proven that a particular action is helpful, at least in the absence of data indicating that it is harmful.

It was this recognition that gave rise to the ongoing qualitative study, some of the early results of which provide an additional research basis for this book. The Bereavement Group LEAP Study (Leader Experiences, Attitudes, and Perceptions, described more fully below) provides many of the anecdotal practice ideas presented here; these notions form many of the nuggets of what I call "clinical wisdom." In other words, where we have no current evidence to support or refute a particular practice, I have contributed the shared wisdom of those who have been shepherding people through groups for decades. I include those ideas here not because clinical and support programs are always correct in their theoretical assumptions and resultant clinical practices. Rather, these ideas form an important "practice" application for this volume because we cannot always wait for the research evidence to compel a practice before we act to support people in pain.

The plan of this book is relatively simple. In the first chapter, I overview the field of bereavement studies as it now stands, providing the reader with a perspective of where we have been in the century since Sigmund Freud first published his paper *Mourning and Melancholia*. Chapter Two examines current thinking about social support as well as how bereavement groups might fit into what we know about family structure, community building, and the dangers of social isolation. In the third chapter, we turn attention to the vital task of recruiting, training, supporting, and supervising group leadership. In my experience, this is one of the most easily overlooked issues in groups, and I have great concern about group leaders who lead groups disconnected from any real opportunities for supervision by more experienced colleagues.

Chapter Four directs the reader's attention to the content of group meetings themselves, offering ideas about the use of guided discussion, writing, and creative arts. The fifth chapter acknowledges that groups do not always proceed according to plan, offering proven practical ideas for managing problematic behaviors, addressing confidentiality, and evaluating effectiveness in group interventions. Chapter Six turns the reader's attention to the unique needs of children and teens, offering the benefit of a robust clinical wisdom paired with strong empirical evidence for effectiveness. As this chapter points out, the evidence for the effectiveness of grief intervention with younger grievers is as strong as any for bereavement intervention.

One of the most discussed concepts in the current bereavement literature focuses on what to do about complicated grief. As Chapter Seven makes clear, this has not been an easy discussion since definitions and descriptions are in constant flux, making research studies and clinical anecdotes difficult to compare. Nevertheless, the chapter maintains, some complicated grief can be expected in virtually every bereavement support group, and this chapter will help readers discover some of the most common ways grief becomes "complex."

Finally, a brief epilogue attempts to shine light on a forward pathway. While the bereavement support group concept is several decades old and we have strong research on some aspects of its effectiveness, this is far from a complete literature on efficacy. The epilogue summarizes some of the challenges ahead in discerning when, where, and under what circumstances bereavement support groups can be most effective.

BEREAVEMENT GROUP LEAP STUDY (LEADER EXPERIENCES, ATTITUDES, AND PERCEPTIONS)

As mentioned earlier in this introduction, the LEAP study endeavored to place the theoretical underpinnings of bereavement support groups and the state of current research about their effectiveness into the context of what is currently happening from the perspective of the people tasked with implementing program ideas: bereavement support group leaders themselves. The idea for the LEAP study evolved after work on this volume had commenced.

The protocol outlined and followed in the study were in compliance with review by the Baylor University Institutional Review Board (IRB). These protocols were developed to protect the integrity of the study and to assure confidentiality of the participants. The LEAP study included semi-structured interviews with both professional and peer volunteers serving in roles of group leaders/facilitators, program coordinators, and clinical supervisors. The respondents represented a wide range of "professional helpers" including nurses, social workers, chaplains, and psychotherapists as well as several peer volunteers whose primary interest in bereavement group leadership was sparked by a loss in their own lives. The intention of this study was not to create a quantifiable and generalizable perspective on groups through probability sampling, although the respondents represented diverse types of programs around the globe. Among other things, the study confirmed what many of us already knew intuitively: asking one set of questions to bereavement group leaders raises an entirely new set of questions; there are far more dimensions to understanding the lived experiences of bereavement support group leaders than this study captured.

The LEAP study fits into a genre of qualitative research known as grounded theory. With its origin in the 1960s study of dying people by sociologists Barney Glaser and Anselm Strauss, grounded theory analyzes interviews looking for common themes to appear in the recounting of the lived experience of the research participants (Glaser & Strauss, 1965, 1967). Possibly in part because Glaser and Strauss developed the research methodology in their quest to understand and describe the experiences of dying people, their method grew in prominence during the latter decades of the 20th century, becoming what Neimeyer and Hogan (2001) referred to as "the most widely used qualitative method in thanatology" (p. 106). Grounded theory has played a pivotal role in some of the most important studies of bereavement including Nadeau's (1998, 2001) research in family bereavement and Hogan, Morse, and Tasón's (1996) grounded theory-informed development of an experiential theory of bereavement. Like all research methodologies, this one has not been without its detractors, but it provides helpful structure for the purposes of this book. Since the interest in the LEAP study was to discover the experiences, attitudes, and perceptions of individuals in the trenches of leading bereavement support groups, grounded theory has provided an ideal methodological framework for this study.

In reporting results of the LEAP study, I have closely adhered to the promise made to participants in the study: that there would be no details provided in publication that could identify them. Since there were no significant patterns noted differentiating, say a group leader from the southern United States from one in the western United States, and since these reports did not markedly differ from those of facilitators in Canada, southern Africa, Asia, or Australia, I have purposefully avoided even geographic region identifiers in reporting this data.

I trust that this volume will not seem too theoretical for practitioners and that readers will find plenty of practical ideas and suggestions throughout. What I believe this volume will do, however, is provide a firm basis for why we choose the group activities we choose, include the individuals we include, and lead the discussions we lead. There are many other bereavement support group manuals (Graves, 2012; Hoy, 2007; Hughes, 1995; Wolfelt, 2004) that provide even more practical tools than this book, and readers who want more clarification may profit greatly in consulting them.

MULTICULTURALISM AND BEREAVEMENT SUPPORT GROUPS

One of the colleagues Routledge looked to for review of the working outline for this book recommended adding a chapter on cross-cultural issues in bereavement support groups. My interest in cross-cultural issues began as an undergraduate student in sociology and has continued through my recently published multicultural examination of funeral rituals (Hoy, 2013). I was attracted to the idea of incorporating multicultural issues in groups and even rewrote the initial outline to incorporate this additional chapter. As the book progressed, however, I realized the inappropriateness of a separate chapter on multiculturalism as an addition to the text. The whole point was to assure that the book accounted for variation and application beyond a European-North American white context.

"Multicultural" means different things to different people, and even scholars have not completely agreed on terminology or definitions. One way to conceptualize multiculturalism is to think about cultures of power and cultures outside the traditional power structures of any society. In every group of people, there are subgroups who are disenfranchised by power systems; in the absence of policies specifically directed at attending to these sub-groups, they are often overlooked in the allocation of public and private resources and even in population counts, which can affect elections and governmental representation (Axelsson, Sköld, Ziker, & Anderson, 2011). My work on a Kenyan public health, education, and agriculture project over recent years has made me aware of how disenfranchised one group can be when another "tribe" wields the power in a society.

In the final analysis, however, participation in bereavement support groups has historically been a choice exercised most often by people primarily of western European lineage. There are certainly exceptions to the rule, but anecdotal evidence points to bereavement support groups being a largely white phenomenon in North America. One LEAP study respondent reported "at least one black" in each of the recent adult bereavement groups in her organization. When pressed about percentages, this leader acknowledged that the last three groups had included approximately 38 people and that three of the participants (7.9%) had been of African lineage. However, a quick check of census statistics for the community revealed the African-American population to be almost 29%.

Much work is yet ahead on finding ways to make bereavement support available to the vast array of cultural groups. One individual interviewed in the LEAP study works in a program with many specialized bereavement groups including one for gay and lesbian individuals dealing with partner loss and another for Spanish speakers, along with the more common groups for bereaved widows, parents, and children. This is an effort to be multicultural, although segregation by cultural group for reasons other than language is a practice open to debate.

In writing this volume, I recognize my position as a white male and hope to have treaded respectfully on matters of multiculturalism. I have grown increasingly skeptical of those who propose easy answers to matters of cultural, ethnic, and racial identity in how social service and health care needs are identified and met. What I have attempted to do in this volume is to offer perspectives from as wide a variety of cultural sources as possible, citing bereavement research from around the world and from many different cultural groups within individual national borders. In interviews for the LEAP study, respondents were asked to evaluate how their programs are doing with incorporating people from non-dominant cultures into their groups.

This book also tries to be consistently respectful of cultural groups. Whenever possible, I have elected to use the most current ethnic categories adopted by catalogers at the National Library of Medicine of the United States Institutes of Health. NLM's medical subject headings (MeSH) are familiar to students and scholars who have conducted literature searches using PubMed, MEDLINE, or many of the other popular database aggregators. The NLM prefers continental ancestry, followed as needed by national identity. In this text, I have tried to follow the NLM's recommendation, so African, European, Asian, and Oceanic serve as the "continental ancestry" identifiers (U.S. National Library of Medicine, 2003). When needed for clarification, I typically have added a national identity such as African American or Asian Canadian.

ABOUT THE "STYLE" OF THIS VOLUME

Early in the writing of this text, I decided to forgo the stiff formalism of third-person language in preference for the less formal first person, much as if I were carrying on a conversation in a seminar room with a handful of students. There are many reasons for that choice. One, of course, is that we labor in a profoundly human field, and third-person language tends to dehumanize the reader and the author; after all, none of us refers to our patients, clients, or group members in the third person when we are in a room with them. Second, I personally find the informality of first person much easier to read if for no other reason than that it is direct and active; fewer words are required to say, "I observed . . ." than are required to say "It was observed that. . . ."

Perhaps most importantly, when we in the social sciences use third-person, passive language, I suspect we are trying to sound like our research is as objective and "scientific" as our colleagues in biology and physics. I recently discovered the work of British social scientist Michael Billig (2013), whose words are helpful on this point:

> By not mentioning the researchers, the writers can avoid the dilemma of choosing how to describe the researchers and also they can avoid implying that the persona of the experimenter might have affected the results. The resulting rhetoric conveys 'objectivity' and 'scientific procedure', but it accomplishes this by being vague.
>
> The writer is following convention by describing the processes of the research in ways that reify them: it is as if the procedures just happen. The readers know perfectly well that this cannot have been the case, but there is a tacit conspiracy between journal editor, writer, and readers to pretend that it is. It might seem strange that social scientists, especially those who pride themselves in being scientific, should systematically describe what has happened in uninformative ways. In this matter, to appear more scientific means giving less information. Researchers have to write as if they have something to hide. (p. 132)

In addition to many years of experience with groups and the interpretation of results from the LEAP Study about the role of groups in grief support, I have tried to take a decidedly "interdisciplinary approach" to this topic. The pages of references at the back of this book will undoubtedly make clear that I have endeavored to read both widely and deeply, not only in the field of bereavement support groups, but in a host of other disciplines whose work might have implication for us. I teach in an interdisciplinary field called "medical humanities" and have always felt, of course, that the field of thanatology itself is an intersection of many fields of study.

Chapters in this volume begin with hypothetical cases. While each includes specific details and names, they are all fictional. The stories are cobbled together from details of many different individuals. Bereavement support groups and volunteers will realize how unfortunately "believable" these accounts are.

What this work is, more than anything else, I believe, is a travel diary, a "journal of journeying" to find the most effective ways to offer group support to bereaved individuals. For me, it has been a profound journey of exploration, and I welcome you to this journey of discovery with me.

CHAPTER 1

Making Sense of Grief

Joan was not the first widow to wonder if she could possibly survive the overwhelming sense of "being lost" that followed her husband's death. Just after their 30th wedding anniversary, Rick had died suddenly at work of a heart attack. He was 52. The autopsy report explained his cause of death as a "proximal lesion of the left anterior descending artery"; their family doctor explained to Joan that her husband had died almost instantly in a cardiac episode known widely as "the Widow Maker." To Joan, more frightening words had never been spoken, and she did not like the term. In one decisive moment, a malfunction in her beloved husband's heart had made her into something she had never wanted to be: a widow.

Now at the urging of a friend from work, she was here: the first evening of a seven-week group called "Exploring Your Grief" in a conference room at a local hospital. When the facilitator greeted Joan at the door, the new widow could already feel the tears welling up in her eyes. It had been almost four months, and she seemed only to get worse, not better. Her anxiety mounted a few weeks earlier when her well-meaning sister-in-law, herself widowed a few years earlier, remarked, "Well, Joan, if you think it's bad now, just wait. The second year is even worse than the first." Somehow, Joan hoped this group of people whom she had never met would help her "explore" her grief. But, in reality, what she hoped more than anything was that in "exploring her grief," she would learn how to get past the overwhelming sense of "lostness" she had felt for the last four months.

Ironically, the quick death of Joan's husband at an early age would have been common rather than unusual in much of the world and throughout much of history. Among early humans, archaeological evidence implies deaths generally came quickly and without warning rather than after the protracted dying so often seen in the Western world today. While we do not know how early humans dealt with grief, we can readily surmise that they did experience it.

Whatever they did with their grief, however, these humans dealt with their dead as a way to deal with their loss. One British scholar writes, "At 10,000 years ago, we have good evidence of elaborate food and decorations inside graves, of the dead being dressed in elaborate ways, of differential burials based on status, or *even possibly the elicited grief*" (Kellehear, 2007, p. 23, emphasis added).

Humans have developed an amazing capacity to adapt to loss. Music in virtually every genre includes references to loss. The words of poets, playwrights, and novelists throughout history have heralded the sentiment of aching human hearts and the solace and hope they found in the face of great sorrow. Novelists in every era have chosen the vagaries of grief to enliven their characters and to draw readers into the sentiment of the story. Perhaps no experience plays on the heartstrings of readers quite like sorrow, if for no other reason than that grief is such a universal human experience.

Perhaps the world's oldest story is that of Gilgamesh, a historical king who reigned in Urek, a Mesopotamian city, around 2750 BCE. The portrayal of inconsolable grief in the life of Gilgamesh is familiar, even if the story's details are unknown to many living in the 21st century. After the death of his friend Enkidu, with whom he had "slain monsters," Gilgamesh, the mythic king-hero of the story, was inconsolable. In the words of the story's narrator, Gilgamesh's grief was beyond understanding, his pain impenetrable, and his sorrow unbearable (Mitchell, 2004).

In similar ways, the poetry of the ancient Hebrews also wrestled with the vagaries of death and the difficult experiences of bereavement. The accounts of the death of the Hebrew patriarch Abraham's wife, Sarah (Genesis 23), and of Jacob, father of famous Hebrew-born Egyptian prime minister, Joseph (Genesis 49–50), portrayed grief and its rituals with poignant words. Perhaps the oldest writing in the Hebrew Bible told the story of Job, a man who lost everything—wife, children, home, possessions, and livelihood. The story is his quest to make meaning of the loss in the context of faith, and in the end, his faith is rebuilt as he found a way to live in a world radically reshaped by his encounter. Incidentally, a large part of the narrative explains the very poor care Job received from his advice-giving, theologically inaccurate friends. Religious literature is replete with references to grief and hope, including perhaps the most quoted text of all time from the Hebrew Bible: "Yea, though I walk through the valley of the shadow of death, I will fear no evil, for Thou art with me; Thy rod and Thy staff, they comfort me" (Psalm 23:4, Jewish Publication Society, 1917).

The Christian New Testament frequently references the experiences of death and loss, in spite of some contemporary Christians insisting that real faith makes grief unnecessary. When Stephen, the first known Christian martyr, died, the response of the community was stated with simplicity: "Godly men buried Stephen and mourned deeply for him" (Acts 8:2, New International Version). In reflecting on the life-threatening illness of his colleague Epaphroditus, Paul, the famous first-century Christian missionary, explained his theological understanding of his friend's recovery: "Indeed he was ill, and almost died. But God had mercy on him, and not on him only but also on me, to spare me sorrow upon sorrow" (Philippians 2:27, New International Version).

Perhaps unlike any group of writers, the Victorians raised "literature of sorrow" to a refined art form. Christ (1995) suggested: "Literature, particularly poetry, was often used to perform a kind of mourning work. Much as the Victorians created material objects that were effigies for the dead, Victorian writers often sought to substitute the literary work for the dead body" (p. 392).

Carman Bliss (1904) dedicated an entire volume of his nine-volume *World's Best Poetry* to the topic of *Sorrow and Consolation*. Among more than 125 poems on death and consolation, he includes 19th-century poet Elizabeth Barrett Browning's appreciation of hopefulness in the light of loss in the words of her sonnet, "Tears." She concluded the work simply:

> Ye who weep only! If, as some have done,
> Ye grope tear-blinded in a desert place,
> And touch but tombs,—look up! Those tears will run
> Soon in long rivers down the lifted face,
> And leave the vision clear for stars and sun.
>
> (Bliss, 1904, p. 126)

In his tragedy *Macbeth*, William Shakespeare placed words into the mouth of his character Malcolm as he informs and then provides support to Macduff in the aftermath of the murder of Macduff's wife and children: "Merciful heaven! What, man! Ne'er pull your hat upon your brows. Give sorrow words. The grief that does not speak whispers the o'er fraught heart and bids it break" (Macbeth, Act 4, Scene 3, lines 210–214).

Paintings, sculpture, and architecture provide a glimpse into the subjective world of how people have experienced loss in history, as well. Eppel (2009) suggests, "Art reveals much of our inner life, the truth about human nature," and then asks rhetorically, "but what is art and why does it resonate so much with us?" He quotes Laplanche and Pontalis' notion of art as "a half-way house between the subjective and objective," suggesting that it is the place where elements of inner emotional life get combined with material elements. While the study of art, Eppel suggests, helps the student better understand the artist's inner life, it likely resonates because of our own identification with that which "strikes a chord with us, because they constitute elements which are universal in human nature" (p. 48).

If classical literature, visual art, and drama all provide windows to the sorrowing soul, these renderings likely describe the subjective inner world of the artists and, by extension, the experienced world of bereaved masses. Nevertheless, developing sociological and psychoanalytical theory desired a more objective description of the bereavement experience, so by the early 20th century, theorists such as Max Weber and Sigmund Freud were examining the experiences of bereavement from an intellectual perspective. Freud's 1917 paper "Mourning and Melancholia" set the stage for the 20th century's voluminous exploration of the bereavement process. Likely responding to a growing desire in his day to pathologize grief, he wrote,

> although mourning involves grave departures from the normal attitude toward life, it never occurs to us to regard it as a pathological condition and to refer it to a medical treatment. We rely on its being overcome after a certain lapse of time, and we look upon any interference with it as useless or even harmful. (Freud, 1957/1917, p. 243)

MODELS: DESCRIBING THE PROCESS OF ADAPTING TO LOSS

In the third decade after Freud's "Mourning and Melancholia" and while the deadliest conflict in history raged in Europe, Asia, the Pacific islands, and North Africa, interest in the role of bereavement intensified. Estimates of total fatalities in World War II range from 50 million to more than 80 million, a number that represents 3% to 5% of the 1939 global population (Duff, 2015; Ferguson, 2006; Rummel, 1994). American psychiatrist Eric Lindemann had been interested in the bereavement experiences of families whose loved ones were military personnel killed in war.

However, it was his work with survivors of the deadly Boston Cocoanut Grove nightclub fire that propelled him to the forefront of conversations about the immediate and long-term effects of grief (Cobb & Lindemann, 1943; Lindemann, 1944).

On Saturday evening, November 28, 1942, fire raced through the famous club; the eight-minute fire would eventually claim 492 lives, including the four Fitzgerald brothers. Like many of the young patrons at the club that night, they and their dates all died at the Grove celebrating the homecoming of Henry, a private in the Army Air Corps (Esposito, 2005). Ironically, this early work of Lindemann's on bereavement represented very complicated stories of loss in that so many of the victims were young people. Many of the victims of the fire that night were celebrating College of the Holy Cross's upset victory in football against cross-town rival Boston College. Like the Fitzgerald brothers, many other young people in the club that night were reveling in the safe return of family members and friends from military service, ironically dying in the celebration marking that their loved ones had survived combat.

As one of the first to systematize the grief process and the ways it can go awry, Lindemann concluded that grief is a "definite syndrome" that might appear immediately after a crisis or after some delay. Through using appropriate techniques, Lindemann (1944) asserted, the "distorted pictures (of bereavement) can be successfully transformed into a normal grief reaction with resolution" (p. 141). Presaging much of the thinking in grief over the next half-century, Lindemann concluded,

> The duration of a grief reaction seems to depend upon the success with which a person does the *grief work,* namely, emancipation from the bondage to the deceased, readjustment to the environment in which the deceased is missing, and the formation of new relationships. One of the big obstacles to this work seems to be the fact that many patients try to avoid the intense distress connected with the grief experience and to avoid the expression of emotion necessary for it. (p. 143)

During World War II and the early postwar years, British psychiatrist John Bowlby was at work trying to understand the influence on young children of an absent mother, studies that gave rise to the attachment theory for which Bowlby is most famous. His research included psychological examination of children accused of theft as well as children hospitalized for various illnesses and injury, the latter project in the late 1940s, in which work the first "phases" of loss were labeled. Along with

James Robertson, a filmmaker Bowlby hired to chronicle the hospitalization experience of children, Bowlby described three phases in this separation process: protest, despair, and denial (Bowlby, 1969; Robertson & Bowlby, 1952). Incidentally, these phases were eventually elaborated into four in Bowlby's collaboration with Collin Murray Parkes, the stage model that predated the now famous work of Elisabeth Kübler-Ross (Bretherton, 1992).

The growing interest in bereavement as a field of inquiry during the mid-20th century gave rise to a need to define terms. Like with most specialized languages, there does not seem to be a "moment in time" when the core terms of bereavement were defined. Rather, there has been a gradual evolution of terminology as the 20th century progressed. *Bereavement* came to be the label assigned to the actual experience of loss, and as interest in non-death losses has grown, the term bereavement seems now to be primarily used in the literature to denote the loss experienced in response to a human death. We can speak of a person as "being bereaved," meaning he or she has suffered this significant death loss. *Grief*, on the other hand, has come to mean the bereaved person's emotional, social, spiritual, cognitive, and physical response to loss, while *mourning* is the term used for the expressive acts or practices of grief that are part of experiencing loss in a particular society or culture (Jakoby, 2012; Stroebe, Hansson, Stroebe, & Schut, 2001).

By the late 1960s, and perhaps influenced by the mounting "body count" in the Vietnam War being played out on the battlefields of the Far East and the televisions of the industrialized West, Europeans and North Americans became intensely interested in death and grief issues. At least across the American landscape, this interest had likely been intensified by the death of the United States' young, idealistic president, John F. Kennedy, in 1963. Less than five years later, civil rights leader Martin Luther King, Jr., was gunned down on a Memphis hotel balcony, to be followed only eight weeks after that by the assassination of another member of the politically iconic clan, presidential hopeful Robert Kennedy.

It is little wonder that when Swiss psychiatrist Elisabeth Kübler-Ross published her book *On Death and Dying* in 1969, it rocketed to the top of bestseller lists, becoming a near-instant cult classic. Within a few years, the popular press, accompanied by many nonspecialists in grief work, applied her seemingly common sense theory to every conceivable loss, and her "five stages" gained prominence in the popular cultural lexicon. Kessler and Kübler-Ross (2005) applied her original five stages of the dying process to post-death grief in a book published after Kübler-Ross' death.

The labels for the five stages made common sense. "Denial," after all, seemed to be the first logical response to bad news, while "acceptance" suggested equanimity, a sighing recognition that all would turn out alright in the end. Whatever "stages" came in between, whether they be Kübler-Ross's "anger," "bargaining," and "depression" or some other scholar's list of five, seven, or nine stages, was really quite beside the point. The picture of grief was one of pathway and journey. If the bereaved person began the "journey of grief," the implied thinking went, there must be a destination. So if "denial" was "Ground Zero," the starting gate and the opening salvo, then "acceptance" must be the destination, the finish line, the *fait accompli*. As bereavement support group leaders know well, the experiences of grief are not so easily compartmentalized.

Kübler-Ross most certainly deserves credit for freeing death from its closet in the urbanized West. Her work became an invaluable gift in the late-20th century, an era in which the dying had been summarily wrested from their most familiar surroundings—the family home—to the hospital or nursing home. There, the predominant thinking seemed to be, these critically ill people could be "properly" cared for by a legion of starched-white-uniformed professionals who bore the credentials of advanced training and who wielded the tools of advanced medical technology. Perhaps Kübler-Ross's greatest contribution to the field lies not in the theory she proposed but in the accessible way she made death OK to discuss. In the nearly five decades since the publication of *On Death and Dying*, dozens of other models have been proposed to describe the grief process.

While Kübler-Ross was conducting her seminars in death and dying for American health care professionals, British psychiatrist Colin Murray Parkes (1964, 1972) was at work on the other side of the Atlantic. A colleague of the aforementioned John Bowlby, Parkes' and his work have enjoyed far greater acceptance in the community of bereavement clinicians and scholars. Likely, this is because of how he employed principles of rigorous scientific investigation to the study of bereavement's effects, a quality absent from Kübler-Ross's stages. In fact, the five stages of the dying process articulated by Kübler-Ross have yet to be validated by research.

In the mind of J. William Worden (1982, 2009), a static set of "stages" or "phases" was simply an inadequate model to describe how bereaved people worked through the emotional, cognitive, physical, social, and spiritual challenges of loss. He suggested rather that grieving people work at the accomplishment of a set of psychological tasks. The first of these four tasks, "to accept the reality of the loss," implies a starting point. Though repeated verbatim in successive editions, in the first edition of his watershed textbook on the subject, Worden (1982) explained: "When someone dies, even if the death is expected, there is always a sense that it hasn't happened. The first task of grieving is to come full face with the reality that the person is dead, that the person is gone and will not return" (p. 11).

The ways Worden has described these tasks has morphed since 1982 when they were first published, but he presently labels the four tasks of mourning as:

1) To accept the reality of the loss
2) To process the pain of the grief
3) To adjust to a world without the deceased
4) To find an enduring connection with the deceased in the midst of embarking on a new life

(Worden, 2009)

Though Worden never intended for his tasks to be viewed as "stages," there is a certain linearity to his system; it is unlikely that one will "find an enduring connection with the deceased in the midst of embarking on a new life" until some time after accepting the "reality of the loss." Worden's tasks have enjoyed wide acceptance among clinicians, likely in part because of the simple, understandable, and practical ways they describe the lived experiences of bereaved individuals. Of the respondents in the LEAP study who talked about a "grief model" or "bereavement framework" forming a foundation for their group program, the vast majority credited Worden's tasks as that model.

During the era Worden was first articulating his theory of the grief process, Simon Rubin (1981) was developing the two-track model of bereavement (not to be confused with Stroebe and Schut's "dual process model" below). Rubin constructed this framework to synthesize the then-dominant psychodynamic (attachment) approach to bereavement articulated by Freud (1957/1917) and Bowlby (1969) with the then-emerging approach understanding bereavement as a change (often growth-producing) in the bereaved person. As expressed earlier, the psychodynamic approach saw grief as fundamentally a process of dissolving the attachment bond between bereaved person and deceased loved one. Citing the trauma work of van der Kolk, McFarlane, and Weisaeth (1996) in a later paper, Rubin (1999) said the second approach saw bereavement primarily in terms of how the bereaved continued to "suffer the aftereffects of bereavement in their various life activities"

(p. 684), seeing grief's effects in biological, behavioral, cognitive, and emotional processes.

A simple way of understanding Rubin's two tracks lay in his "bifocal" approach, demonstrated in a two-column chart displayed in his "overview, retrospect, and prospect" paper. There, he referred to track one as the "functioning" axis, including the bereaved individual's abilities to cope with anxiety, depression, and somatic concerns, interact relationally in the family and other significant relationships, manage the stresses of work, and invest in life's tasks. On the other hand, Rubin's second track evaluated the bereaved individual's relationship to the deceased in terms of imagery, emotional distance, positive and negative affect vis-à-vis the deceased person, the tendency to idealize the deceased, and the activities of memorialization as the relationship with the deceased and loss was transformed (see Rubin, 1999, p. 685, Figure 1). This second track, Rubin wrote, "is concerned with how people are involved in maintaining and changing their relationships with the deceased" (p. 685).

Reflecting primarily on the experience of grief for bereaved parents, Rubin (1989–90) wrote, "In sum, for our sample of bereaved parents in Israel, the natural course of mourning is difficult, pronounced, and demonstrably persistent" (p. 335). For grief to "proceed normally," Rubin indicated a belief that two processes had to occur (hence, the two-track model). First, parents had to be able to carry on both conscious and unconscious grieving for their child. Second, he wrote, parents had to find a way to move eventually from the "overbearing preoccupation with the loss and the lost to a renewed focus upon living" (p. 335). Interestingly, in Rubin's perspective, this is made possible through the pull from society and family (i.e., social support), as well as the simple ongoing responsibilities of day-to-day living. What Rubin did not address, however, was exactly how this process happens without these well-meaning family members and friends disenfranchising the loss of bereaved parents by telling them—verbally or nonverbally—to get on with life.

European scholars Margaret Stroebe and Henk Schut (1999) have suggested still another lens for examining the bereavement process, one that has informed much controlled, clinical research on grieving individuals. Stroebe and Schut (2010) described a grief process anchored by two ways of coping: loss-focused and restoration-focused. They defined loss orientation as "concentration on, appraising and processing of some aspect . . . (involving) a painful dwelling on, even searching for the lost person, a phenomenon that lies at the heart of grieving" (p. 277). The restoration orientation they envisioned is one of attending to the changes that occur in the bereaved individual's life as he or she reorients to living "in a changed world without the deceased" and includes "rethinking and replanning one's life in the face of bereavement" (p. 277). From the very earliest moments of loss, Stroebe and Schut contended, bereaved people are participating in both processes (hence, the name, "dual process,") whether remembering life with the deceased and all that has been lost (loss focus) or planning the funeral and thinking about future financial implications of the death (restoration focus).

Stroebe and Schut made a further observation about bereaved individuals. Not only do they participate in these two distinct ways of coping, the theory goes, bereaved individuals "oscillate" between the two, working for a time at one process and then for a time at the other. Presumably, as time elapses since the death, these oscillations become less pronounced. In early grief, bereaved people tend to react like pinballs bounced to and fro with exaggerated expressions of emotion and behavior. As the bereaved person continues to adapt to the loss through the use of restoration-focused coping, grief might gradually become more akin to the quiet rocking of a boat on an inland lake.

From the first time I saw it in publication, I have been intrigued by the notion of oscillation between processes; I consider it to be a helpful way to think about what I have observed in my own clients through the years. As I began formulating my own "model" of the bereavement process in the early 1990s, it was the work of Collin Murray Parkes and of my own counseling mentor, J. William Worden, that influenced me most; since first encountering their work as an undergraduate, I have been attracted to the organized ways they talked about accommodating loss. My own thinking, now articulated in what I have come to call the "compass model," developed first in a congregational ministry context, which was then refined over nearly two decades in a hospice and community bereavement setting (Hoy, 1996, 2008). I am gratified that this simple tool for thinking about grief has been embraced now by a wide variety of clinical and lay caregivers in hospices, congregations, hospitals, and private practice. Caregiving professionals and volunteers often report they appreciate its practical usefulness both in understanding the grief process and in communicating with bereaved individuals and families.

This lens describes bereavement through four interrelated *adaptive processes*, each beginning with the letter "R," situated on and around a quad-directional compass (Figure 1.1): *remembering, reaffirming, realizing,* and *releasing.* I have never been at ease with the notion of grief "recovery," even though a plethora of books and bereavement support

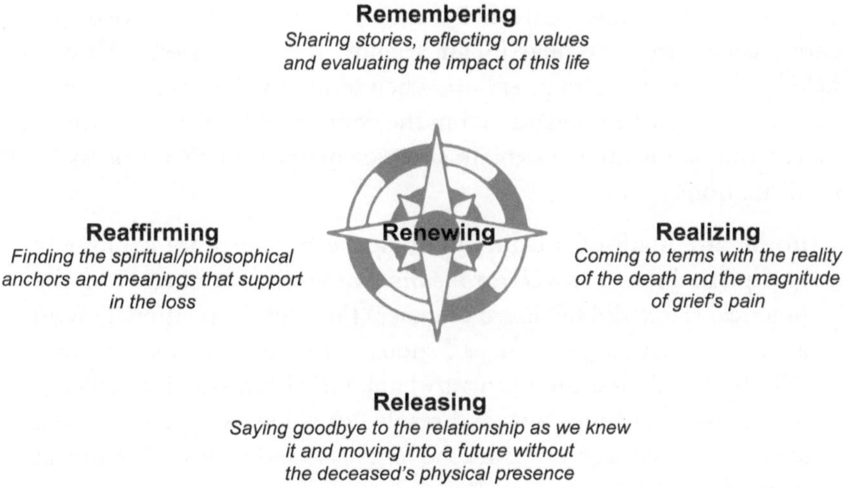

Figure 1.1 Compass Model of Bereavement

programs in the last few decades suggested such was the goal of grief. In response, around 2010, I started talking about *renewing* as a fifth process integrated with the other four.

Remembering is fundamental to the grief process as the bereaved person shares stories and reflects on the values that underlie those stories. An especially important aspect of bereavement work as reflected in grief groups, this "storytelling" can become an important tool for previously unacquainted group members to get to glimpse the lives of other group members and, vicariously, the lives of those who have died. The model encourages bereaved individuals to share details of the relationship and also to get behind the details of the stories to actually talk about (and/or write about) the values that characterized their loved one's life. A widower who describes his deceased wife's work in a community food pantry is talking not just about the details of her life but the character values of compassion and perhaps generosity.

Most bereaved individuals also engage in *reaffirming,* a process for adapting their spiritual and/or philosophical anchors in the context of making meaning in the loss. For most grieving individuals, spiritual matters do not remain unchanged in the face of loss. Frequently called "worldview" in the literature, these beliefs are deeply—though often unconsciously—held and may be so deeply imbedded in one's way of thinking that they are taken for granted (Mills, Bonner, & Francis, 2006). Sometimes, deeply held beliefs are reinforced in the experience of loss, and the individual's belief in a loving God is solidified by the care received from compassionate friends. In other cases, even deeply held beliefs do not seem to endure when tested by the apparent vagaries of loss and must be renegotiated in the context of life's experience. Neimeyer and Sands (2011) explain some of nuances of this process I call reaffirmation:

> In the aftermath of life-altering loss, the bereaved are commonly precipitated into a *search for meaning* at levels that range from the practical (*How* did my loved one die?) through the relational (*Who* am I, now that I am no longer a spouse?) to the spiritual or existential (*Why* did God allow this to happen?). How—and whether—we engage these questions and resolve or simply stop asking them shapes how we accommodate the loss itself and who we become in light of it. (p. 11)

The professional or volunteer helper might be inclined to think that the bereaved individual with no religious belief omits the adaptive process of reaffirmation. However, in practice, what I have seen is that for people whose worldview does not include adherence to an organized religious system, this tool may look more like an affirmation of the intrinsic value of life and a celebration of the deceased's most memorable characteristics (similar to the formulation in the adaptive tool of *remembering* above). In my clinical work with many dozens of bereaved parents in the latter years of work in a secular bereavement program in southern California, I found that for none of these parents did their child's death imply annihilation. While they may not have ascribed conventional religious language of an afterlife to their child's continued existence, they would not endorse an idea that their child had ceased to exist. Rather, the child might now be a "star shining down from above" or "a spirit all around me." This meaning-making work of continuing a bond with the deceased child seems to be very significant utilization of the tool of reaffirming.

Neimeyer (2010) reminded counselors and others that "a good deal of evidence" points to the importance of meaning reconstruction as a "centrally relevant process" in individuals working through their bereavement experiences. He continues that the evidence indicates an inability to reconstruct meaning in the face of loss accounts more significantly for "persistent grief symptomatology" than such "objective" factors as the cause of death, the amount of time passing since the death, and perhaps even the additional difficulties presented by violent death (p. 14). In a study of how families negotiate meaning in the face of death, Nadeau (1998) wrote:

> The meanings thus articulated relate to how well families manage after the deaths—how difficult it is for them to go on living without the lost family members. . . . It could be argued that a search for meaning comes out of the perturbation caused by a death. The status quo is upset. Existential questions are raised. The struggle to find answers to these existential questions, which is the search for meaning, is central to the grieving process. In the families who inspired this study, the ability to attach meaning and to share these meanings within the families and with others greatly affected how the families coped. (p. 3)

Realizing calls the bereaved person to admit the reality of the loss and to come full-face with the pain of grief. Rarely does a person persist for many weeks or months in the belief that his or her loved one is coming back, but the initial response to death is most often one of disbelief. For those whose religious and cultural customs permit it, seeing the body can be important in this process, especially when death came unexpectedly (Hoy, 2013). However, caregivers must be aware that the conflict between "reality" and "denial" is not a once-and-done process. One bereaved mother spoke on behalf of many when reporting: "I heard a car door slam outside and jumped up expecting to see him come through the door; within seconds, I collapsed into my chair in sobs, suddenly aware that it could not be him; he is dead." One role of the bereavement group in the face of such stories of realization is to normalize the process, reassuring group participants that they are not losing their minds.

As the bereaved person gradually lets go of *physical* connections with the deceased, the compass model posits, she is making the adaptation of *releasing*. This is not "closure" or "moving on"; rather, it is a gradual loosening of ties to the physical presence and the gradual process of thinking of the dead in terms of *psychological memory* rather than *physical presence*.

In every society thus far studied, humans do this initially through the rituals that surround death as well as in rituals enacted on anniversaries and special occasions. Whether or not the bereaved planning the rituals consider themselves religious, these ceremonies are filled with spiritual content and can be invaluable in the bereavement process. Doka (2015) wrote, "Certainly, rituals after the death can be critically important to families and others as they cope with loss" (p. 239). Then, citing the work of Rando (1984), Doka continued, "Funerals can allow mourners a sense of the reality of death, they offer a chance to ventilate feelings, to provide meaningful actions in a disorganized time, present opportunities to remember the deceased, foster a coming together of supportive others, and create an interpretation of the death according to their own philosophical or spiritual background" (p. 239).

The body is removed from the place of death, sometimes before and sometimes after preparation by family, friends, or professionals. Within days—or sometimes hours—family and community participate in anciently rooted rituals characterized by five common anchors: significant symbols, gathered community, ritual action, cultural heritage, and body's presence. These initial rituals are often revisited at significant points in the bereaved person's or family's experience, such as the unveiling of the tombstone around the first anniversary of the death observed in traditional Jewish societies (Hoy, 2013; Pine, 2015).

These four adaptive processes of the compass model are different from the linear notion of "stages" in that they are not even implied to occur in a sequential order. Moreover, bereavement is a continuous process of adaptation, so remembering, reaffirming, realizing, and releasing continue, at least in some ways, for the remaining life of the bereaved person. One happily remarried widow said, almost 30 years after her first husband's death, that on his birthday, she found herself fondly recalling the birthdays they shared in the early years of their marriage. Ironically, she had been married to her first husband for only 10 years when he died but had been married to her second husband for nearly 25 years when she reported these experiences. Especially around significant holidays and anniversaries (birthdays, wedding anniversaries, anniversaries of death, etc.), these adaptations of grief are faced afresh (Rando, 1993).

Recovery does not seem to be exactly the right word to describe the "goal" of the bereavement experience. In the aftermath of a serious injury, recovery is thought to be achieved when the patient returns to a pre-injury state of functioning. Eventually, strength and dexterity return, and at some future point, there is little if any residual damage from the injury. Terms like "full recovery" seem right to describe this process of injury from healing.

However, the grief occasioned by a death in one's family or friendship circle does not lead to recovery, to a return to pre-loss functioning. Rather than the death of a loved one being a contusion or fracture from which one recovers, the death of a loved person is more like an amputation to which one must adapt. In the compass model, *renewing* is the name given to this discovery of how one lives in a world radically changed by loss. Far from the notion of "recovery" or "closure," renewal implies a transformed worldview, a changed way of being in the world once that assumptive world is deeply shaken by the "earthquake" of profound loss (Janoff-Bulman, 1992). Rubin (1999) said his research findings and clinical practice with bereaved parents "were in line with the need to redefine loss and mourning as a process whose impact is neither clearly time-limited nor leads to a complete separation from the deceased" (pp. 688–689). In a report longitudinally examining the bereavement experiences of parents over ten years, Rubin (1989–1990) found that a degree of continuing mourning characterized parents whose young children had died and parents whose sons had died in military service. Interviews with bereaved parents demonstrated that for parents of adult sons, the loss represented a relationship nurtured over many years, consuming extensive emotional energy and relational investment. Parental grief in such cases, Rubin found, meant mourning decades of interaction. Among parents grieving the death of a younger child, the experience meant mourning a potential relationship. Through the years, grief over additional aspects of that potential relationship had to be mourned, especially corresponding to developmental milestones in the child's life.

There has been growing scholarly and clinical support for jettisoning the word *recovery* from the grief support worker's vocabulary; its presence in the first place likely grew out of the growing medicalization of bereavement in the late 20th century. Recovery is one of the terms Neimeyer, Keesee, and Fortner (2000) object to in their analysis of contemporary understandings of bereavement. Tedeschi and Calhoun (2008), whose work has been seminal in seeing traumatic events as potentially growth-inducing experiences, have also taken exception to this terminology, which they believe implies a "leaving behind of their connections to their loved ones, a connection that carries much meaning and comfort. Moreover, the term "in recovery," they posit, now carries with it a strong connection to people who are coping with addictions, at least in the West (p. 28). After dismissing other possible terms to signal the progress of bereaved people in the process, Tedeschi and Calhoun consider the word "resolution" to be a good compromise. In introducing their 814-page tome on bereavement research, Stroebe et al. (2001) wrote, "It is also important to note the general view these days that bereaved individuals do not 'get over' their loss and back to normal but rather adapt and adjust to the changed situation. Thus, labels such as 'resolution' or 'completion' of grief are deemed inappropriate" (pp. 9–10).

For its strengths in practical usefulness in clinical counseling, one shortfall of the compass model is its reliance on metaphors related to journey, and these images likely imply a fixed destination. Bereavement, however, is more like an ongoing pilgrimage without a destination, which is why the notion of "stages" does not work to describe it. The emerging consensus belief seems to be that loss is an experience that alters the rest of the bereaved person's life. The death of a parent to a young child or an adult child changes the way that child or adult encounters subsequent life experiences. Even though healthy grieving implies not organizing one's life around the loss forever, grief is a lifelong process of change, adaptation, and renewal.

THE SCIENCE OF GRIEF

The late 20th century witnessed the development of dozens of empirical instruments to measure the effects of grief on the well-being of bereaved individuals. While space does not allow a full examination of this multitude, I have noticed three instruments cited with significant regularity in the literature of bereavement research: the Texas (Revised) Inventory of Grief, the Grief Experience Inventory, and the Inventory of Complicated Grief (ICG).

Developed at the University of Texas (Houston) Medical School, the Texas Inventory of Grief was first introduced by Faschingbauer, Devaul, and Zisook (1977) and updated with revisions a few years later (Faschingbauer, 1981). Known for its simplicity, the TRIG is comprised of 13 items measuring present grief and eight items assessing life disruption due to grief in the past. The instrument has been validated with a diversity of age groups and ethnic populations, demonstrating a high degree of differentiation between uncomplicated and complicated grief (Futterman, Brown, Holland, Thompason, & Gallagher-Thompson, 2010; Nam & Eack, 2012; Sandler, Ayers, et al., 2010; Sandler, Ma, et al., 2010; Servaty-Seib & Pistole, 2007; Wilson, 2007).

Also extensively used in empirical research with bereaved individuals, the Grief Experience Inventory (Sanders, 1999; Sanders, Mauger, & Strong, 1985) includes 135 true-false items that are scored to nine bereavement scales (despair, anger/hostility, guilt, social isolation, loss of control, rumination, depersonalization, somatization, and death anxiety). Additionally, there are three validity scales to measure levels of denial, atypical responses, and social desirability and six exploratory research scales not recommended for clinical use.

A third assessment instrument frequently used in research with bereaved individuals is the Inventory of Complicated Grief (ICG), originally a 19-item Likert-scale instrument that now consists of 15 items (O'Connor, Lasgaard, Shevlin, & Guldin, 2010; Prigerson et al., 1995).

Often, it is difficult to establish an empirical basis in a growing field that has developed out of the need to help people. Much like the history of medicine, bereavement caregiving has responded to "felt needs" first and allowed its empirical results to catch up in time. Much like the interventions used in early medicine, sometimes intuition and application of studies interpolated from other fields of inquiry provided just the right mix for bereaved people to be helped. At other times, unfortunately, bereaved people were undoubtedly subjected to the same kinds of unscientific interventions as bloodletting and surgery without anesthesia. Following up on an work published a decade earlier (Silver & Wortman, 1980), Wortman and Silver (1989) reported what they considered to be pervasive myths shared by researchers, clinicians, lay caregivers, and, because of social norms, the bereaved themselves:

> Individuals who encounter a loss are expected to go through a period of intense distress; failure to experience such distress is thought to be indicative of a problem. Moreover, it is assumed that successful adjustment to loss requires that individuals "work through" or deal with their feelings of grief rather than "denying" or "repressing" them. Within a relatively brief period of time, however, people are expected to resolve their loss and recover their earlier level of functioning. (Wortman & Silver, 1989, p. 349)

One concern the authors raised was that if laypersons held unrealistic expectations about the normal course of grieving, they may be less likely to offer appropriate support to family members and friends. Their work has been widely cited for beginning the conversation about "myths" in grief, though not all theorists, clinicians, or researchers agreed with all of their premises or conclusions (Stroebe, van den Bout, & Schut, 1994; Worden, 2015). One person whose research findings did support the perspective of Wortman and Silver was Columbia scholar George Bonanno (2009). In *The Other Side of Sadness*, Bonanno suggested many bereaved individuals did not experience the debilitating distress from loss that had often been directly stated or implied in the literature. Instead, Bonanno suggested, many bereaved people demonstrate great resilience in the face of loss, though critics have rightly questioned why distress and resilience could not coexist in the same individual.

Some of Bonanno's earliest work in bereavement focused on the relationship between emotional expression and emotional repression, as well as how this relationship might affect long-term outcomes in bereavement (Horowitz, Bonanno, & Holen, 1993). This was a particularly important line of research, since predominant clinical wisdom at the time suggested verbal expression of emotion was virtually essential to make "progress" in one's grief. I remember the dominant grief *mantras* of the early 1980s, suggesting "You've got to feel it to heal it" and "Get it out or it will kill you"; Middleton, Moylan, Raphael, Burnett, and Martinek (1993) corroborated my memory a few years later. In their international study of bereavement professionals, they found that most endorsed attachment and psychodynamic perspectives on grief from which the notion of necessary catharsis has grown. Furthermore, 65% of their respondents endorsed the notion of "absent grief," generally arising from denial or from an emotional inability to express the negative aspects of the loss. Among their respondents, 76% believed that this absent grief generally gives rise to delayed grief.

In a longitudinal study of 42 conjugally bereaved individuals, Bonanno and colleagues explored these notions, attempting to better understand the relationship between emotional expression and positive outcomes in bereavement. The beginning phrase of the title of their paper in *Journal of Personality and Social Psychology* is a fair representation of their findings: "When Avoiding Unpleasant Emotions Might Not Be Such a Bad Thing" (Bonanno, Keltner, Holen, & Horowitz, 1995). Readers will find a more nuanced discussion of these findings in Chapter Seven's analysis of treatment protocols for complicated grief. Among other things, these point to the potential efficacy of exposure therapy, a well-substantiated therapeutic protocol for addressing trauma (Bryant et al., 2014).

A subsequently published report from the same study explored how observed facial expressions among widowed individuals at six months after their loss might predict long-term bereavement outcome (Bonanno & Keltner, 1997). In the study, researchers observed and video recorded the facial expression of widowed individuals during semi-structured interviews as the bereaved individuals talked about their relationship with their deceased spouse. Then, participants completed several psychological instruments, including the Texas Revised Inventory of Grief (Faschingbauer, 1981). The researchers found that positive facial expression (surprise, enjoyment, and amusement) predicted better grief adjustment at 14 and 25 months post-loss, while negative facial expression (anger, contempt, disgust, fear, and sadness) predicted worse grief adjustment at

14 and 25 months. Negative facial expression at the six-month post-loss interview also predicted poorer perceived health on the part of participants at the 14-month assessment (Bonanno & Keltner, 1997).

While these early papers did not mention the concept of resilience for which Bonanno is now so widely known, the seeds of his later thinking were certainly present. Of special interest to readers of this volume is an interpretation of these results Bonanno and Keltner (1997) expressed in the "discussion" section of their study results. There, they surmised that the minimization of negative expression and the maximization of positive communication might actually encourage better social support from the friends and family members of bereaved individuals.

Bonanno's studies have consistently shown a large percentage of bereaved individuals displaying what he and colleagues came to call the "resilience trajectory" (Bonanno, 2012, p. 755). One study examined the grief responses of 205 widowed individuals from the Changing Lives of Older Couples (CLOC) study whose spouses had died after the interviews with both husband and wife conducted in 1987 and 1988. Bonanno et al. (2002) found that 45.9% of these widowed individuals displayed this resilient pattern, exhibiting "low levels of depression both prior to the loss and through 18 months of bereavement, and had relatively few grief symptoms (e.g., intense yearning for the spouse) during bereavement" (Bonanno, 2004, p. 23). Bonanno explained further that these individuals did not exhibit such things as emotional coldness, marital dissatisfaction, or dismissive attachment when at the initial couple interview. The individuals did, however, score high on measures administered in that initial interview that predicted they would adapt well to loss, including, Bonanno reported, "acceptance of death, belief in a just world, (and) instrumental support" (p. 23). These individuals did not escape all symptoms of grief, and most reported some transient cognitive disruption, sleep disturbance, rumination, emotional yearning, and other typical manifestations of conjugal loss. However, as Bonanno pointed out, these symptoms were temporary and did not generally disrupt day-to-day functioning for these resilient bereaved individuals (Bonanno, 2004). In a more recent paper, Bonanno (2012) proposed criteria and frameworks for continuing research into the factors that might predict resilience among adults facing potentially traumatic events.

Like many paradigm-shifting notions, Bonanno's perspective was met with resistance by bereavement caregivers in some quarters. The notion that nearly half of bereaved people might exhibit this "resilient" quality, paired with the idea that "talking through" grief could actually portend difficulties in the process, turned many treasured beliefs on their heads. Nevertheless, in the fourth edition of his text, pioneer in the bereavement counseling movement J. William Worden (2009) mentioned Bonanno's resilience work in passing and then concluded, "I think this focus is overdue" (p. 6).

DO GRIEF INTERVENTIONS HELP?

One of the most vexing questions of the early 21st century has been, "Does grief counseling help bereaved people?" In a continuing quest to ground supportive interventions in the best empirical evidence, it is right to question the efficacy of the supportive strategies that have become conventional wisdom in the bereavement support community.

In one early review of then-current studies, Jordan and Neimeyer (2003) write:

> It is a part of the assumptive world of most bereavement caregivers that their interventions work. Most practitioners believe that what they do is helpful and necessary and that it does no harm. Moreover, most grief counselors would probably argue that most mourners would benefit from the services they offer. Understandably, caregivers in the helping professions want to believe that their work is valuable and their competence is recognized. (p. 765)

One issue that clouds the interpretation of bereavement research data is the widely-held belief by bereavement professionals that most grief is self-limiting. In other words, the vast majority of bereaved individuals eventually move adaptively through the loss so that they are able to function well emotionally, socially, and physically in their chosen daily activities (Bonanno, 2009; Jordan & Neimeyer, 2003; Stroebe et al., 2001). Whatever else can be said about these bereaved, at some point after their loss, they have adapted to the experience; in the task language of Worden (2009), these bereaved have adjusted to a world without the deceased (task 3) and have found "an enduring connection with the deceased in the midst of embarking on a new life" (task 4) (pp. 46, 50). Worden goes on to explain that the noncompletion of this task is "perhaps not living. One's life has stopped with the death and has not resumed" (p. 52).

There are several implications of this debate for professional and volunteer helpers who seek to align their interventions with the best available research findings. First, there are manifold ethical and procedural issues with bereavement outcomes research. In a provocative article on research ethics, Balk (1995) questions the issues of assigning people with clear bereavement-related distress to a nonintervention control group. He reviews a study of bereaved college students in which an unexpectedly large portion of students assigned to the nonintervention control group showed distress about the loss and then quoted a colleague who wondered if some simply could not bear the rekindling of distress without hope of help. He laments the National Institute of Mental Health review committee's rejection of what he saw as a plausible solution to the problem. He further reminds researchers and clinicians alike that in bereavement research, the well-intended effort to protect research participants from risk while also contributing to the scientific knowledge of a field can appear, at least at times, to be at cross-purposes.

Second, research results are not always as clear cut as they might seem. Larson and Hoyt (2007) refer to an oft-cited study reporting that 38% of bereaved individuals actually were worse off because of their grief treatment. The frequency of citation in subsequent literature was primarily from a paper by Robert Neimeyer (2000), a leading figure in bereavement studies. However, as Larson and Hoyt note, the actual implications drawn by Neimeyer in the cited paper rely on a brief unpublished dissertation by one of his students (Fortner, 1999) who actually introduced the notion of treatment-induced deterioration effects (TIDE) findings. Larson and Hoyt further point out that this "evidence" relies on a suspicious methodology developed in a master's thesis; they write, "The TIDE technique represents an unorthodox statistical analysis—one that has never been subjected to peer review" (p. 349) and which they suggest, based on further investigation, would not pass the tests of blind peer review.

The advice given to beginning researchers to trace their conclusions back to the original source seem more important than ever in this light. Several years after writing the dissertation, Fortner (2008) corrected a formulaic error from the paper without retracting the original conclusion. More than a decade after the original dissertation and the citation by Neimeyer (2000) the "dust" had not completely settled. Without agreeing with Larson and Hoyt's assumption that grief interventions are helpful, Schut (2010) concluded, "Considering the impact of this original message (of grief counseling's harmful effects), we can only be thankful to Larson and Hoyt for scrutinizing the scientific basis of that claim. It is safe to say now that claims of deterioration effects of grief interventions have no sound empirical basis" (p. 8).

Third, analyses purporting to investigate the efficacy of bereavement interventions often fall prey to their own biases and failure to control variables. For example, the previously mentioned study by Fortner (1999) mixes analysis of varied bereavement interventions implemented by a wide range of caregivers including both lay peer support group leaders on one end of the continuum and highly trained and experienced mental health clinicians on the other. Incidentally, 18 of the 23 studies Fortner examined were interventions led by professional therapists, while anecdotal observation indicates these are rarely the people leading the kinds of community-based bereavement support programs considered in this volume.

Fourth, I am reminded of the decades-old sociological principle to which I referred in the introduction to this book: "However, not everything that can be counted counts, and not everything that counts can be counted" (Cameron, 1963, p. 13). Bereaved individuals who flock to bereavement support groups and apparently find therein enough help to refer their newly bereaved friends, and even, on occasion, become leaders of groups themselves, are not likely swayed by the conflicting research reports about whether or not various kinds of bereavement interventions work.

Many bereaved individuals attend a group session or two only to determine "This is not for me" and, therefore, never attend again. But for countless others, whether because of something that happens in the interpersonal dynamic of shared social support, the educational content that normalizes the bereavement experience and points a way forward, and the sense that here is a place where my life situation is understood, grief groups work. Just because we have not yet found the best ways to measure effectiveness does not prove that interventions among the bereaved are therefore ineffective.

GLOBAL VILLAGE: THE ROLE OF CULTURE IN BEREAVEMENT

Like many of the theoretical formulations and practice concepts surrounding contemporary psychology, much of the early thinking in bereavement developed out of a European-American framework (Sue, Bingham, Porché-Burke, & Vasquez, 1999). This worldview prizes individualism and privacy while seeing the work of grief as the severing of attachment bonds (Vasquez, 2015). Both through the LEAP study and in my own connections with clinical colleagues through the years, I have heard the oft-observed notion that bereavement support groups are overwhelmingly white, meaning that the participants in groups, at least across the North American landscape, tends to not include representatives from many minority people groups. There are exceptions, of course. Nearly 25 years ago, I interacted with the bereavement leadership of a large African-American congregation in our city, and their group, made up mostly of bereaved African Americans, was providing important support to members of their congregation and community. One respondent of the LEAP study working in a multicultural community where nearly half of the population is Latino/a reported about half of the participants in her bereavement groups were also Latino/a. While these are important examples, they do not represent the experiences of most LEAP study respondents or my own observations of bereavement groups in the multicultural milieu of the Los Angeles area.

Limited access to services is one possible reason for this "lack of color" in bereavement services. In discussing the locations where groups are held, LEAP study respondents frequently described the location of their groups with language similar to one respondent: "You will find our groups all out in the 'Lily white suburbs.' " The implication of this group leader and others interviewed is that suburban locations are often far away from the communities where underserved populations live. In contrast, one LEAP study respondent pointed out that participants in the groups she oversees tend to come from lower socioeconomic strata, owing, she believes, to the fact that higher-income bereaved have access to professional psychotherapy because they have private insurance or the means to pay. Whether her assessment is correct or not is beyond the scope of this book, but it is almost without doubt that bereaved individuals with less economic resources are most dependent on the typically free services of bereavement support groups. If transportation is limited, the chance of individuals and families participating in groups is significantly reduced. Moreover, people want to fit in, and they will often not accept services if sensing "I am the only one like me here."

Another respondent in the LEAP study described efforts to build relationships between the organization's child program coordinator and school counselors at sites in the inner city. This agency runs several dozen school-based groups for bereaved children and teens every year, and the program coordinator indicated they are mostly in schools serving communities where many underserved families live. "These are parents who would have to ride the bus five or ten miles to come to our evening program, a trip that could easily take an hour each way and cost their family $15. Our experience over the last 20 years is that is not going to happen." As an outgrowth from the school-based program for children, one of the agency's clinicians regularly offers workshops for parent groups at the same schools. In contrast to the stereotyped notion that "those schools" cannot engage parents, these programs are exceptionally well attended.

Over the last decade or two, this organization has received many accolades from local school and community officials for the agency's laudable efforts at helping underserved communities. This LEAP respondent pointed out one more "fringe benefit" that could easily be overlooked by readers: "We depend on contributions and grants. Foundations want to know what you are doing for the underserved. We can point to this program and the families we have helped. Case closed."

Another important issue at the intersection of multiculturalism and bereavement is that customs, practices, and beliefs about death and bereavement are likely culturally bound constructs. In contrast to the "dominant culture" ideas expressed above, ethnically diverse practices often focus on creating new relationships with the deceased, treating the dead with respect, connecting the spiritual and material worlds, and observing characteristically longer mourning periods (Sue et al., 1999; Vasquez, 2015). Professional and volunteer caregivers alike must guard against easy stereotyping and implicit bias, which often insidiously works its way into practice. Though priorities may be shifting, Hall (1997) suggested that ethnic researchers and clinicians have had little option other than to extrapolate data and find culturally appropriate interventions based on research with Europeans given that so little research has focused on ethnic groups.

In her closing keynote address at the 37th annual conference of the Association for Death Education and Counseling, Melba J.T. Vasquez (2015) challenged listeners with a humble appraisal of her own struggles with bias. Pointing out that she is a fourth-generation Mexican immigrant to the United States, Vasquez reminded listeners that we must constantly develop our own skills at becoming open to the different ways of coping with death. Sometimes, she indicated, our biases are not against people of other nationalities and ethnicities. She illustrated the principle through a captivating story from the waning weeks of her 83-year-old grandmother's life. Children and grandchildren gathered for an early fall Thanksgiving feast. A Catholic Mass began the day, but since the son hosting the party had become a Baptist, he and his wife invited their minister to preach what Vasquez described as a Spanish language "hellfire and brimstone" sermon. "Most of us politely observed at a distance," she remarked, "and tried not to roll our elitist judgmental eyes."

After the sermon, however, the minister led a profoundly meaningful ritual, offering a quiet time for each adult child to speak private words to their mother, providing the dying matriarch with oil to dab on the forehead of each adult child. Vasquez thoughtfully told the gathered conference goers, "That day, I observed the most effective and powerful resolution and closure activity ever conducted by any mental health expert. It was humbling to acknowledge that someone whom I had negatively appraised out of my unfamiliarity had something so amazing to provide this family in pain" (Vasquez, 2015 cited in Hoy, 2015).

The population of a geographical area changes due to two forces: from natural population change (births and deaths) and from migration. If the sum of births and in-migrations exceeds the sum of deaths and out-migrations, the population grows. English-speaking Western nations (the United Kingdom, Canada, the United States, Australia, and New Zealand as examples) have experienced in-migration throughout their histories. Americans like to think of the United States as a "melting pot," but in historical reality, many nations, including those of the developing world, have been "melting pots" at some point in their history. I observed this on my first trip to Kenya; while in Kisumu, I found a large population of Indian business owners whose parents and grandparents had emigrated from that British colony at the beginning of the 20th century. Sometimes, the population of immigrants overwhelms the indigenous population, resulting all too often in dramatic demonstrations of racial violence and genocide.

In addition to intentional policies that institutionalize prejudice against minority people, individuals who are not part of the dominant culture often simply get overlooked for services. In the LEAP study, I was curious to know about the attempts being made by organizations to reach out to bereaved individuals who were part of these often-overlooked groups. What I found were "spotty" efforts, including the organization above that reaches out intentionally to inner city schools and one group that monitors ethnic involvement in its programs and closely compares it to the community's population. However, others reported neither efforts nor, in some cases, much interest in reaching underserved communities. One program administrator pointed out that the organization's programs were advertised widely and all were welcome, regardless of ethnicity or culture. "We don't worry much about who comes and who doesn't."

The debates that have raged about the nature of bereavement in the last few decades are far from over. How grief is experienced and how much of that modeling is influenced by culture is a topic of continuing discussion. To be sure, some manifestations of grief are normal and predict no rising risk of long-term disability. On the other hand, mounting research evidence demonstrates that some grief goes seriously awry, and determining what those indicators and risk factors are must be a subject of continuing inquiry. How this latter class of bereavements is addressed in bereavement groups will be the subject of Chapter Seven, whether these experiences with bereavement are labeled as "complicated grief," "prolonged grief," or, in the recent publication of the *Diagnostic and Statistical Manual (DSM-5)*, "Complex Bereavement Related Disorder."

One significant need for both the bereaved and for the caregiving professionals and volunteers who provide support to them is an organizational framework, a way to make sense of the process of grief. The various models of bereavement all attempt to provide just that framework. Whether one is a member of the dominant cultural group within a geographical place or is part of a minority group, whether one has said goodbye to a child, parent, spouse, sibling, or friend, what bereaved people desire is a way to make sense. How that desire for sense making relates to the human needs for support, especially in the context of a bereavement support group, is the topic to which we next turn.

QUESTIONS FOR REFLECTION AND DISCUSSION

- In your early experiences or training about loss, what did you learn about grief? How have those views changed?
- To which grief model or combination of models are you most drawn? What factors in that model (those models) help you understand bereavement most clearly? Why?
- What do you make of the debates about the science of bereavement? Are there parts of this conversation to which you feel drawn to pursue in your own learning?
- What are some of your own customs and beliefs about death, loss, and grief that you assume to be "universal"? Is there any evidence they might be culturally bound?

CHAPTER 2

Social Groups and the Support of Bereaved Individuals

When Robert walked into the local chapter meeting of the Compassionate Friends, he was a bereaved single father. After he and his wife, Kate, divorced eight years earlier, they had remained "on good terms," but that was mostly, he later admitted, to make life better for the kids, who were 11 and 14 at the time. The investment in acting "civil" to one another "for the sake of the children" had seemingly paid off. Their daughter, Amanda, had recently graduated college and taught third grade at an elementary school nearby. She and her fiancé were planning their wedding for later in the year.

Seven months ago, their son, Devin, now age 19, died in a horrific high-speed crash while driving the motorcycle that Kate and her new husband gave Devin for Christmas. Robert was devastated at the death of his only son, in whom he had invested so much. Robert and Kate's youngest son was a "great kid," the proud dad recounted. He was an okay student, but he was a fantastic mechanic. Most of all, Robert told the other bereaved parents that night, "Devin had a soft spot for anybody in need. He would give you the shirt off his back. He never met someone he couldn't get along with."

Though Robert's need to connect with a caring support network is a human characteristic as old as humankind, the *formal* network of other bereaved parents is a recent innovation in the scope of human history. As an organization, the small British group that would become the Compassionate Friends is less than five decades old, though it counts nearly 700 local chapters in more than 31 nations, including Argentina, Australia, Belgium, Peru, France, the Netherlands, Poland, Canada, and the United States (Compassionate Friends, 2015). At a loss for how to provide support for two couples whose children died days apart in the

British hospital where he was a young chaplain, Rev. Simon Stephens struck on the idea of getting these parents together around a kitchen table. That was in 1969 (Loder, 2010). The local chapter of the Compassionate Friends Robert joined was one of the first begun in Canada in the late 1970s.

Robert's experience receiving strong social support from his Compassionate Friends group was mirrored by what Rosemary discovered after her husband's death. Less than a month after Rosemary's husband died, a volunteer from the Community Together support service in her town reached out to provide social support to this newly bereaved widow. Marge, the volunteer, explained that she had been amazed by the help she had gotten from her Community Together volunteer three years earlier when her own husband died. As different as are the experiences of widows from bereaved parents, what both Robert and Rosemary discovered is that social support is invaluable, especially when it comes from people who have also experienced a similar loss. The support both received owed its genesis to the same period of history; about the same time Rev. Stephens was experimenting with the best ways to support bereaved parents in the United Kingdom, Phyllis Silverman (1967, 1969, 2004) was discovering ways to support widows in the United States. Elder and Burke (2015) trace the origin of the contemporary bereavement support group to Silverman's widow-to-widow work, and the community organization from which Rosemary received such caring support had been modeled after Silverman's program.

After the September 11, 2001, terrorist attacks, many questioned the need for intervention for most bereaved individuals, suggesting instead that people only need the care of their community. To their credit, these critics reminded the general public and professional caregivers alike that humans are an incredibly resilient lot and that most, even when exposed to harrowing circumstances, will not need the intervention of a mental health professional (Sommers & Satel, 2005). Unfortunately, these critics often mix together grief interventions with trauma counseling and depend on the forum afforded by major media's op-ed pages to broker their opinions. In response to events like the Columbine (Colorado) school shooting, Satel (1999) suggested a prescription that is difficult to access for many suffering individuals: "Most people, in fact, are quite resilient and don't need registered experts to deal with anguish. Are our priests and rabbis not up to the task? Are our families' instincts to comfort not keen enough?" (p. A25). Her rhetorical question implies that most bereaved individuals sense the supportive helpfulness of caring family members and attentive clergy. Unfortunately, this is all too often not the case.

From the vantage point of 35 years, Silverman (2004) wrote that the detractors made a valid point, one she had been making for many years. In introducing the second edition of her helpful volume on widowhood, she wrote, "I join in the debate with this book on the side that recognizes the importance of social support from peers. Perhaps these issues should not be posed as a competition. (Everyone needs) a 'little help from a friend.' This book is about the role of a particular friend, one who has been down the same road before" (p. xiv). Silverman was not practicing revisionist history; she had suggested the same truism in her original report about the success of the widow-to-widow program. In that paper, she concluded, "I believe that the base for preventive work is not the mental health clinic, which should reserve its highly skilled services for those who are seriously disturbed and require special care; prevention should be the work of people and agencies that deal with people as they move through the normal phases of a life cycle" (Silverman, 1969, p. 337).

Her initial widow-to-widow program utilized the services of five "aides," who all had been widowed for a period between two and five years. After obtaining contact information from death certificate data, the aides wrote an informal note to each widow offering to visit in the home. The results were impressive; of the 91 widows contacted in the first seven months, 70% accepted the offer of the aide's support, with half receiving visits at home and the other half interacting by telephone. Eleven simply declined further contact, while 12 others acknowledged the program sounded like a good idea but that they did not see themselves in need of help.

In the first month, aides reported that widows primarily wanted to talk. They shared details of their husbands' deaths, expressed fears about the unknown future, wondered aloud about how to raise children alone, and articulated concerns about financial matters. About the work of these widowed peers, Silverman (1969) wrote, "Most people are quite able to care for themselves and really need only the special help that comes from having a friendly ear to listen and a shoulder on which they can, in a sense, cry without feeling that they are imposing or being told to 'keep a stiff upper lip' and to control themselves" (p. 335). The needs of widows to have friendly ears and shoulders inspired the first widow-to-widow support groups Silverman began to complement the individual support work being done.

For some of her target audience, three and one-half decades had not changed the expectation of some bereaved individuals' family and friends for the grieving to "control themselves." Silverman (2004) quoted one young widow who voiced a need for others who understood the dilemmas. Noting she had been on antidepressant medication since her husband's illness, she recounted experience with her own family members. When she was having a particularly bad day, family members would ask, "Have you had your pills today?" apparently assuming antidepressants to be a "magic potion" (p. 34).

BETTER TOGETHER THAN APART

Recently, Kosminsky and Jordan (2016) have joined the chorus of bereavement caregivers to assert that the empirical evidence is considerable in demonstrating that social support is a key factor in the experiences of bereavement and trauma. They wrote that social support is important in helping protect individuals from difficult life experiences. Likely, this social support would have been a major factor in the helpful experiences recounted by individuals like Robert and Rosemary who join bereavement support groups.

This need for social support Robert and Rosemary experienced, however, is part of a much older tradition. For as long as our ancestors have walked on two feet, evidence suggests that humans have gathered themselves in groups. The terms kinship, tribe, and nation used widely in anthropology demonstrate the ubiquitous presence of such people groupings across the globe (Bailey & Peoples, 2014). However, this "grouping" behavior is not only a human trait; it is present among other species, as well. Sumpter (2010) writes:

> Animal groups provide many key examples of collective phenomena. They also provide some of the most spectacular and fascinating sights in the natural world. Flocks of birds turning in unison or migrating in well ordered formation; fish shoals splitting and reforming as they outmaneuver a predator; swarms of honeybees settled on a branch of a tree while colony members use dances to debate where they will fly; and the long bifurcating trails along which ants transport food and materials have all long fascinated scientists. There is something captivating about the patterns these groups create. They are neither entirely regular, nor are they entirely random. They are, quite simply, complex. (p. 2)

Animal individuals gather in groups to achieve a number of purposes, including the sharing of information and resources. Ants, honeybees, and naked mole rats are just a few of the species that communicate between individuals to encourage the sharing of food. For example, naked mole rats have been observed to leave odor trails and chirp loudly on the way back to the nest from a discovered food source. Investigators have watched as the rats display their discovered food for nestmates to see, apparently with a desire to altruistically share their newfound resources (Sumpter, 2010).

Seemingly altruistic behavior among species is understandable as individuals incorporate a pattern of mutual interdependence. Only in solidarity with other members of the community, the theory posits, is the chance of long-term survival increased and the risk of starvation or predator reduced. Though not living in the risk category of naked mole rats, bereaved humans do encounter specific, quantifiable risk. Bereavement has been shown in numerous studies to increase the individual's risk for significant mental and physical health impairments (Shear, Ghesquiere, & Glickman, 2013; Stroebe, Schut, & Stroebe, 2007). Studies are ongoing to discover how social support may be a buffer against some of these risks for illness and mortality.

Bereaved individuals frequently derive their primary social support from their own kinship circle of people drawn together by birth or marriage. However, kinship does not always mean "official" relationship, as Nuttal (2000) pointed out in his illustration from Greenland. In that society, when a relationship does not already exist, one can be created, and individuals can withdraw from kinship relationships if they regard them as unhelpful.

What matters most is not how one is related by lineage; what seems to make the most difference across cultures is the degree of relationship present. Many small-scale societies look after the needs of the bereaved collectively, whether one is "in the family" or not. As individuals move farther away from their nuclear family and affiliate with networks, they usually choose those network affiliations to join with people who share ideological, economic, or life-stage interests. Studying the ways in which individuals choose to affiliate in these groups is likely the most instructive for understanding how bereavement groups begin, thrive, and eventually, decline and die.

Carl Rogers (1970) made a clear distinction between natural kinship groups and those whose purpose is business tasks, education, or in this context, therapeutic intervention. This latter kind of group is a "planned, intensive group experience" (p. 1). Rogers traced the origin of this planned, intensive group experience to the midcentury education groups of Massachusetts Institute of Technology psychologist Karl

Lewin. Lewin's colleagues and students continued these "T-Groups" (for "training") after his death in 1947. These groups were certainly intended to develop more effective business practices, but they did so by helping business leaders develop interpersonal skills.

Meanwhile, Rogers and his colleagues at the University of Chicago Counseling Center were at work developing a Veterans Administration-sponsored model for training counselors to support veterans returning from World War II. Rogers reflected that the counseling center staff felt that the training needed to be more than cognitive, so they set out to provide an intensive group experience for trainees in order to create better self-awareness, to discover attitudes that would prove counterproductive in the counseling experience, and to create relationships between colleagues that they could carry into their work.

Arguably, the father of groups designed for psychosocial support was Joseph Hershey Pratt. In his treatment of patients with advanced tuberculosis, the Boston, Massachusetts, internist determined that effective treatment must attend to more than physical symptoms that portrayed the advancement of the disease. The tuberculosis support "classes" he developed consisted of sharing from the journals each patient kept and testimonials from successful patients. Apparently, the mutual support enjoyed by the patients helped manage the depression and isolation that were so common with the disease. (Raphael & Wilson, 2000; Yalom, 1995).

The encounter group model Carl Rogers developed in the 1960s created a structure for the deep interpersonal sharing kinds of group work he envisioned. Late into his life, Rogers used the encounter group model to bring together people from varied political factions and worldviews. He used it in work with Catholics and Protestants in Northern Ireland and in the interactions between blacks and whites in South Africa (Goleman, 1987). From the perspective of more than a half-century of history, it seems that Rogers' early work in these "encounter" groups paired with his significant contribution of client-centered therapy made a significant contribution to what we know today as the bereavement support group. From my perspective, most of the techniques and strategies used in developing groups for grieving people today had their origin in Rogers' work.

In my own practice in southern California during the 1990s, I led a weekly group for widows and widowers in a local senior citizen community center. Many of the participants knew each other from other activities at the center, whether they were dance classes, exercise activities, travel clubs, or congregate meals. The shared community was significant. They connected generationally; participants were all older than 50, and most were in their 70s or 80s. They connected according to their psychological/emotional state; they all had become widows in recent months. Not every recently widowed senior who participated in the activities of the senior center joined our group; some looked to their faith community or their own nuclear family as their "support group." Nevertheless, the senior center's staff kept regular center users aware of the varied opportunities for groups, including the one I led for widowed older adults.

Quite anecdotally, I observed that the majority of older widowed individuals who joined this group were not in close, personal contact with their nuclear family. In many cases, adult children had moved from the area, even if that geographical mobility had taken them only to another part of southern California. Adult children, for example, who had moved from our coastal community in the southern part of Los Angeles County to the San Fernando Valley in the northwest faced travel times to visit their widowed parents that could easily exceed two hours. With the crowded schedules that are frequently part of middle- and upper-income families—dance lessons, gymnastics, soccer, and a host of school activities—paired with working single parents or two working parents, widowed elders were often left alone. This phenomenon might be one reason so many people referred to this group as their "lifeline."

Fors and Lennartsson (2008) observed a similar pattern in their analysis of data from a large Swedish sample of adults. Adults working in or retired from nonmanual occupations were less likely than their so-called blue collar colleagues to live close to or have weekly contact with their families. This social construction of the grief experience is essential to understanding the historical rise and potential usefulness of bereavement support groups. As Lofland (1985) understood it, grief "is an emotion, however much based in biological capacities, which touches directly on the mutual interdependence of selves and societies, of actors and others, of me and you" (p. 181). In short, bereavement is experienced both individually and socially.

The urban mobility of humans has not diminished the need for social connection; if anything, it has increased that need. While an examination of contemporary social theories such as cosmopolitanism (Appiah, 2007), postmodernity (Best & Kellner, 1997; Butler, 2002), second modernity (Beck, Bonss, & Lau, 2003), and globalization (James & Steger, 2014) are beyond the scope of this book, these theories share an appreciation for the increasing role of social networks in the lives of individuals. In a provocative study of adolescents in Sydney, Australia, Turner, Halse, and Sriprakash (2014) found that their primarily immigrant sample placed high priority on connections with family, community, and religious community. Interestingly, they wrote,

> While the experience of migration, geographic mobility and family dispersal provided a strong foundation for a global awareness and a cosmopolitan identity, the everyday experience and consciousness of these young people focused overwhelmingly on their local neighbourhood. Further, despite living amidst a diverse range of cultures, communities and ethnic groups and in a multicultural society, the cultural spaces occupied by these young people were defined by family, kinship and ethnic groups in ways that appeared strongly separated and bounded from other ethnic groups. (p. 88)

Turner et al. (2014) noted the paradox that can be present in such tight-knit communities. Such connections can, in fact, intensify social isolation because the time and energy invested in maintaining and growing family relationships can hinder development of relationships with peers in the larger community. They wrote, "This, in turn, limits young people's capacity to establish the social capital required for their longer-term social and economic well-being" (p. 95) including the ability to get jobs and to connect with other people in facing crisis.

There are limits to the ability of one's natural social group to provide support in a crisis. Especially when multiple family members suffer the same devastating loss, they often need resources outside of themselves to cope with the experience (Nadeau, 1998; Shapiro, 1994; Walsh & McGoldrick, 2004). Entire communities grieve, and while the shared history can make storytelling and remembrance more robust, the downside to such exclusive reliance on internal, existing support is that it can be very difficult for members of the social group to reach outside. The shame and loss of "face" can simply be too overwhelming. Most of us who grew up in the American South heard the adage, "Don't air your dirty laundry in public," but this maxim is part of the cultural expectation of many groups around the world. Seemingly, the more kinship-oriented a society is, the more unlikely individuals will reach outside of that kinship circle for support, even when it might be in their best interest.

As a cultural group, firefighters are well known for getting their primary community belonging needs met within the "brotherhood." At least in departments like the Fire Department of New York (FDNY), the high number of firefighters from Irish and Italian descent, coupled with the prejudice these immigrant groups historically faced from politicians and the then-dominant communities, helped fuel an insular camaraderie within the department (Greene, Kane, Christ, Lynch, & Corrigan, 2006). In addition to serving in a stressful, high-intensity occupation, these individuals spend large quantities of time together waiting to work, amplified by time together on hobbies and projects of mutual interest in their off-duty time. While this camaraderie potentially creates a strong social support system in the face of crisis, that natural system can be overwhelmed in the face of group-wide crisis and trauma (Cowman, Ferrari, & Liao-Troth, 2004).

In an event like the 9/11 terrorist attacks, where more than 340 New York City firefighters died, any natural support system would be overwhelmed, leaving high prevalence of posttraumatic stress disorder and depression in its wake (Caramanica, Brackbill, Liao, & Stellman, 2014; Chiu et al., 2011). Grief and trauma are not the same experiences, though in cases like the terror attacks they generally co-exist. Moreover, traumatic experiences potentially complicate bereavement in significant ways; trauma in the bereavement support group will be addressed in Chapter 7.

In their study of the Scottish Tak Tent cancer support program, Deans, Bennett-Emslie, Weir, Smith, and Kaye (1988) observed that support group members came mostly from people with higher socioeconomic status. But while higher income people seem to be more ready to join support groups than people with lower levels of economic resources, it is likely that people in traditional immigrant communities and in much of the developing world possess more refined natural support systems. Rosales (2013) observed a deep connection between Mexican and Guatemalan *fruteros* (street fruit vendors) in Los Angeles, determining that the network of *paisanos* provides important functions, often providing immigration information, storage for fruit carts, equipment purchase information, and micro-financing. In other words, the perceived need for social support outside one's natural networks observed among middle-income and higher-income lifestyles might be needs that are not perceived to be lacking in the first place among people of lower socioeconomic status.

Socioeconomic status and ethnicity are certainly not causally related to one another; immigrants to any society are not all among the poorest strata of society. However, the observations of Turner et al. (2014), paired with the results discovered by Fors and Lennartsson (2008), may provide important considerations for program leaders who attempt to build a group for people outside of the dominant support group crowd.

As a social group with an identified purpose, the bereavement support group movement, it should be noted, grew up in a North American context among people of northern and northwestern European descent. Possibly, the frustration many Caucasian bereavement program leaders express with their inability to attract large numbers of nonwhite participants to support groups is at least in part because there is a tighter social circle already in place among some of these groups.

Social networks have undergone somewhat of a metamorphosis as the world has become more urbanized; whether urbanization has actually caused the change is a matter of some speculation. As individuals have moved away from family farms and small interrelated villages toward cities, where production and social roles are more specialized, individuals choose the social groups of which they will be a part. Workmates and housing neighbors are theoretically part of one's social network, but whether one chooses to actually socialize with those individuals is an entirely different matter. This differentiation of social roles and relationships into groups one joins because of interest is very different than the society where one is born into relationships. There is truth in the old tongue-and-cheek axiom, "You choose your friends, but you're stuck with your family."

Bereavement support groups enjoy this "affinity group of choice" status. While no individuals participating in a bereavement support group are happy to be bereaved, they generally express gratitude that they have found a group of people who understand. They sense affinity with that group, perhaps because of a common relationship to the deceased (bereaved parents or widows), because of a common kind of loss (Survivors of Suicide or Parents of Murdered Children), or because of common beliefs and values (church bereavement group). Except for those rare cases where a court has ordered individuals to "get bereavement counseling" and they have found their way into the group, people voluntarily affiliate with bereavement groups. Incidentally, because the clinic I served in Los Angeles was a favorite referral center for the county family court, we received many of those court-ordered counseling cases. In my experience, individuals participating in groups because of court order were frequently less engaged with the group experience than those individuals who came of their own free volition.

Urban life also provides far more opportunity for individuals to "specialize" in the types of support they receive. How this works is clear in bereavement support groups. A remote rural community of 800 individuals is unlikely to be able to support a widows group, a bereaved parents group, and a suicide survivors group. Individuals in a city of 500,000 are far more likely to find such specialization.

Grief-related social support is activated almost immediately after the death in most societies, though the first formal opportunity for communal social support occurs in the organized funeral rituals. Kellehear (2007) cited the work of Emile Durkheim to support his notion that funeral rites help integrate and reintegrate people in the midst of crisis by restoring order and control in the midst of emotional chaos. Kellehear wrote,

> Death and dying rites in particular helped people to let go of the dead and presumably helped the dying let go of the living. These rites also permitted the development of a structure or plan for the orderly expression of powerful emotions, allowing potential chaos to be controlled but with the social and emotional support of others. In fact, it is the presence of others that performs the actual control because they can physically support, encourage and help with the emotional and social work by sharing the task of control. (p. 114)

For his part, Durkheim (1982/1895) considered the role of social groups to be paramount in truly understanding the psychology of the individual.

> Whenever elements of any kind combine, by virtue of this combination they give rise to new phenomena. One is therefore forced to conceive of these phenomena as residing, not in the elements, but in the entity formed by the union of these elements . . . what we maintain regarding life could be reaffirmed for every possible kind of synthesis. The hardness of bronze lies neither in the copper, nor in the tin, nor in the lead which have been used to form it, which are all soft or malleable bodies. The hardness arises from the mixing of them. The liquidity of water, its sustaining and other properties, are not in the two gases of which it is composed, but in the complex substance which they form by coming together. (p. 39)

What draws groups of people together in such a way that the synergy Durkheim observed is greater than the sum of the parts? Individuals get their belonging needs met in a diversity of ways, but they seem to gravitate to groups based on three interrelated factors: shared history, shared values, and shared purpose. Theoretically, group cohesion is greater with significant overlap among these three factors.

A sense of shared *history* at least partially explains the connection between members of families. Lineage is a strong shared history. Weil (2013) suggested that the interest in genealogy engages people of "all origins and persuasions, who join hundreds of genealogical organizations and spend a significant portion of their time and money researching their roots in libraries and archival repositories or at home on the Internet" (p. 2). Identity is the substance genealogical hobbyists are exploring, Weil argued, and the quest seems more concerned with discovering their own identities rather than those of their ancestors. This shared sense of historical identity is present in virtually all social groups, and it is a core component of a sense of belonging. However, even community bereavement groups of individuals previously unrelated to each other quickly develop a sense of shared history simply because of the similarity of life experiences and loss.

Social groups also seem to be drawn together by a sense of shared *values*. Political organizations, faith communities, and an array of nonprofit[1] entities exemplify the grouping together of people because they share a common set of values. Among bereavement groups, this component of belonging is likely most often seen in groups that are developed by faith communities or by individuals and organizations particularly concerned about a particular kind of commonly disenfranchised grief such as miscarriage, death by suicide, or gay/lesbian partner loss. The shared values observed in these groups consist of core beliefs about the nature of the relationship and or the loss as well as a value of compassion toward those commonly on the "outside" of traditional structures of social support.

Finally, social groups can be drawn together by shared *purposes*. Dageid (2014) asked 49 participants in support groups for persons living with HIV/AIDS in South Africa why they were part of the group. Fifty-nine percent indicated they participated in the group to gain information, and 53% indicated they were part of the group for the social support they derived from it. Deans and colleagues (1988) saw similar results in their study of Scottish individuals involved in cancer support groups, with participants indicating satisfaction the groups had allowed them to make new friends, learn more about cancer, and connect with other individuals dealing with similar illness. Interestingly, one of the often-articulated purposes of participants was that they would sense their presence in the group would be helpful to others, and this was a purpose not generally seen as fulfilled.

Participants in bereavement groups describe their goals in joining a group with such terms as making sure one's experience with loss is "normal," establishing connections with understanding others, and gaining information/education/resources about the grief process. Hughes (1995) helpfully reminded group leaders that though bereaved people attending groups may have difficulty articulating their goals and expectations, they definitely have them: "They do not attend support groups because they have nothing else to do" (p. 75). However, she continued, the goals and expectations of the prospective participants might be very different from the intended purpose of the group, and the screening interview is the appropriate time for facilitator and prospective participant to discuss those differences.

The confluence of shared history, values, and purpose may partially explain the growing interest in bereavement support groups based in faith communities. Representatives from churches and temples of all sizes, doctrinal perspectives, and worship styles have contacted me increasingly in recent years seeking advice and resources related to establishing bereavement groups. The leaders in some faith communities seem to think loss needs to be dealt with through a specifically spiritual framework and that the individual's own faith community will do that with more consonance than a community-wide bereavement group. The reading of sacred scripture and the offering of prayers are sometimes seen as essential ingredients in such groups, and locating the group meeting within the structure of the faith community seems to be an easier way to offer a tailor-made spiritual experience to mourners.

Undoubtedly, the meteoric growth of the GriefShare model in recent years is an example of the desire for some Christian churches to provide for their own participants through a ready-made grief support program. The program consists of 13 DVD presentations featuring a diversity of individuals offering perspectives and insight on their own grief journey and providing practical guidance for bereaved people. According to the organization's website, "thousands" of GriefShare support groups meet across the United States, Canada, and 10 other countries, led by "people who understand what you are going through and want to help. You'll gain access to valuable GriefShare resources to help you recover from your loss and look forward to rebuilding your life" (Church Initiative, 2015). Respondents in the LEAP study ranged from leaders of GriefShare groups to at least a few who were sharply critical of the model. One respondent indicated distaste for the proselytizing efforts he had seen exhibited in these groups in years past, a fact somewhat corroborated by one LEAP study participant who indicated that GriefShare had been an important part in the enlargement activities of the congregation.

HOW GRIEF GROUPS DIFFER FROM OTHER GROUPS

Bereavement support groups share many things in common with other kinds of human groupings, and yet they also stand apart, almost as an entirely different species. One frequently cited text for group therapeutic interventions is the 650-page tome of psychiatrist Irvin Yalom. Now in its fifth edition, *The Theory and Practice of Group Psychotherapy* includes the contribution of a co-author, Molyn Leszcz. For his part, Yalom has been a preeminent voice in the practice of group psychotherapy at least since the first edition of his book was published in 1970. The volume is cited in many later books on group therapy and is a standard text in training psychotherapists in the principles of group work.

Yalom and Leszcz (2005) have suggested that the therapeutic experience in general and groups in particular include 11 primary factors, including phrases that will sound like familiar goals to experienced bereavement support group leaders: instillation of hope, imparting information, imitative behavior, group cohesiveness, and catharsis (pp. 1–2). The research evidence is compelling, Yalom asserts, that group psychotherapy is as effective on the whole as individual therapy, with 80% of people receiving psychotherapy being better off than those who do not (Yalom, 1995).

However, while bereavement groups share many things in common with Yalom's (and others') perspectives on psychotherapeutic groups, they also differ markedly. Most notably, while much therapeutic work is done in a bereavement support group, the kind of group I envision is not a psychotherapy group. In its policy statement affirming the effectiveness of psychotherapy, the American Psychological Association (2012) includes several characteristics in its definition of psychotherapy. It affirms that psychological treatment (psychotherapy) is delivered by trained providers in response to a condition of illness and affirms an earlier definition that psychotherapy seeks "to provide symptom relief and personality change, reduce future symptomatic episodes, enhance quality of life, promote adaptive functioning in work/school and relationships, increase the likelihood of making healthy life choices, and offer other benefits established by the collaboration between client/patient and psychologist" (Introduction, paragraph 2).

First, observation indicates that the vast majority of bereavement support groups are not led by psychotherapists and therefore, by definition, are not psychotherapy groups. Though exact numbers are unknown, anecdotal evidence suggests that most bereavement support groups are led by peer volunteers and by a variety of caregiving professionals other than psychotherapists. While not intended to be a representative sample, the LEAP study found many bereavement support groups to be led by caring peer volunteers with varying amounts of training and experience.

An even larger number of respondents in the LEAP study reported groups led by caregiving professionals with varying amounts of training, most frequently with graduate degrees in professional fields such as social work and practical theology; hospice social workers usually hold master of social work (MSW) degrees, and hospice chaplains generally hold master of divinity (MDiv) degrees. Most hospice bereavement coordinators seem to come from the ranks of these two professional specializations. The central premise of this book is that bereavement support groups can be effectively led by a wide range of professionals and volunteers including, but certainly not limited to, licensed mental health professionals. However, this diversity of leadership does make quantitative assessment of bereavement support group effectiveness more difficult.

Second, psychotherapy groups frequently address clinical issues that can clearly be labeled as psychological disorders: major depressive disorder, posttraumatic stress disorder, and panic anxiety disorder, to name just a few. Each of these disorders is characterized by clear, demarcated clinical criteria for diagnosis. In other words, a patient is not diagnosed with major depressive disorder because a psychotherapist says the patient is depressed. That diagnosis is made on the basis of the sound clinical judgment of a trained health care professional in evaluation of the patient against a specific set of criteria.

At this writing, bereavement is not categorized as a "disorder" in the dominant diagnostic systems used around the world, namely, the World Health Organization's *International Classification of Disease* or the American Psychological Association's *Diagnostic and Statistical Manual of Mental Disorders*. "Complicated bereavement," is, by definition, a disorder, though researchers and clinicians hold widely divergent opinions about what line of demarcation is crossed between "normal" and "complicated" bereavement.

In any case, bereavement support groups have as their focused tasks the helping of otherwise psychologically healthy individuals cope with a normal life event. In part, bereavement support groups hopefully perform in the lives of grieving individuals some of the same roles that caring extended family and close friends would have a few generations ago. Normal grief is not a disorder for which individuals need (or likely benefit from) psychotherapy. Furthermore, when grief meets whatever diagnostic criteria is chosen to label it as "complicated," the difficulties of the experience are not likely to be adequately addressed in a peer-led bereavement support group. What does seem promising in the case of complicated grief are manualized group interventions developed by Shear, Frank, Houck, and Reynolds (2005) and Shear et al. (2014), discussed more fully in Chapter Seven.

ETHICAL CHALLENGES

In their seminal work on the ethics of grief counseling, Gamino and Ritter (2009) suggested that much grief counseling has proceeded without it being particularly tethered to an ethical approach. The frequently decentralized and grass-roots approaches common to bereavement support groups make ethical grounding an even more important consideration.

One challenge in grief groups may resemble a caveat offered by Shevellar, Sherwin, and Barringham (2014) in their study of belonging needs among Australian mental health patients. Through a semi-structured qualitative interview study, the investigators discovered that "a significant risk in the context of social isolation and loneliness is having a service take the place of having a life. Or, in other words, a service agency offering felicity and fellowship might become community life for people rather than introducing them to community life" (p. 6). While this study involved mentally disabled individuals rather than bereaved people, one must consider whether it is helpful for the bereavement support group to become the community of choice rather than helping bereaved individuals reconnect with their primary supportive community.

Moreover, bereavement group sponsors and leaders must carefully evaluate their motives for working with individuals in groups. Professional codes of ethics remind persons practicing in virtually all helping fields to avoid conflicts of interest in the ways they connect with individuals as vulnerable as many bereaved individuals are. In at least one powerful way, every sponsored bereavement support group has a built-in conflict of interest. A hospital may begin a bereavement support group primarily to boost quality assurance scores or the institution's image in the community. Funeral homes sponsoring bereavement support groups may be expecting to build goodwill and future business through groups. Hospices potentially see groups as an opportunity for fundraising as well as a way to satisfy governmental requirements for follow-up with the families of patients served. Many faith communities undertaking bereavement groups may fundamentally view them through the lens of outreach and congregational growth. Even individual clinicians hosting bereavement groups in their practices might see groups as a way to attract potential clients (Gamino & Ritter, 2009).

Bereavement support group leaders and program coordinators must work together to assure ethical appropriateness in ways that groups are promoted, in the disclosure provided by leaders about the limits of their training and skills, and about the purposes of the group.

IS SOCIAL SUPPORT IMPORTANT IN BEREAVEMENT?

In their examination of the "science" behind spa treatments, mineral baths, and warm water therapy for sore joints, Bender et al. (2005) acknowledge that sometimes, it is difficult to find empirical verifiability for the health habits individuals develop. Acknowledging the role of "placebo effects," the researchers posited, "The placebo effect is therefore considerable; if it 'pleases', the pain is reduced, and the patient's general well-being improves, then arguably it is of value irrespective of trial results from randomized, controlled trials" (pp. 221–222). This book takes its place in the quest for the science behind the role of social support in general and of bereavement groups specifically. Herein, I acknowledge the very possible role "placebo effects" have on participants' reported satisfaction. However much like spa treatments, if bereaved individuals perceive they are better able to function in adapting to their loss as a result of participation in groups and the social support they receive, it will take compelling evidence of harm to persuade most caregivers to eliminate the practice.

Clinicians and peer volunteers assume that social support improves bereavement outcomes, and some studies have pointed in that direction. In their analysis of interviews with 30 dementia caregivers in the months after the patients' deaths, Grafstrom, Winblad, and Almberg (2000) found a recurrent theme of the perceived value of social support, both before and after the death. Bereaved individuals reported most satisfaction with a combination of professional support (nurses, counselors), emotional support from extended family and friends, and practical support such as help with house and yard work.

Dimond, Lund, and Caserta (1987) found a correlation between social support networks and mental health outcomes. Among their 192 widowed respondents between the ages of 50 and 93, higher quality and larger social networks were correlated with lower levels of depression and higher overall satisfaction with life.

After reviewing several existing studies on the role of social support and bereavement, Vanderwerker and Prigerson (2004) acknowledged the deleterious effects of negative social support and assumed the role of positive social support in their study of Internet, email, and mobile phone usage by bereaved individuals. While results were mixed concerning the use of technology as a means of gaining social support, they found the presence of social support to be "consistently protective against (Complicated Grief) across timepoints. These results suggest that ensuring adequate social support for bereaved individuals is an effective means of mitigating some of the negative outcomes associated with the loss of a loved one" (p. 54).

However, not all research supports the notion that high levels of perceived social support actually contribute to better outcomes in bereavement. Analyzing previous studies as well as data from the Changing Lives of Older Couples (CLOC) study, Stroebe, Zech, Stroebe, and Abakoumkin (2005) suggested that social support neither appears to buffer bereavement's negative effects nor accelerate recovery.

While the CLOC study represents a very detailed collection of data on a large group of individuals, it should be noted that its respondents were overwhelmingly white (88.1%) and all respondents lived in the Detroit, Michigan, metropolitan area (Nesse, Wortman, House, Kessler, & Lepkowski, 2003). Stroebe et al. (2005) pointed out the inconsistency of their findings with those of Okabayashi et al. (1997), conceding that one explanation could be the differences between cultural collectivism and individualism, especially considering the latter's Japanese study sample.

The analysis conducted by Stroebe et al. (2005) apparently did not consider racial differences in the results of the CLOC study itself, an understandable analytical decision in light of its overwhelmingly white sample. Lack of ethnic and/or cultural diversity is a limitation in much of the research examining social support in bereavement. However, Carr (2004) did analyze ethnic differences in the CLOC study, finding that African Americans had significantly lower levels of anger and despair than their European-American counterparts. In discussing the data behind these findings, she wrote, "Blacks' lower levels of anger are attributable partly to their higher levels of religious participation and coping and also are explained partially by Blacks' greater reliance on their children for social support, . . . underscoring the importance of having a broad and varied base of social support" (p. 615). In her research report, Carr surmised that African Americans "have developed a stronger and more varied web of social relationships, including extended family and the church; it is precisely these resources that may buffer against symptoms such as anger in the face of spousal loss" (p. 615).

Social support was also found to play an important role in bereavement experiences in the study conducted by Burke, Neimeyer, and McDevitt-Murphy (2010). Their study examined 54 homicidally bereaved African-American individuals and found larger reported support networks than among Caucasian bereaved individuals in similar existing studies. In analyzing their data in light of the previous studies' mixed results on the buffering effects of social support on bereavement, these authors suggested that their study is "broadly consistent" with the "optimistic" interpretation of social support's efficacy (p. 17).

Like all studies that seek to parse data according to racial or other cultural categories, this analysis must be considered carefully, a point Carr (2004) makes in her conclusion. The point of inclusion here is not to suggest that whites and blacks inherently grieve the death of a mate differently; the dramatic difference in the size of the two groups in this analysis would make that a spurious conclusion in any case. Rather, the point is to note that there are groups of bereaved individuals for whom, clearly, social support plays a vital role in their bereavement experience, and predicting which individuals for whom it will or will not be important will required more fine-grained analysis than the CLOC data supports.

QUESTIONS FOR REFLECTION AND DISCUSSION

- What do you suppose are the ways altruistic or cooperative behavior actually encourage social connection?
- How do you evaluate the author's claim that there are limits to how much a bereaved individual's family and friends can do to help? What are the reasons for your response?
- The author suggests that groups are drawn together by one or more of a shared history, shared values, and shared purposes. Do you agree? Why?
- Do you believe social support is really important in bereavement? Why or why not?

NOTE

1. Around the world, a plethora of terms labels the not-for-profit activities of charitable organizations for which surplus funds are invested in the mission of the organization rather than returned to members or stockholders. A few of the more common terms are nonprofit, nongovernmental organization, civil society, third sector, charitable organization, and nonprofit. For the sake of simplicity, this book generally uses the term *nonprofit* to subsume all of these types of organizations and activities.

CHAPTER 3

Recruiting and Training Group Leadership

One difficulty both of conducting research into the structure of bereavement support groups and of writing about them is in defining terms. *Bereavement support group* or a similar title is the name used to label a diversity of models and structures located along a continuum. On one end, a peer leader, an individual who might be a year or two along in working through a significant personal loss, leads some bereavement support groups. These groups often operate on a model influenced by the self-help model of the 12 steps of Alcoholics Anonymous. They typically function with neither oversight by nor input from professionals trained in bereavement, counseling, or any other related discipline.

Bereavement support group also is the label chosen by groups led by a clinically-trained psychotherapist, sometimes sponsored by an organization that provides oversight and accountability. Social work, licensed professional counseling, pastoral counseling, and family therapy are the professional disciplines that seem most often tasked with leading the bereavement support groups offered in abundance by local hospices, bereavement centers for children and families, and palliative care organizations. Small agencies may have one or two support groups meeting regularly, while large hospices often host a dozen or more. One respondent in the LEAP study works for a hospice-sponsored community bereavement center that hosts more than 15 bereavement support groups.

In between these extremes, bereavement support groups also include networks of peer-led groups without professional oversight or consultation linked together through a network such as the Compassionate Friends. While group leaders are free to structure their local groups to meet the needs of group participants, TCF actively encourages facilitators to avail themselves of the significant quantities of resources and training offered by the organization.

Some organizations prefer to staff bereavement groups with co-leaders, including both a peer facilitator and a professional co-leader. Organizations that utilize their services will often staff groups with interns in the last year of their degree plans leading to master of social work or master of counseling.

This brief summary of the diversity of groups only examines one detail: the leadership. Additionally, a researcher or program planner who wants to rely on the best evidence for program practices must consider all of the other variables in the sample examined in the individual research report. Even the LEAP study, a research project providing one piece of the evidence for this book, interviewed a relatively small sample of group facilitators, with widely varied levels of experience, training, geographical situation, and cultural background. One can readily surmise what makes it so difficult to evaluate evidence about the benefits—or potential harm—of bereavement support groups.

QUALIFICATIONS OF BEREAVEMENT SUPPORT GROUP LEADERS

The pathways to support group leadership are many. Here are just a few of the stories offered by leaders participating in the LEAP study.

> About two years after L's brother died of suicide, L began leading the suicide survivor's group that had provided profound support to L after the loss. Though taking a few-year break, this leader has been facilitating this monthly support group for more than 20 years.
>
> After a successful 20-year career in business, B decided to return to school to earn a master of social work degree. During B's second internship placement at an inner city school, B gained some experience leading a group for bereaved adolescents and "was hooked." Following the completion of the degree, B worked in medical social work and school social work, eventually gaining the supervised hours needed to sit for the social work licensing exam. As a licensed clinical social worker, B now leads two bereavement groups for a large community hospital and supervises two interns from the same university program where B received the MSW degree.
>
> K spent the first several years of a "helping career" in the role of congregational minister. During this period, K realized that "gifts and passions were best lived out" in the context of the counseling part of the pastoral role. After a job transition, K followed the desire to get more training in bereavement support. K attended a four-day workshop to earn certification in facilitating a "turn-key"

> system of bereavement support and began leading several groups each year.
>
> After five years as a hospice chaplain, the agency director approached J about taking on the role of bereavement coordinator. Though sensing a lack of experience for the task, J reluctantly agreed and began attending every grief counseling workshop available. Even when attending the national chaplain's meeting each year, J sought out sessions related to bereavement. A retired psychotherapist living in the community agreed to be J's supervisor in developing bereavement support groups, and J worked under his mentorship for more than three years.

As will be no surprise to experienced bereavement program administrators, the LEAP study revealed a diversity of opinions about the qualities needed in a bereavement support group leader. Some program administrators utilize only trained and experienced clinicians or well-supervised clinical interns (such as second-year master of social work degree interns working under the supervision of a licensed clinical social worker). Other program administrators welcome and—in at least a few cases—actually prefer peer volunteers to lead groups. One organizational leader, for example, believes that psychotherapists make bereavement support groups into something they were not intended to be: psychotherapy groups. This program leader was adamant in the interview that since bereaved individuals "need models to look up to," a middle-aged widow who "is a few years down the road" is a better support group leader than a 23-year-old intern. Indeed, if the purpose is to provide peer support, this program administrator's perspective is accurate, since a young adult would rarely share the life experience of a middle-aged widow.

Earlier in my career, I embraced this model. Our program did not actively recruit as potential leaders for groups those individuals who had not worked through a significant loss. We utilized counseling interns and college students preparing for careers in the helping professions, but I generally thought these individuals to be less effective than those who had successfully negotiated a significant loss in their own lives. I now believe that thinking has significant downsides. Patients rarely expect their oncologist to have survived breast cancer in order to be effective in determining an appropriate course of chemotherapy for her patient, for example, and a dentist need not have suffered a dental abscess in order to be technically competent to perform a root canal. Personal experience is a good qualification in some cases, but it is neither mandatory nor even preferred, in all.

During the years I supervised a support group program staffed by peer volunteers, I observed that some of our most passionate child bereavement group leaders were people who had experienced a deep loss during their own childhood or adolescence. As a general rule, these individuals understood the risks to children of experiencing losses without support and, in many cases, these leaders had suffered from lack of meaningful support themselves. The passion that accompanied these volunteers to the work we shared, however, always had to be tempered by their training and their collegiality with other volunteers and our clinical team.

Though experiencing a loss may not be a prerequisite for effective bereavement support group leadership, there are some qualifications that are imperative. Interestingly, these are the qualifications that were raised multiple times in the interviews with other bereavement support group leaders and program administrators in the LEAP study.

Eagerness to Learn

In a mid-20th century talk to students, Indian philosopher Jiddu Krishnamurti taught, "There is no end to education. It is not that you read a book, pass an examination, and finish with education. The whole of life, from the moment you are born (un)til the moment you die, is a process of learning. Learning has no end and that is the timeless quality of learning" (Krishnamurti, 1954, ch. 8, para. 6). Regardless of their life experience and level of training, the most effective bereavement support group leaders seem to be individuals who apply Krishnamurti's perspective: They are learning in "the whole of life."

This can be an overwhelming proposition; bereavement support group leaders, whether full-time professional counselor or peer volunteer facilitator, could never absorb even a small portion of the plethora of new material available each year. Scholarly articles in the half-dozen leading bereavement journals[1] numbered more than 200 in a recent year. In addition, there are hundreds of bereavement-related articles published in an average year in the journals of other fields, such as recent articles in *European Journal of Public Health*, *Palliative Medicine*, and *Journal of Community Nursing*. Hundreds of new grief-related books are published annually, and there is no shortage of seminars, workshops, and lectures addressing issues of bereavement. One LEAP study participant explained: "Working with the group, attending classes, reading everything I could—well, it just became a learning journey for me."

Another group leader interviewed stressed the importance of learning from group members, noting that in nearly 18 years of group leadership, this leader learns something new about grief from virtually every person participating in a group. At the first meeting of each new six-week group this leader facilitates, participants stand together on an unfinished quilt laid out on the floor. As they stand together, the leader tells them, "There are no experts on grief. I might have some educational credentials, but that does not make me an 'expert' on your grief. Each of you has something to teach the others in our group, and every one of you has something to teach me."

What does seem important to characterize bereavement support group leaders, however, is a willingness to learn continually. When interviewing potential group leaders, one bereavement program director asks what the potential leader is reading and attending related to grief. This program leader is then better able to assess the potential leader's level of interest in the field by discovering the amount of input the individual is voluntarily seeking.

Compassion

Individuals use the word "compassion" to label many behaviors, but the twin components that emerge in the literature are being emotionally moved at the suffering of another welded to a desire to help (Klimecki, Leiberg, Lamm, & Singer, 2013; Simon-Thomas, 2012). While historically thought to be a matter of genetics—either one has compassion or she does not—a growing research literature indicates that compassion can be learned.

The beginning of "learned compassion" seems to be in the parent-child relationship, the attachment bonding that Bowlby (1969) popularized. Over the life course, compassion is experienced as the individual encounters both big and little setbacks. This element of compassion experience is likely triggered in potential group leaders who articulate their desire to help others by "giving back." Emerging research on neural plasticity, the ability of the brain to change, indicates that compassion can actually be taught. Meditation and mindfulness techniques offer great promise in helping individuals become more compassionate in their care of others (Klimecki et al., 2013).

Whether learning it in their own experiences with loss or in hearing the stories of others, compassion is a vital quality to effectiveness among the bereavement group leaders surveyed in the LEAP study. Program administrators must assure that group leaders learn ways to manage their compassion in a self-caring way in order to avoid what is variously referred to as "compassion fatigue," "burnout," and "empathy overload." Nevertheless, some level of pre-existing care for hurting people seems obvious. One would wonder why an individual would volunteer to lead a bereavement group in the absence of compassion for bereaved individuals. To assess compassion in interviews or training activities, program administrators can inquire about how the potential group leader defines compassion, how he or she "sets limits" on how care is offered, and how he or she has specifically acted in compassionate ways toward others in the past.

Reliability

One LEAP study respondent expressed the sentiment of many interviewees: "Bereaved people have so much going on, so many people who have 'failed them' relationally. The last thing we need is a group facilitator who might show up, who might not, who might be prepared, or who might not be. That shoots our program in the foot." Another respondent expressed a similar notion: "People are already grieving; they don't need you to be 'flakey.' "

Reliability—doing what one says when one says it—is a skill expected in most places of employment. However, with bereavement support group leaders, workers are often volunteers rather than paid employees. Nevertheless, program coordinators can emphasize the importance of regular, punctual attendance with reminders of how specifically bereavement can be further complicated by unreliable group leadership.

Authenticity

Another characteristic mentioned by multiple respondents in the LEAP study is the value of authenticity or genuineness. According to one leader who mentioned this characteristic, there is no room in the bereavement support group for a person trying to impress participants with credentials or experiences he or she does not have. A colleague once said she had discovered that "grieving people have a finely-tuned B.S. detector," a colloquial way of saying that bereaved individuals have an uncanny ability to spot people who are less than genuine in their approach.

Collaborative Style

Arrogance, a "know-it-all" attitude, condescension toward others, and a sense of superiority are attitudes that do not bode well for bereavement support group leaders. By virtue of their leadership role in the group, facilitators may already be perceived by group members as the "experts" on all matters related to loss. Because they are fundamentally mutual-help groups, bereavement support groups demand leaders who are collaborative in their approach to problem solving. Inquire about a person's experience working on a team (committee, community group, task force) to study and solve a problem. With more than 20 years of group leadership, one participant in the LEAP Study explained, "The group isn't about me. I'm so happy people in our group aren't talking to me, they're talking to each other."

How the support group room is set up likely contributes to (or detracts from) this collaborative style. One support group leader described group members gathered in a half circle with the leader's chair in the center facing the others and a flipchart next to the leader's chair. The training this leader had received was where the leader learned to set the room this way; it was described as the "preferred setup." Such an arrangement likely sets the leader in the role of expert teacher. Questions will likely be directed to the leader, and group members will wait to offer their input until after the leader responds.

Though the ability to play well with others is a skill ideally learned in childhood, individuals uncover nuances to teamwork throughout their lives. In groups, participants inevitably raise questions such as "How do I get a good night's sleep when all I think about is Bob?" If the facilitator responds immediately, he or she will reinforce the concept of "leader-expert." If instead the leader turns to the entire group and says, "Some of you have been grappling with your loss for a while now. Tell us what you have done to get to sleep," the facilitator encourages the group to become a community of individuals helping each other through loss. If leaders become the all-knowing "sage on the stage," they will squelch meaningful problem-solving dialogue among participants.

Flexibility

Few qualities would seem to be more important on the part of group leaders than the characteristic of flexibility. This willingness to bend to the circumstances is needed in matters of group organization and group content. Participants in the LEAP study recounted numerous examples of plans gone awry because a more pressing need presented itself.

On Monday, one leader went to bed with a plan for content in Tuesday's group meeting, only to awaken Tuesday morning to the awful news emanating from New York, Pennsylvania, and Washington, DC, as the events of the 9/11 terror attacks unfolded. This leader decided to proceed with the group as planned, assuming some of the nine regular attendees would not be in attendance. In fact, they all showed up, apparently needing the care of the group of people they had learned over their early weeks together would be most supportive in such a tragedy. However, the group leader intuitively determined to lay aside well-intentioned plans to talk about grief at the holidays as the group discussed how the day's events triggered memories and exacerbated their own experiences with loss. A bereavement group leader cannot become flummoxed at the "derailment" of a tightly conceived plan.

Emotional Stability

While using standardized formal assessments to quantify the psychological stability of potential leaders may seem extreme, a minimal level of emotional maturity seems to be an important characteristic for group leaders. The level of emotional upheaval present for many participants in bereavement support groups implies the need for facilitators who possess stability in their own psychological selves.

In their attempt to develop a standardized instrument for assessing emotional stability, Chaturvedi and Chander (2010) surveyed professional, experienced psychologists to develop a list of opposing characteristics that qualify levels of emotional stability. Their five traits pointing toward emotional stability were: optimism (vs. pessimism), empathy (vs. apathy), autonomy (vs. independence), calm (vs. anxiety), and tolerance (vs. aggression). Though both authors were working as psychologists in Bhopal, India, at the time of their research, what these authors do not report is the cultural context of either the psychologists surveyed for their consensus trait list nor for the 200 college students on whom the emotional stability scale was tested.

Viewing emotional stability as a necessary function of organizational leadership, Li, Ahlstrom, and Ashkanasy (2010) and Li, Chun, Ashkanasy, and Ahlstrom (2012) investigated their construct in the context of Chinese business. Their 10-item emotional stability questionnaire inquired about the respondent's self-assessment of panic, anxiety, recovery from unhappiness, ability to self-calm in anxious experiences, and ability to recover quickly from upsetting circumstances.

For program coordinators who interview potential support group leadership, a possible practice application of these two studies is to ask open-ended questions about such matters as how the applicant exhibits optimism, self-calms in anxious experiences, and works toward recovery after upsetting experiences. Inquiring about the potential leader's self-assessment presents an added benefit of being able to more easily assess the individual's level of personal reflectiveness and self-awareness.

Effective group leaders require a combination of personal qualities and leadership skills. Without question, leadership skills can be taught through an effective training program, good mentorship, and ongoing supervision. Qualities like compassion, collaboration, and flexibility are developed over a lifetime, but they can almost certainly be enhanced in an effective training program. The characteristics of effective group leader training are the topic to which we next turn.

RECRUITING AND RETAINING GROUP FACILITATORS

At this writing, it has been well over a quarter century since I led my first bereavement support group. I had led teaching and training experiences many times in both large groups and small groups; interacting with individuals and families facing the crisis of a loved one's death was "all in a day's work." What I had never done—nor been specifically trained to do—was to lead a support group for bereaved people. From the vantage point of three decades, I now realize how little I knew about what I was doing.

At that time, I think I might have been too overwhelmed to realize how little I really knew about what I was doing. In any case, there had been precious little instruction in my educational training about how to lead a group. In fact, the closest I got to such training was a very fine course I took in college on small group communication. The principles I learned there, it seems to me from this vantage point all these years later, must have been instrumental in helping me get through that first experience leading a group.

When a program coordinator must begin a bereavement support group, he or she frequently acts as the first group leader. When I began at Pathways in 1996, I inherited a small family bereavement program begun by my predecessor, who had apparently always led the parents group during the age-grouped seven-week program for children, teens, and their families. The next seven-week session was a few weeks from beginning, and the assumption was that our experienced volunteers would lead the children's groups and I would lead the parents' group. With three or four seven-week groups each year, it was a manageable pace. As we began to add school groups during the day and additional adult groups in the evening, it was immediately clear that I could not effectively lead all the new groups we would be beginning. So where does a program director look to find potential bereavement facilitators?

Recruiting new group leaders will be a different process if the program philosophy demands peer volunteers rather than trained clinicians. Some respondents in the LEAP study insist on trained clinicians to lead groups and only consider fully credentialed (licensed) mental health professionals. One respondent described recruiting through her own network in the local counseling association. She indicated that this task was becoming more difficult and supposed that falling reimbursement rates had forced private practitioners to spend more time on "billable" clients, resulting in less time for volunteer work. She also noted that agencies (including her own) had reduced staff and that administrators tended to expect "more results for the same money."

Volunteers are vital to the bereavement support group work of most organizations interviewed in the LEAP study. Most faith community bereavement groups seem to be led by volunteers who are not clinical counselors, as are groups that are part of networks such as Compassionate Friends, Bereaved Parents USA, Parents of Murdered Children, and Survivors of Suicide. The administrator for one grief camp for grieving children, who participated in the study, indicated that a typical weekend camp in her organization engages about 100 volunteers to look after about 60 youngsters. Community volunteers were engaged, leading groups in every child/teen-focused family bereavement program whose leaders or group leaders participated in the study.

The utilization of volunteers in bereavement support programs is a global phenomenon. Though much research about recruiting and retaining volunteers has been conducted with European-American participants in the United States, studies of volunteer work, both inside and outside of bereavement programs, is increasing. Several LEAP study participants indicated concerns about engaging volunteers from nondominant cultural groups in an effort to serve increasingly diverse communities more effectively.

Though not focused on bereavement programs, one Chinese study examined the role of volunteers in the burgeoning nonprofit sector of China. These scholars noted the vital role volunteers play in that:

> Since the 1990s, the Chinese government had gradually reduced its social service provision, as part of the accelerated transition from a centrally planned economy to a market economy. To compensate for the lack of public services, the Chinese government encouraged the founding and development of service-oriented organizations. (Zhang, Guo, & Cai, 2011, p. 20)

In one study of 1,361 nonprofits sampled from nearly 215,000 submitting a nonprofit tax return (Form 990) to the United States Internal Revenue Service, Hager and Brudney (2011) examined volunteer recruitment difficulties. Some nonprofits inevitably struggle with recruiting volunteers because of the nature of the organization's work. All things being equal, they suggested, it is more difficult to recruit volunteers to work with individuals with chronic illness or intravenous drug users than it is to recruit volunteers to work with suburban children. These attributes likely evolve from potential volunteers' understanding of the organization's mission, perhaps at times as a factor of whether this group "deserves" the attention it is getting. If we believe the commonly held notion that Westerners deny or at least emotionally run from interactions with death, bereavement programs may struggle with some of these "difficult mission" issues in recruiting volunteers. One program's volunteer resource manager opined, "I've quit going to volunteer fairs to recruit people. All I ever hear is, 'Oh that work must be terrible; I could never do that; it's just so depressing.' "

Hager and Brudney (2011) also suggested that some volunteer recruitment problems can be addressed by endorsing different recruitment (and retention) strategies. Volunteer "intensiveness" is one of those measurements. Most nonprofit organizations ask volunteers to report the number of hours they invest in organizational pursuits. Nonprofits use that data in writing grant proposals and in reporting the work they do. Virtually anyone who has worked in volunteer recruitment, however, knows that organizations have a small group of volunteers who on a regular basis invest large numbers of hours in the organization and a much larger group of volunteers who give relatively few hours. Contrary to their hypothesis that high levels of intensiveness (many hours required) would make recruitment harder, the researchers found the opposite to be true; high expectations correlated with less difficulty in recruiting.

Reflecting on the work of Heidrich's (1990) four types of volunteer service (direct service, leadership, general support, and member at large), Hager and Brudney hypothesized that providing a large array of volunteer opportunities from which the potential volunteer could choose is one important element in recruitment and retention. Their study results initially appeared to contradict the thesis, implying the counterintuitive notion that an array of opportunities would actually make recruiting more difficult. They reported, however, that further examination showed mixed results.

Even bereavement group leadership can require varying amounts of time (volunteer intensiveness), depending on expectations regarding continuing education and organizational meetings as well as the time required to facilitate a group. If Heidrich's division of volunteer work types is correct, in programs for which group work is their primary mission (such as many child/family-focused bereavement centers), there is still an array of volunteer opportunities available including office work, fundraising, communication, board leadership, and advocacy. However, Hager and Brudney (2011) found that regardless of organization size, high levels of intensiveness (hours worked) actually made it easier to recruit volunteers rather than making it more difficult.

Collegial networks have always been an important source for program leaders to learn about potential volunteers, whether they are clinicians or lay volunteers open to training. Quotah (2008) suggested that Hispanic chambers of commerce and Hispanic employee groups may be effective places for recruiting Latinos(as). Ethnic communities that are relationship-focused tend to depend on personal, direct communication, and potential volunteers will be most receptive to organizations that seek to utilize all of the skills volunteers offer (not limited to speaking a language).

Hager and Brudney (2011) found that using a wide array of marketing strategies to recruit volunteers was counterproductive in that organizations reporting the most difficulty recruiting volunteers were also the organizations that employed so-called shotgun approaches in marketing. They echoed Bradner's (1995) warning that "the wise recruiter needs to decide which [method] might be most effective for the job in mind" (p. 68), saying their empirical results portray a similar picture. Hager and Brudney asserted, "Recruitment problems may lead to the use of more recruitment approaches, but this strategy does not necessarily lead to fewer problems" (p. 152). Instead, they suggested studying which methods work best and then focusing attention on developing those methods to increase the chances of recruiting enough volunteers with the needed abilities and skills.

The *news media*, via health and community calendars in print newspapers and local Internet sites (such as the local volunteer center online bulletin board), often provide nonprofit groups with free listings in their community calendar. These avenues can be useful for promoting groups and for recruiting potential leaders.

During my years at Pathways Hospice, we often utilized our relationships with *faith communities* to help recruit volunteers to lead our programs. At least in the United States, there is a correlation between religiosity and volunteerism. We developed a relationship with one large predominantly European-American congregation from the Assemblies of God denomination. The church made a generous contribution to our program costs, hosted our family bereavement program for more than a year, and provided a cadre of volunteers, not only in our bereavement program but in our hospice and senior caregiving programs, as well. Citing several recent research studies, Mencken and Fitz (2013) wrote,

> Religious individuals are twice as likely to volunteer for the community, and 80% more likely to be engaged in secular causes than secular people. . . . Many scholars who have studied this pattern have argued that the religious message (compassion, sacrifice, loving one's neighbor) instills in adherents an obligation to help those in need. (p. 492)

Reviewing the deep heritage of African-American religion in community causes, Gutierrez and Mattis (2014) found the link between church and community volunteering to be significant in their study of urban African-American women in a northeastern American city. Though neither childhood experiences in faith communities, education, nor income predicted voluntary activities, current membership in a religious institution "emerged as a significant and positive predictor of volunteer engagement," with church members in their study 3.87 times more likely to volunteer than non-church members (p. 609). Moreover, African Americans are more likely to look to their congregation and clergy for information related to bereavement, leading Dansby-Giles, Giles, Haralson, and Johnson (2014) to suggest that this resource is pivotal in program development.

Bereavement program leaders with whom I have consulted have often expressed concern about whether religious people can "check their beliefs at the door," as one hospice bereavement coordinator put it. In one sense, this is a fair question, though it may expose potential religious bigotry unless program directors express the same level of concern about volunteers being able to "check their political beliefs" or "check their economic philosophy" at the door, as well. The question might turn out to be of less concern than on first glance. Mencken and Fitz (2013) found that religious conservatives who also held a theological view of God as judgmental were significantly less likely to volunteer outside of their place of worship than individuals who held a more open theological stance.

In their study of the volunteer recruitment and retention efforts of 1,361 nonprofits in the United States, Hager and Brudney (2011) found that organizations who actively engaged *current volunteers* in the recruitment of new ones had less difficulty with recruitment than organizations that did not. Presumably, existing volunteers know the organization's mission and strategies. They are also likely to know individuals who share their passions, values, and skills. One LEAP study participant said, "Many of our new volunteers, maybe close to half of them, are friends of current volunteers. They tell their friends at church and at work, 'Hey, I'm doing this work with grieving kids. Why don't you come help us?' " Quotah's (2008) perspective on recruiting Hispanic volunteers is helpful here, owing to the notion that many nondominant cultural groups in any society are focused on relationships with others from their own community.

Several respondents from the LEAP study indicated they consider using *individuals who once participated in their program* to lead groups. This happened most openly in the groups sponsored by faith communities. In two cases with these faith-based programs, the bereavement support group relies on a 25–30 minute video presentation at each meeting; participants view the program as a large group. Following the large group viewing of the video, the group divides into smaller discussion groups of four to eight participants; these groups are led by veterans of the program who receive several hours of training in leading group discussion.

Other LEAP study participants also reported recruiting volunteers from the ranks of former program participants, though most did not seem interested in using volunteers who had not passed the first-year anniversary of their loss. As a general rule, the more formal training in counseling and bereavement education the LEAP study respondents had completed, the more eager they seemed to be to utilize only well-trained volunteers who had been carefully selected and screened.

RETAINING EXISTING VOLUNTEERS

Though not a focus of their study, Hager and Brudney (2011) noted earlier research corroborated results in their current study:

> In our studies of retention, we make a point of noting the value of volunteer management capacity that focuses specifically on the interests of volunteers. Recognition activities, training and professional development for volunteers, screening and matching to appropriate assignments, and using volunteers to recruit other volunteers were all positively related to retention of volunteers. (p. 151)

Miller (2010) offered five simple strategies for empowering volunteers to keep them engaged in the organization's work: set clear expectations, assume they will get it right, be flexible, let them do what they love, and express gratitude. Volunteers are smart people who bring valuable skills to the organization, Miller suggested, but they do not need volunteer managers to "hover" over them. Helping volunteers connect their passion to the organization's mission is an important strategy for keeping individuals engaged (pp. 186–187).

One possible conclusion from experience supported by the LEAP study is that every group facilitator needs a basic understanding of the nature of the bereavement process as well as fundamental understanding of how groups function. However, just because these are important concepts with which new leaders need to be familiar does not mean classroom instruction is the most effective way to teach them. Even with more than 600 pages of "instruction" in his book on group psychotherapy, Yalom (1995) observed, "Though some introductory didactic sessions are useful, I find much of the material presented in this book can be best discussed with students around appropriate clinical material that arises over several months of an observed group" (pp. 513–514). Leader training programs might include orientation to such matters as the basics of bereavement, the interaction of people in groups, and the importance of leader self-care.

PROVIDING TRAINING TO GROUP LEADERSHIP

In the opinion of LEAP study respondents and on the basis of my own experience leading a group-oriented bereavement support program, good training paired with strong supervision is vital to success. Poorly trained group facilitators are a liability to the organization. More importantly, however, evidence is growing that they burn out more quickly and provide sub-standard care to bereaved individuals.

Bereavement Basics for Leader Training

Reconstruction of meaning is a central activity of the grief experience. "What does all of this mean?" and "Who am I now that this person has died?" are fundamental questions bereaved people explore. Robert Neimeyer and colleagues have been instrumental in exploring this arena and in developing theoretical models of how meaning reconstruction functions in the lives of bereaved individuals (Gillies & Neimeyer, 2006; Neimeyer, 2000; Neimeyer & Sands, 2011).

Also of importance for bereavement group leaders is an understanding of the context of ongoing attachment to the deceased. While death ends a physical life, it does not erase the relationship to the person who died. The work of Klass, Silverman, and Nickman (1996) on *continuing bonds* has assisted clinical helpers and peer volunteers alike in understanding the texture of an ongoing connection to the deceased. Another area of basic knowledge for group facilitators is in the ongoing discussions about the relationship between gender and grief. While hypotheses abound about this connection, a helpful construct with growing empirical support is the notion of instrumental vs. intuitive "styles" of grief described by Ken Doka and Terry Martin (2010).

In their training, group leaders should also be helped to shed their overreliance on culturally popular approaches to *simplifying grief into a set of stages or phases* that proceed predictably from one to the next. While such models provide clean, easily compartmentalized understandings of the bereavement experience, they fail to grasp the nuances of individual experiences with loss and the utter unpredictability inherent in much of the process (Neimeyer, Keesee, & Fortner, 2000; Stroebe & Schut, 1999, 2010; Worden, 2009).

Twin concepts bereavement group leaders must grasp in their training are the *importance of social support and the nature of disenfranchised grief* (Doka, 2002). Social support as a vital component for the effective negotiation of the bereavement process is a central premise of this book and of the vision to develop bereavement support groups. This support is lacking for many individuals, in part, because of the presence of culturally disenfranchised grief, a term coined by Kenneth Doka. The loss experience can become disenfranchised because the loss is not recognized in the mourner's cultural group (such as the loss of a pregnancy) or because the mourner is not acknowledged (business partners and ex-spouses are two examples).

Program coordinators will want to insure that bereavement group leaders are well versed in the *diversity of cultural beliefs and customs* related to loss. Especially in urban environments, bereavement leaders are likely to work with individuals whose cultural customs are dissimilar to those of the facilitator; fascination with and a desire to learn about differing funeral rituals, beliefs about loss, and religious tenets are helpful attributes for group leaders. One helpful strand of conversation for members of bereavement groups is a discussion about how their various families and communities observed funeral ceremonies for their loved ones. When invited to do so, group participants bring funeral memorabilia to share, including such items as symbols used, printed memorial tributes, and photos (Hoy, 2013; Lewis & Hoy, 2011).

The assessment and recognition of complicated grief among group participants is also essential for group leaders. Both the language labeling the phenomenon of *complicated grief* and the way symptoms are classified have changed dramatically over the last 30 years. In its fifth edition published in 2013, the editors updating the *Diagnostic and Statistical Manual of Mental Disorders* stopped short of calling complicated grief a clearly defined clinical disorder, but the editors did provide a framework for encouraging further research. By categorizing complicated grief as a "condition for further study," the *DSM-5*'s nomenclature for "Persistent Complex Bereavement Related Disorder" delineates "normal grief from persistent grief" (American Psychiatric Association, 2013, p. 790). In theory, this distinction should result in more effective intervention for the estimated 8 to 15% of bereaved people whose grief does not proceed in an expected fashion (Keyes et al., 2014; Prigerson et al., 1995; Rando, 1993; Shear et al., 2011; Worden, 2009).

Some clinical scholars see complicated bereavement as a much wider issue than the ongoing chronicity of loss envisioned in the "persistence" notation of the *DSM-5*. Worden (2009) has categorized four types of complicated grief, only one of which ("chronic grief") seems to be subsumed under the current model of complicated grief. He believes delayed grief, exaggerated grief, and masked grief are three other often-overlooked constructs not specifically addressed in the emerging diagnostic criteria for persistent complex bereavement disorder. Current conceptualizations of bereavement indicate a continuum of loss, "a continuous relationship between normal and abnormal grief reactions, between the complicated and uncomplicated, and that pathology is more related to the intensity of a reaction or the duration of a reaction than to the simple presence of absence of a specific symptom or behavior (Worden, 2009, p. 134).

Unanimity is further away than might otherwise be readily apparent. In the context of the American Psychiatric Association's publication of the *DSM-5*, many deplored the apparent overmedicalization of normal human existence, suggesting in almost conspiratorial language that "Big Pharma," the often-maligned pharmaceutical industry, was pushing for expanded diagnoses in an effort to drive revenues and profits from psychotropic medications (Frances, 2013).

A Standardized Patient Model to Help Train Interpersonal Skills

Many training programs utilize role-play where one (or several) trainees take on the role of bereaved individual, family, or group while another one or two trainees assume the role of counselor. Worden (2009) provides a dozen vignettes as an appendix to his book that use just such an approach to the training of bereavement counselors. Consensus among

LEAP study respondents who oversee volunteer programs as well as several group leaders themselves reported that needed interpersonal and group management skills are best taught through role-play and practice group sessions.

Clinical training programs have increasingly used standardized patients to train clinicians in practical skills, and the educational method has enjoyed strong empirical support for its effectiveness (Pastor, Cunningham, & Kuiper, 2015). May, Park, and Lee (2009) define standardized patients as individuals coached to demonstrate characteristics of specific patients presented in a consistent way to different learners. Medical and nursing schools, for example, hire individuals from the community and train them as actors to help teach skills such as physical examination. In some cases, the standardized patients are clinicians hired specifically to teach clinical skills to students (Hodges, Regehr, Hanson, & McNaughton, 1997). Fussell, Lewy, and McFarland (2009) studied the use of standardized patients in training substance abuse counselors, finding trainees evaluated the standardized patients as authentic in their portrayal of symptoms and behaviors. A similar model holds promise for training bereavement support group leaders, although the LEAP study did not reveal a program where professional group members act as standardized patients.

However, several LEAP study respondents who train group leaders indicated they use role-play extensively in training new group leaders and sometimes in supervision of experienced leaders. One respondent indicated that in group leader training, "We throw everything we can at them in role-play. I want them to know how to handle the worst situation you can imagine."

Leader Responsibilities

Though writing specifically about training groups for mental health professionals rather than bereavement support groups, Aveline's (1993) suggestion of a group leader's five primary tasks is instructional. These responsibilities are to: 1) to contain the anxiety of the group; 2) to establish a therapeutic environment in the group by shaping norms of support, acceptance, and group autonomy; 3) to guide the group toward issues that can be addressed in the time allotted; 4) to guard against damaging self-disclosure or loss of self-esteem on the part of group participants; and 5) to end well. To use Aveline's metaphor, a group leader is like a mountain guide who uses familiarity with the terrain to both encourage and to protect group members.

All five tasks are vital, but my experience with bereavement support groups points to the first as clearly primary: containing group anxiety. Individuals attending bereavement support groups seem naturally ill at ease. They are usually psychologically fragile, reeling from a significant loss and desperately trying to find ways to put life back together. One of the greatest experienced needs of these individuals is that they want to feel safe. Aveline (1993) has suggested that the establishment of ground rules and the assurance of confidentiality are two important ways this anxiety is relieved. Confidentiality is addressed more fully in Chapter Five.

EFFECTIVE LEADERSHIP OF GROUPS

Ineffective leadership will sink a group faster than any other factor. According to respondents from the LEAP study, effective group leaders seem to share some particular characteristics. First, group leaders must focus on the people who actually attend. Bereavement groups work, in part, because individual attendees realize their story is important. One seasoned group leader said it this way: "Whether you have a few in attendance or a whole room full, never forget that the people who matter are the people who come." Showing (or voicing) disappointment to the group causes those in attendance to feel their participation is of less importance.

Even the innocent rhetorical question asked when there are three people in the room instead of the customary eight, "Well, I wonder where everybody is?" communicates subtly to the three who are present that their attendance is not as important as the five who have not arrived. If the group is not closed and there is space in the room, group leaders can offer a quiet suggestion at the end of meetings to invite participants to invite their bereaved friends to attend. Otherwise, leaders need to concentrate only on the individuals who do attend.

People want to know their part in the group is important. Group members seem to appreciate a brief phone call after they attend their first meeting. Thanking participants for coming and asking if there are any questions about the group can be an important way to acknowledge the participants' importance. If a "regular" misses more than a meeting or two, following up can reveal if an illness, family crisis, or some other factor is keeping the participant away from the group.

LEADER SELF-CARE IN TRAINING PROGRAMS

An old adage speaks volumes to potential group leaders: "We cannot give that which we do not possess." As imperative as strong understandings of the bereavement process and of group dynamics and leadership skills are, it seems equally imperative for potential group leaders to learn the importance of good self-care. Professionals and volunteers who provide care to bereaved individuals share the same risks for compassion fatigue and burnout witnessed among other caregivers. Research studies have generally focused on populations of professional caregivers who are employed full-time in caregiving roles. However, lay caregivers can experience many of the same factors that have been isolated as risks for compassion fatigue and burnout—many high intensity cases, perceived need that outstrips resources, and limited peer support (Sprang, Clark, & Whitt-Woosley, 2007).

A simple starting point in good leader self-care is the affirming of a *clear sense of purpose* in the work of supporting bereaved individuals and families. For many, the sense of purpose and the meaning they derive from their work with bereaved individuals take on an almost religious quality, with language mirroring that used frequently by members of the clergy. In conversations with support group leaders over the years, I have frequently heard individuals intone their "sense of call" or the "sacred vocation" with which they view their work. Steven Covey (1989) wrote, "It's incredibly easy to get caught up in an activity trap, in the busy-ness of life, to work harder and harder at climbing the ladder of success only to discover it's leaning against the wrong wall. It is possible to be busy—very busy—without being very effective (p. 98).

Awareness of one's own losses is paramount, also. Worden (2009) suggested that working with the bereaved raises one's awareness of personal losses and that that awareness sometimes comes with great pain. Working through one's own losses provides credibility and confidence for the bereavement group leader who wants to help others. While providing care to a widowed individual would likely be overwhelming for a group leader whose own mate had recently died, the group leader effectively working through that loss will likely produce a more compassionate, more credible, and more helpful caregiver.

Bereavement support group leaders must be vigilant in monitoring countertransference in their work with bereaved individuals. The concept of countertransference owes its genesis to the psychoanalytic work of Sigmund Freud, but it essentially includes the "counselor's unconscious feelings that emerge as a result of working with the client" (Murphy, 2013, n.p.). In their text about the transformative impact clients potentially have on psychotherapists, Kottler and Carlson (2005) remind professional counselors of their training to avoid at all costs the goal of getting one's own needs met through the counseling relationship.

Conceded as "easier-said-than-done," they prefer therapists to learn skills for becoming aware of and managing this countertransference, in part through taking stock of what one is learning through clients (and group members).

While bereavement group leaders can be powerful role models in groups because they have suffered a similar loss to the individuals in the group, they must be vigilant in not allowing the group to become focused on their own experiences. As a practical matter, when people have asked me as a group leader, "What do you do to manage the stupid things people say?" or "How do you recommend dealing with lonely evenings?" I have tried to practice the art of first asking others in the group to respond. I believe this accomplishes two objectives. First, it demonstrates that the collective wisdom of the group surpasses my own knowledge, even though I will likely add my own ideas to the conversation. Second, such an approach gives me time to consider how much self-disclosure on my part as the group leader is in the best interest of the group. In my experience, a quick answer from me almost always results in more disclosure of my own story than is likely helpful.

Another means to self-care is participating in *continual learning and development*. Attending workshops, reading books and papers, and participation in ongoing training are essential for bereavement group leaders to continue developing skills and to expand their knowledge of the field. The Association for Death Education and Counseling (ADEC) is the preeminent organization of individuals studying and supporting bereaved people. The credentialing program, leading to the certification in thanatology (CT), affirms that the credentialed individual is in possession of a body of knowledge about the field. Some might consider it overkill, but I think it is a reasonable goal for people who invest significant amounts of time in supporting bereaved people.

Program leaders might think about shaping their training by the body of knowledge matrix and sponsoring individual volunteers by paying a portion of the costs to complete the credentialing process. Employers wanting well-versed bereavement support staff (including competent group leaders) should consider requiring certification during the first year or two of employment. Both group leaders and program coordinators will want to beware of "quick" training programs that provide a certificate for a weekend or weeklong training experience. They are often expensive endeavors and, in my experience, reflect the philosophy of one or two entrepreneurial individuals while not necessarily being grounded in current research and thinking about the bereavement process.

Developing habits of physical self-care are equal in importance to such things as ascertaining purpose and continuing one's education. Physical self-care includes *adequate nutrition*, *restful sleep*, and *challenging exercise* to provide the physical strength and endurance to do the emotionally challenging work of supporting bereaved individuals.

THE VITAL ROLE OF SUPERVISION AND APPRENTICESHIP

Without ongoing, intentional supervision, errors in understanding and technique simply are reinforced to become habits. Every reader has likely met a colleague who does not have 20 years of experience; this individual has one year of experience repeated 20 times. While not a panacea, supervision helps to reduce the risk of that happening.

Respondents in the LEAP study sometimes felt adrift in their work. One leader who had completed a four-day intensive training program that was supposed to have "certified" this facilitator for group leadership acknowledged a fear of not knowing "how to spot a person truly in trouble in grief." Having heard and read some of the ongoing debate in the leader's first annual meeting of the Association for Death Education and Counseling about the definitions, clinical significance, and breadth of complicated grief, this leader questioned a personal ability to effectively screen participants.

My own clinical training and experience caused me to wonder about some other group leaders I interviewed, even when the leaders themselves did not seem to recognize a need for professional support and supervision. In the case of several leaders facilitating groups in self-help groups or faith communities, there seemed to be an overall scarcity of training in the fundamentals of bereavement, group leadership skills, or screening/assessment abilities. Even among those who listed workshops attended and books read, I found myself with concerns about what I have come to call the "untethered" nature of their work in bereavement support groups.

Seemingly everyone agrees now that most bereaved individuals do not require the intervention of a trained clinical counselor; the point made throughout this book is that likely only one in five or one in six bereaved individuals need professional help in negotiating the process. Among colleagues, the way I have articulated this fact is to say grief is normal—until it is not. Then things can go badly very quickly. The supervision, or at least consultation, of a skilled counselor with whom leaders can discuss their group participants seems essential, in my view.

Advanced training and licensure is no guarantee of competence in death-related loss, either. Some clinical professionals have maintained a fierce allegiance to one or another model of the bereavement process significantly lacking in either empirical or clinical evidence to support it. Not an insignificant number of practicing professionals with whom I have interacted in seminars across the United States and Canada indicate that they have not read a journal article or a book nor attended a workshop specifically related to bereavement in at least a decade. If the study completed by Beckett and Dykeman (2015) can be generalized beyond the six studied counselor training programs in the Pacific Northwest region of the United States, counseling students may still be generally getting sparse training related to bereavement.

I would not knowingly refer bereaved individuals to a group led by peer volunteers or inexperienced professional counselors unless those group's leaders were connected to experienced counselors thoroughly versed in contemporary understandings of bereavement work. Even after 15 years of leading bereavement groups, I continued participating in a monthly group of extraordinarily well-trained colleagues under the leadership of our mentor, J. William Worden.

Bereavement support group leaders are likely best trained through an apprenticeship approach. After leaders-in-training gain some basic education about current perspectives on bereavement and the role of death and grief in the lives of individuals, families, and communities, these group facilitators-in-training can profitably observe the work of seasoned leaders. One program coordinator interviewed in the LEAP study said the model followed in that agency requires each observation to be followed by an experience that requires the trainees to reflect on their observations in writing and orally. When the newly-trained leaders have completed their required observations (15 hours or 10 group meetings), the new leader is assigned as a group co-leader working with an experienced group leader. Veteran group facilitators are taught about how to be effective mentors, expecting trainees to "watch first and then take on more and more responsibility as the group progresses."

These experienced leaders provide moral support and a "calm hand," thereby reducing anxiety. Occasionally, the program leader noted, the veteran leader needs to step in to "rescue" a fledgling trainee, but generally the new facilitators provide excellent leadership to the group. The program leader noted one unexpected benefit from the experience: "Members of the group feel a real sense of satisfaction that their grief has benefited others by helping to train a new counselor."

One of the challenges in training and supervising group leaders/facilitators is in helping them set and maintain appropriate boundaries regarding the involvement of their own stories and expressions of grief in the group. One could argue that group facilitators need to keep some "professional detachment" so that the group does not become focused on helping the leader cope with his or her own loss.

We must expect group leaders to potentially become "overinvolved" in the group process. The individuals responding to invitations to be trained as a bereavement group leader most likely possess unusually high levels of caring attitudes and behaviors. If these potential leaders were to complete a behavioral style instrument, their empathy scores would likely be off the chart. Program leaders can help considerably by discussing and modeling boundaries with group facilitators.

QUESTIONS FOR REFLECTION AND DISCUSSION

- What essential qualities of a bereavement leader would you add to the author's list? Why do you think they are important? Are there any on the author's list that you believe are secondary or even unnecessary? Why?
- If you were creating a training program for bereavement support group leaders, how many hours would your training program last? What would you include, and how much time would you give to each topic? How would you mix together lecture, small group discussion, role-play, and other activities in the training program you envision?
- How do you manage your own self-care? What strategies to you employ? Do you believe your strategies work? How have you reached that conclusion?

NOTE

1. Scholarly (peer-reviewed) journals specifically addressing the bereavement field include *Death Studies; Omega: Journal of Death and Dying; Mortality; Illness, Crisis, & Loss; Bereavement Care; Journal of Loss & Trauma; and Grief Matters: The Australian Journal of Grief and Bereavement* (Wittkowski et al., 2015).

CHAPTER 4

What Goes On Here? Developing Content for Adult Groups

At the conclusion of an educational conference on suicide in October 1982 at Illinois' Aurora College, nursing student Ernie Brasher stood and asked where the group for suicide survivors met. The speaker told Ernie, whose own 20-year-old daughter had died by suicide only 10 months earlier, that there was not one. As the story goes, Ernie would not sit down. Stephanie Weber, a college intern and conference organizer whose mother had died by suicide 13 months earlier replied, "If you are a survivor interested in a group, return this Monday at 7:00 pm." Eight women attended that first meeting, beginning a group that has been meeting on the third Monday of each month for nearly 35 years. Stephanie Weber still facilitates that group (Suicide Prevention Services of America, 2012).

Like many other Survivors of Suicide (SOS) groups, that original group in Aurora, Illinois, begins each monthly meeting with this passage:

> Welcome to this circle where we hope you may find space to grieve, to search, to listen, and to reach out.
>
> Each one of us brings here a story: the story of our brokenness and sorrow, the story of our survival, our need to get more out of life.
>
> We come here to be with people who understand our struggle and our hurt: they too have tears in their hands and pain in their hearts.
>
> This is a sacred place where we can explore our feelings: our loneliness, our shock, our anger, our guilt, our sadness or whatever is hurting us inside. This is a place where we can share our humanity and find strength and inspiration in each other. . . .
>
> Although we remain deeply wounded people, let us find comfort and healing in what we believe and in our ability to care for each other. (Pangrazzi, n.d.)

Bereavement support groups use a diversity of ways to introduce their meetings. One leader interviewed in the LEAP study lights a candle in the center of the table around which the group meets and invites individuals arriving for the meeting to each light a candle in memory of their loved ones. Another makes certain that the smell of coffee and freshly baked cookies permeates the meeting room to "welcome and encourage those who are uncertain whether they have the strength to attend the meeting." Some of the leaders of groups hosted by faith communities interviewed for the LEAP study offer a prayer at the beginning (or the end) of the meeting, while others do not.

FORMATTING A GROUP MEETING

Results from the LEAP study show amazing similarity in the general format of adult groups among the leaders interviewed. In spite of the diversity among leaders interviewed in terms of their own background and training, these leaders generally begin their groups by welcoming participants and introducing the meeting's format, providing opportunities for participants to "tell their story," and offering some content guidance through an educational piece. In interviews, the basic format of adult bereavement support groups was highly similar in spite of diversity in geography, group sponsorship (church, hospice, bereavement center, etc.), participant constituencies, and meeting themes.

Group leaders who spoke specifically about the topic were unanimous in their perspective that leaders should arrive ahead of participants; the consensus perspective is that group leaders are responsible for welcoming participants as they arrive, even in groups where there are designated volunteers who share this task. "Soft start" is a good term to describe the beginning of some group meetings, wherein group participants gather in an informal time for members to mingle before the leader actually calls participants to order. Group leaders interviewed for the study as well as those I have observed throughout my career rarely begin meetings at the exact minute of the published beginning time; some leaders admitted they frequently began the organized activities of their groups ten minutes or more after the official starting time.

One experienced bereavement group leader explained a simple perspective on organizing the content of a support group. Though the four-point outline for group meetings represented the perspective of this respondent, there was striking similarity between this plan and those offered by other group leaders. According to this respondent, group meetings include:

Welcome—the facilitator warmly greets each participant on arrival and then welcomes the entire group with a brief overview of the meeting theme and content.

Engagement—the facilitator introduces an activity relating to the theme of the meeting. When addressing anxiety, for example, participants are given a few minutes to make a list of their fears; when the group meeting focuses on memories, participants make their own "memory boxes."

Discussion—after participants have worked on an individual project or activity, the facilitator leads a large-group discussion or gives instructions to work in groups of two or three to talk about what the participants have done or to share elements of their personal stories that relate to the theme.

Education—During the group discussion or in a brief concluding section, the facilitator points out two or three principles related to the meeting's theme. When the focus of the group has been on physical well-being, for example, the group leader either shares practical ideas about physical fitness or reiterates ideas that members have already discussed. This facilitator might say, "I think Margie had a great idea when she said she found it easiest to walk with others; there is a walking group that meets at the mall at 6:30 every weekday morning." The facilitator who shared this outline pointed out a high priority on the education section, indicating that every meeting needs to have an educational component so that participants should leave with an idea to try.

ROOM CONFIGURATION

The group leaders interviewed in the LEAP study nearly all indicated a preference for group participants sitting around a circle of chairs; there was a mixture of preferences for the presence of a table or group of tables around which members sit. Some leaders offered explanations for their preferences, ranging from practical to psychological. While one leader preferred tables because of the expressive arts activities used in the group, another remarked: "I like the 'safety' a table provides. Grieving people already feel so vulnerable, and I just think this gives them a bit of a safety net." Another leader offered a nearly opposite opinion: "I don't like a table; I think it feels like a barrier. People just share better when there isn't this giant piece of furniture between us."

One group leader interviewed received training from a commercial grief training organization that the leader said insists on "standard practices."

In this case, the respondent said, he participated in a four-day training conference leading to his becoming "certified" as a specialist in the organization's group process. In this case, he reported, the organization prescribes that groups be set up as a semi-circle, with the facilitator in the center of the half-circle facing the group. Since in this model the leader sits next to a flipchart to illustrate or notate parts of the opening "presentation," this leader noted the likelihood that group participants would see the facilitator as "the expert." Even though the arrangement is what the respondent believes is required as part of the "franchise" of using the training organization's "brand," this leader explained his misgivings about this arrangement. Of those leading formalized talk-related groups, this was the only respondent whose group seating arrangement differed from the general pattern of the group in a circle and the leader as part of that circle.

Educational researchers have studied the role classroom configuration has on learning outcomes as well as the comfort and psychological well-being of students, demonstrating that room configurations that encourage interaction accompanied by interactive activities increase learning retention from 5% in lecture formats to 50% in discussion formats and 75% in "learning by doing" (activity) formats (Herman Miller, n.d.). Research efforts are ongoing to determine how room configuration affects group dynamics in focus group research, thereby raising questions about the reliability of some studies (Farnsworth & Boon, 2010). However, while research efforts have been ongoing to determine best configurations for educational spaces and focus groups used in market research, apparently no study to date has examined the effects on group dynamics or participant outcomes emanating from the configuration of furnishings in a support group meeting. Leaders interviewed in the LEAP study generally have strong opinions about room configuration, so it seems important to empirically examine the effects this variable may have on bereavement outcomes for individual participants.

GROUP ACTIVITIES

Guided Discussion

Like their cousins, psychotherapy groups, bereavement support groups for adults tend to focus on the verbal expression of grief through storytelling, oral descriptions of experiences, and discussion of emotions. Because so much of what happens in adult bereavement groups is based on verbal communication, the greatest problems leaders describe center around verbal issues, including such matters as group members who monopolize the discussion and those who attempt to solve every problem offered by other group members. These and other group problems are discussed in Chapter Five.

Among leaders interviewed in the LEAP study, a common theme was the importance of guiding the discussion among group participants. Though many of the respondents indicated that they provide opportunity for "check in," where group members have a free opportunity to talk about a high point or low point in life since the last meeting, preference among those interviewed is toward clear, open-ended questions that invite sharing of bereavement experiences. Several of the respondents create questions that invite group participants to talk about a specific topic. In other words, rather than asking, "How are things going for you in your grief?" these leaders use questions such as "How are you managing the anger in your grief?" or "What are the parts of your loss experience that seem to provoke the most anger in you?"

Journaling Activities

While some individuals talk through their grief, others seem best able to express the impact grief has on their life through writing. One group leader in the LEAP study reported providing a simple bound journal containing 80 pages of blank, lined sheets to each member of the group, along with a list of "journal starting" questions. Though they were originally intended to help adolescents learn to keep a personal bereavement journal, the following "journal starters" are useful for any age group:

- Today, I am thinking about the holiday when we . . .
- Today, I am thinking about when I first learned of the death . . .
- Today, I am thinking about the time when we went . . .
- Today I am thinking how grateful I am for . . .
- Today, I am thinking about how angry/guilty/sad/lonely/scared I am because . . .
- Today, I find the hardest part of this experience to be . . .

(Hoy, 2007, pp. 64–65)

Though tested most thoroughly with substance abuse groups, the technique of *interactive journaling* (Miller, 2014) shows promise for work with bereavement groups. The technique begins with written therapeutic content (printed or online) that is then embedded with guided questions for reflective writing. Conceivably, short passages of bereavement educational content could be offered to group members either in the group or as homework assignments. The interactive questions embedded in the text could then be used as discussion starters when the group resumes conversation during that session or when it meets at a subsequent session.

The week before planning to discuss ideas for managing holidays in bereavement, for example, the group leader might give to each participant the following passage with the accompanying reflective questions:

> Sights, sounds, and smells of the holidays remind you this year that things are very different. In fact, you may find yourself dreading the holiday season more than any other period since you became a bereaved person.
>
> The holidays are especially hard in grief because they are occasions of great sentiment. Everywhere we go—the shopping mall, worship, even banks and other places of business—remind us that someone very special has died. Familiar music reminds us of days gone by. The aroma of holiday spices causes bells to ring in our heads. Someone you love has died and your world is changed forever.
>
> Holidays are also hard in grief because they are built around relationships. Family gatherings cannot ever be the same. And of course, memories of bad relationships cause us to realize the past cannot be changed.
>
> In preparation for our next meeting, think about this passage and write a brief response to these questions in your journal. Be sure to bring your journal along to "jog" your memory during our discussion. (Hoy, 2014/2000, p. 1)
>
> - What sights, sounds, and smells are most poignant reminders of the holidays for me?
> - Which traditions do I expect are going to change most this year?
> - What about the approaching holidays do I most dread?

Miller (2014) reports that over a 25-year period, interactive journal materials have been distributed to more than 20 million individuals, with high endorsement from participants and therapists for their usefulness. Though randomized clinical trial results are just recently beginning to emerge, early results show promise. One study examined 183 jailed inmates in North Carolina whose offenses were alcohol or drug related and who had at least one prior incarceration. The study provided interactive journaling to 98 inmates and provided the standard government-issued booklet on the connections between substance abuse and criminal behavior to the control group of 85. Recidivism rates for the interactive journaling group was 51% and for the non-journaling control group was 66%, a result that demonstrates statistical (and clinical) significance (Proctor, Hoffman, & Allison, 2012).

Creative Arts

Several of the respondents in the LEAP study pointed to the use of various creative arts activities with adults in their groups. While participants in child support groups have used art activities since the first groups began, those interview respondents who reported using creative arts generally indicated a recent embracing of these strategies. One respondent indicated a growing awareness about learning theory emphasizing the varied learning styles of individuals. In the understanding of this leader, some individuals enjoy talk-focused groups, while others learn better in active ways. Her choice to use a combination of guided discussion and creative arts in her groups was based on her understanding of how different individuals receive information.

The use of creative arts in health care enjoys a growing evidence base. In a review of the scholarly literature of the value of creative arts in health care in general and mental health specifically, Clift (2012) reported beneficial effects for the use of choral singing with Parkinson's disease and chronic obstructive pulmonary disease (COPD) patients as well as visual arts creation projects with soldiers diagnosed with posttraumatic stress disorder (PTSD). In addressing the question of evidence for effectiveness, Clift continued:

> In discussing evidence in relation to arts and health, it is important to recognize that the growth, scope and variety of practical initiatives in this field should, in itself, be regarded as important evidence of the feasibility, acceptability, flexibility and vitality of working through the creative arts in supporting health care and promoting health. Such activities would not happen and certainly would not continue to happen, if their value was not recognized and if the experiences of such initiatives on the part of artists, health professionals, and participants did not point to tangible benefits. (p. 123)

Creative arts have shown promise in improving psychological and physical well-being in patients with serious diseases, including cancer, as well as patients coping with chronic disease. In their survey of online written communication between 155 rural women living with chronic illness, Kelly, Cudney, and Weinert (2012) found 37.7% referred without prompting to their use of creative arts as a coping strategy, reporting that such use helped in coping with pain, relaxation/quality of life, and encouragement to give back to others. Nainis et al. (2006) examined patients with cancer before and after a one-hour art therapy intervention. Researchers used the Edmonton Symptom Assessment Scale (ESAS) to assess pain, tiredness, nausea, depression, anxiety, drowsiness, lack of appetite, well-being, and shortness of breath before and after the intervention. Results showed statistically significant improvement after the intervention on every symptom except nausea.

On the basis of his research review, Clift (2012) suggested that creative arts are "benign" and "carry few, if any, risks to health" as opposed to many forms of invasive treatment. "The experiences of people who feel they have benefited from participation in arts-based interventions for health deserve to be taken seriously, not as anecdotal evidence but as serious personal testimony" (p. 124).

Craft boxes and *holiday ornaments* made from paper maché have become a widely-used medium for artistic expression of emotion, storytelling, and permanent memorabilia keeping. One group leader described an "experiment" in which he provides these inexpensive boxes to group participants at the first meeting, with the instruction to make a memory box over the course of their six-week group. He reminds group participants to bring their boxes to the last meeting and provides opportunities for group members to show their boxes to the group and explain the significance—both of the box decorations and the items collected to go inside. This leader described a bereaved father who decorated the box in patriotic colors in memory of his son who had died in military service; when he opened the box to show it to other group members, it contained the service medals his son had received.

Rather than group members decorating their memory boxes on their own, other respondents described group box-decorating activities taking as much as an entire group meeting. One group leader reported providing markers, stickers, and other decorative materials, while another group facilitator in the LEAP study indicated she provides a few items and asks group members to bring decorative items to share. Those who have used box decorating as a group activity report a high degree of quiet conversation and collaboration as the group members work on their boxes around a common table. One respondent whose organization provides age-divided groups for children and teens with a simultaneously meeting parents' group reported that all groups decorated memory boxes at the same meeting. The benefit to this arrangement of the activity, this leader reported, is that families have a discussion point as they share their boxes, not only with their support group friends but with their own family members, as well. Though varied kinds of wood boxes are also available, respondents who use memory box-making as part of their group experience indicated a preference for the stiff paper boxes that are widely available at craft stores and through online sellers by searching "paper maché craft boxes."

Some respondents in the LEAP study described creative art projects focused on the creation of photo collages. In one case, group members are invited to bring photos to the group meeting to use in creating the collages, while another respondent discussed using magazines from which to cut photos and headline words. This bereavement group leader provides old magazines, glue sticks, and poster board; she said she marveled at how group members work so diligently on their collages, which, in turn, become the "visual aid" as group members tell the stories of their loved ones' lives. This leader recounted the story of a mother attending the group following the death of her infant daughter. In making the photo collage, this mother chose to create a collage around the theme of "dreams I had for my daughter," assembling photos of children playing, prom dresses, and wedding photos.

For the group leader with an "arts and crafts" knack, there is no end to ideas; a few hours browsing in a physical or online craft store will likely produce dozens of project ideas. Colored glass, candles, decorative picture frames, and scrapbooks all hold promise for creative ways to engage adult bereavement support group participants in active expressions of their grief experiences or the story of a loved one's life.

During the literature review and interviews with practitioners leading to this volume, I found dozens of creative activities and discussion starters that facilitators have used in their bereavement support groups (some are contained in the eight-session group outline in the appendix). One very helpful compendium provides descriptions and instructions on using more than 90 techniques, including guided journal activities, body art, visualization interventions, memory boxes, and music practices (Neimeyer, 2012); that volume's sequel (Neimeyer, 2015) includes 50 additional techniques. With the plethora of good ideas abounding for helping group members adapt to their experiences of loss, practitioners must constantly choose which activities or ideas to implement in their groups.

Borrowed Narratives

An often-overlooked resource for bereavement support groups is the use of what Harold Ivan Smith (2012) calls "borrowed narratives." The biographies of famous individuals and the ways they coped with loss can be, according to Smith, a model for the more "common" bereavement experiences of everyday people. For many years, I have skimmed biographies for details about how a famous individual coped with the death of someone loved, and Smith's volume is replete with examples of famous individuals whose names are known around the world. Inspirational stories emerge from the grief experiences of Corazon Aquino, Eleanor Roosevelt, Barbara Bush, Caroline Kennedy, Arthur Ashe, Lady Bird Johnson, Colin Powell, and C. S. Lewis.

Owing the idea to Smith's work, I have occasionally begun groups with the story of a famous person and described how he or she coped with loss. To build suspense, I usually share details of the person's life and loss first, only adding their well-recognized name at the end of the story. When addressing a grief group in a Christian congregation several years ago, I began with words similar to this:

> He had waited a lifetime for the right person to come along; in fact, his colleagues had long sense given up on matchmaking, considering the man to be beyond hope for romance. When at long-last, he met the woman of his dreams and married her, he was 57 years old. Just more than four years later, the beloved for whom he had waited a lifetime died. If he were alive today, he would undoubtedly have used the term "soulmate" to describe their relationship. Though he did not want the rawness of his grief to be associated with his then-famous reputation as a Christian teacher and philosopher, he fortunately published excerpts from his journal, words from which have been inspirational to millions as they cope with loss. For the gift of modeling how to grieve deeply while wrestling with faith, we all owe a debt of gratitude to the legendary Cambridge Christian scholar, C.S. Lewis and his little 70-page treatise, *A Grief Observed.*

A GROUP'S FIRST MEETING: GETTING STARTED RIGHT

As mentioned in Chapter Three, Aveline (1993) has suggested that one of a group leader's most important tasks is to contain anxiety for group participants. Though Aveline did not specifically have bereavement groups in sight in his writing, the principle holds true for groups of people seeking support after the death of a loved one. A sense of psychological safety must be infused into every group meeting, but it is essential that it begin as the group first gathers. Greeting participants warmly, working with group members to establish ground rules, discussing confidentiality, and providing a clear overview of how group meetings will work are all vital to creating a sense of psychological safety.

Individuals attending their first bereavement support group meeting are understandably anxious. Unless an individual is there having been coerced by a parent, spouse, or other loved one to attend, he or she is coping with what is apprised to be a significant loss. I remember a woman nearing 80 years of age who made her way into our group. She could barely get the words out of her mouth that her husband had died after nearly 60 years of marriage. She later told me that she was frightened of what might happen in this room, but she was even more frightened she was losing her mind. Her anxiety was palpable.

Every group needs a greeter. At the first meeting, the group leader (or one of the co-leaders) will usually assume that role, but at subsequent meetings, other participants might volunteer for the task if invited. All individuals attending for the first time will wonder if they "fit in" or even if they have found the right room. I vividly remember a group meeting when we did not have a group greeter, and about 15 minutes into the group, a gentleman stood to his feet and exclaimed, "I think I'm in the wrong place; everybody in my life is still alive!" A greeter could have saved us all some embarrassment. Whether drinks and snacks are offered is a matter of personal taste and local custom, but the aroma of coffee brewing and fresh cookies arranged on platter provides a very inviting atmosphere.

While many bereavement groups operate in facilities designed for other purposes (classrooms, church parlors, and hospital conference rooms, to name a few), several respondents in the LEAP study work with organizations that operate free-standing bereavement centers. One described the "living room" in the center where she works, suggesting that it is a welcoming space that allows individuals and families to relax and focus on the emotional work of grieving. "People come and sit awhile," this respondent said.

> For those with strong family of origin memories, it often helps them remember those family dinners, you know, the holidays and birthdays. For those who don't have such great memories, the living room maybe helps them write a new script. Inevitably, people tell us that this entry to our house makes it seem they have "come home."

Establishing "ground rules" at the first meeting is another way to relieve anxiety. Bereavement is often a chaotic experience, so established ground rules can suggest a sense of stability for participants. Group leaders who were interviewed in the LEAP study offered several rules their groups had established:

- one person talks at a time
- no advice giving unless it is asked for
- since we only meet for *x* weeks, we agree to make every effort to attend every meeting.
- what is said in our group stays in our group
- no put-downs of others
- you only have to talk if you want to
- no monopolizing the conversation

The important element is for the group leader to guide the group in setting rules to which participants agree; several LEAP study respondents indicated they believe group participants should be given a voice in establishing those rules.

Thirdly, group member anxiety can be reduced through the agreement of complete confidentiality on the part of every individual participating in the group. One LEAP study participant explains the importance of confidentiality to every new group and repeats the message at most group meetings. Even though this agency operates in a large urban area, the respondent explained, word can get around. Group members are encouraged to talk about their own loss experiences with others outside the group but never to tell personal information about others in the group. Some LEAP study participants discourage the use of last names at group meetings so that group members feel more emotionally safe. The role of confidentiality is treated in detail in Chapter Five.

A fourth way to manage participant anxiety is to provide a verbal (or written) "road map" of how groups will be structured. One way to do this at the first meeting is to follow a script such as this one:

> I am so glad each of you has chosen to become part of our group. It takes a lot of courage to come to an unfamiliar place and talk with unknown people about such a difficult topic; thank you for honoring us with your participation. Let me tell you a little about how I see our group working.
>
> Each week when we gather, we will take a few minutes to enjoy coffee and snacks; I hope you will feel free to come a few minutes

> early when you can. You can sign up on the sheet over by the coffee pot if you would like to bring a snack one week.
>
> Right at 2 o'clock, I will call us together here at the table. We will start with a quick "go-around," when I will ask each person to share the name you want to be called and a sentence about the loss that brought you here. It will take a few weeks to learn everybody's name and story, but doing that each time we meet will be a big help. Then, each week, I will talk briefly about a topic of interest to most bereaved people; I have a schedule here so you can see where I see us headed. Before we leave today, we will talk about other topics that might be of interest, too. After I make that brief introduction to the topic, I will try to get our conversation going with a few questions I have thought about. That will help us get to know each other and provide support to each other. I hope you will never feel pressured to talk, but my job is to guide us in such a way that everyone who wants to gets the chance.
>
> One of the tasks that I think is vital is for us to agree with each other about confidentiality and for us to work together to establish what we want the ground rules of our group to be for the next eight weeks. That will be our focus today, okay?

This information can also be shared in prescreening interviews as interested individuals learn more about the bereavement support group and the group facilitator or program leader assesses the individual's appropriateness for the group. Nevertheless, repetition is a friend, so it may be helpful to repeat the same introduction at the first group meeting. Over my years of leading groups, I have gravitated toward an opening to every meeting in which I explain the simple outline of the meeting, thinking that a little direction at the beginning helped our group stay "on track" and helped relieve the anxiety of individuals unsure about being in a bereavement support group.

How punctually to start and end group meetings seems to be of perennial concern for leaders. One school of thought is that most of what we do in the Western world operates on a fixed time system; when the university announces that my class begins at 8:00 a.m., I am in the classroom and ready to go at 8:00 a.m. Even at that early hour, I expect students to do likewise. The perspective I share with students on the first day of class is they should not agree to take a class at that hour if they are not planning to arrive on time every day. I have colleagues who lock the classroom door at the published start time of their classes and do not allow students to enter even one minute late.

Another reason for starting on time is that most people arrive on time and some arrive quite a bit early, especially at the first meeting. Several LEAP study respondents indicated a reluctance to punish the people who arrive on time by waiting for those who show up late. Moreover, a sure recipe for individuals to arrive later and later for subsequent meetings is to wait for latecomers. Week two may begin 10 minutes late, and by week four, people will still be straggling in at 20 minutes after the published time. It just seems to be human nature. Nevertheless, time and punctuality are cultural constructs rather than universal, invariable concepts. Local customs typically dictate how rigorous a schedule must be kept.

PLANNING GROUP "THEMES"

The LEAP study uncovered a number of "themes" that seem to be common among group facilitators as they plan meeting content. Most of those interviewed indicated a preference for meeting topics, even though they might have few tactics to keep the meeting focused on that topic. There is wide agreement about some essential topics that all groups should address, whether as "sessions" of a six-, eight-, or 10-week group or as topics to be addressed periodically throughout the year in an ongoing group. For example, helping group members face holidays in grief was a common meeting topic among the LEAP study respondents. For those who lead time-limited groups, they tended to set aside one session for discussing the difficulties of and strategies for facing special days; most included cultural holidays, birthdays, family events, and anniversaries in this session.

For those facilitators leading ongoing groups, most address grief at holidays and special occasions throughout the year, but usually just before "holiday clusters." One American LEAP study participant said in his ongoing group, he addressed the traditional winter holidays in mid-November, and the "family days" of Mother's Day, Father's Day, school commencement, and summer family reunions at the last meeting in April or the first meeting in May. Since which holidays are seen as significant varies by cultural tradition, religious heritage, and personal preference, group leaders will want to consider the demographic constituency of the group or ask group members to suggest the special days they find most problematic.

When asked to provide the topics discussed in groups, LEAP study participants listed several topics they assure get addressed in the course of groups they lead. The emotional components of grief (anger, guilt, sadness, etc.) were most often listed first among respondents, with several indicating they work to create a "safe place" where difficult emotions can be expressed and discussed. Study participants make sure to talk about what Yalom (1995) called the "new unpalatable life role" (p. 454), with group leaders describing it variously as "adapting to the new normal" and "learning to live in a changed world." Most LEAP study respondents also make sure their groups discuss relationships with families and old friends, the possibilities for personal growth through grief, and the holistic nature of grief, explaining that the bereavement experience includes emotional, cognitive, physical, social, and spiritual elements. Most group leaders address the importance of delaying major decisions and the formation of new relationships, whether as friends or as possible romantic partners.

A somewhat surprising number of group leaders interviewed in the LEAP study indicated a preference for what one called a "free-for-all." One respondent explained that grieving individuals know best what they need, so she allows the topic of the group to evolve each night. This strategy requires active leadership, however, in that a vocal group participant can easily steer the group topic at every session in the direction he or she wants it to go.

In my first book about leading support groups (Hoy, 2007), I included a plan for an eight-session group. Though that book is now out of print, those ideas for leading guided discussions in the bereavement support group are included in the Appendix. However, some topics for inclusion in grief support groups merit more attention than either that provided by the eight-session group in the appendix or the summary list from participants of the LEAP study.

Emotional Expression

For many years, I have referred to anger, fear, guilt, loneliness, and sadness as the emotional "Big Five" of grief. While bereaved individuals are likely to experience any emotion for which we have a label, these five seem to be the emotional experiences most labeled by the bereaved individuals with whom I have worked. In interviewing respondents to the LEAP study, I encountered these emotions repeatedly.

"Recovery"

While many groups use the word "recovery" in their names, leaders will want to choose vocabulary carefully, a concept briefly discussed in Chapter One. In their objection to the use of the word "recovery," for example, Tedeschi and Calhoun (2008) have reminded readers that words have power and that "language is a living organism" (p. 28). Though these researchers suggest a survey be undertaken to discover the terminology most preferred by bereaved people themselves, it would likely be a profitable discussion in a bereavement support group meeting to begin in this way:

> There have been many people—including some professionals who study and support bereaved people—who have debated whether or not the word "recovery" is a good word to use in talking about the grief process. While some would say that a word is just a label or a symbol, others believe that language is intensely powerful in helping us aspire and set goals about the future. What do you think about the word "recovery," and do you see it as a good term to describe what your hope is for your experience with loss?

As the group meeting proceeds, the leader can invite group members to suggest other words or terms that they find objectionable. Group members may very well discuss their dissatisfaction with popular terminology such as *closure*, *moving on*, *putting this behind you*, and *getting over it*.

Continuing Bonds

One discussion in the bereavement literature in recent decades details what have come to be called *continuing bonds* (Silverman & Klass, 1996). Along with their co-editor Stephen Nickman, Phyllis Silverman and Dennis Klass describe a "new paradigm," one that does not see the goal of the bereavement process to sever the attachment bond with the deceased. Rather, the model they propose is based on substantial data that "suggest that the bereaved remain involved and connected to the deceased, and that the bereaved actively construct an inner representation of the deceased that is part of the normal grieving process" (p. 16). After reviewing several studies on the role of these maintained attachments with the deceased, Wortman and Silver (2001) helpfully reminded clinicians that these links can be perceived as comforting or frightening; several studies with bereaved children, for example, indicate some children find a "watching parent" as a scary notion and/or are afraid of a parental "ghost" (p. 417).

Kosminsky and Jordan (2016) concluded that the development of a continuing bond with a deceased child is especially important for bereaved parents as they renegotiate the attachment bond that is so much a part of the parent-child relationship. They quoted Klass (1997, 1999) in suggesting that bereavement support groups such as the Compassionate Friends can be powerful tools in effecting these newly reconstructed bonds.

Instrumental Grieving

The late 20th century witnessed a growing interest in understanding gender differences in bereavement, suggesting that men and women grieve in predictably different ways (Golden, 2000; Staudacher, 1991). In some cases, the perspective went so far as to suggest that with their reticence to share emotion, Western men grieved deficiently. In his overview of masculine grief, Golden (2000) wrote,

> The masculine side of healing is not as accepted a mode of healing as the more traditional verbal and emotional expressions. It tends to be quieter and less visible, less connected with the past and more connected with the future; less connected with passivity and more aligned with action. As a consequence, I have noticed repeatedly that people who use a predominance of this masculine side of healing are suspected even by mental health professionals of "not really healing." (p. 1)

Doka and Martin (2010) proposed that a large subset of bereaved individuals do not process the experience of grief in primarily emotional tasks. Rather, they suggested a continuum of grief styles ranging from "intuitive grief," the widely regarded emotional processing, to a much more action-oriented style they called "instrumental grief." While Doka and Martin acknowledged that social assumptions about gender roles influence grief styles, they asserted that the way individuals grieve is bigger than stereotyped gender roles.

In their study of 99 counseling students, Beckett and Dykeman (2015) found that 93.9% were unaware of the theoretical construct of instrumental grief. What they deemed as possibly the most clinically significant finding of the study is that 66% of their respondents indicated they would often, very often, or always encourage emotional catharsis in treatment of a patient in a video vignette of instrumental grief. This finding, they concluded, indicated that instrumental grievers were likely to be treated with interventions that may be inappropriate. While this could be due to a lack of awareness, the authors seem to think the problem is "lack of fit" between the clinical tools provided to counselors-in-training and the needs of the bereaved individual operating within an instrumental style. "If most counselor education and supervision is weighted heavily toward emotional expression," they pointed out, "then the high likelihood of utilization may simply be an illustration of the proverb, 'If the only tool you have is a hammer, then everything you encounter is going to be treated like a nail' " (p. 229).

Physical Well-Being

Stahl and Schulz (2014) conducted an extensive review of the research on influence of bereavement on the health behaviors of older adults. The authors reviewed what they call six behavioral domains or "modifiable risk factors" that are important for maintaining health: physical activity, nutrition, sleep quality, alcohol consumption, tobacco use, and body weight status. Their review examined 32 research studies published between 1980 and 2011, finding varying levels of effect in the relationship between bereavement and health.

For example, the researchers found strong evidence for a link between bereavement and nutritional risk as well as involuntary weight loss; nutritional risk is usually defined in the literature as poor eating habits such as consumption of the wrong food (junk food, highly processed food) or simply not eating enough to maintain weight and vitality. The researchers also found moderate evidence for impaired sleep quality and increased alcohol consumption. The relationship between bereavement and physical activity was unclear in the studies reviewed.

Other scholars have explored the relationship between bereavement and physical health on youngsters, reporting similar findings (J. Li et al., 2012; Morin, 2014). Of special interest to bereavement support group leaders is the findings by Weinberg et al. (2013). In their study of 123 bereaved youths and a matched nonbereaved control group, and after controlling for mental health history and pre-existing illness, they found that the bereaved young people showed a significantly higher risk for obesity five years later than did their nonbereaved counterparts. Though their recommendations were primarily addressed to their physician-psychiatrist readers, they suggested that bereaved youths be monitored for weight changes, that youths and surviving parents be provided with educational content on healthy eating, and that support groups address the "associations between negative emotions, stress, and eating behavior" (p. 839).

Just because there are correlations between bereavement and poorer physical health does not mean they are causally related. Like other researchers, Stahl and Schulz (2014) recommend ideas for studies to further examine elements of the relationship between bereavement and physical health. But they also note the importance of attending to physical health in the assessment and intervention of those who interact with bereaved older adults.

Few bereavement groups I have observed over my career fully address the importance of nutrition, sleep, and exercise, and fewer still seem to teach self-management strategies to their participants. With habits of nutrition, rest, and activity having such a profound effect on mental health as well as making such an important contribution to overall physical well-being, bereavement support group leaders must lead the efforts to teach bereaved people how to cook for one, make good food choices, limit unhealthy foods, and interact around healthy food. Perhaps we can even model the behavior in our bereavement groups by replacing high calorie, sweet, fatty commercially prepared baked goods with healthy snacks like granola bars, apples, bananas, and nuts.

ONLINE BEREAVEMENT SUPPORT GROUPS

From the earliest days of Internet development, some individuals have been interested in providing and receiving bereavement support from an online community. In one of the earliest analyses of the use of Internet technology with bereavement, Sofka (1997) produced a review of the then-current resources online, concluding that ethical questions abound in the reliability of materials and the protection afforded to individuals participating in support groups. Interestingly, Sofka provided background and definitions for terms that have now become part of the vocabulary of most English-speakers—World Wide Web and URL, for example.

Sofka (1997) pointed out, for example, the ethical issues implicit in conducting observational research based only on reading the postings of online bereavement forum users, in part because the intention of the bereaved individuals' postings in Internet forums was not that their stories be used for research projects such as content analysis. "Lurking," the reading of individual users' postings as an observer without joining the online discussion, Sofka pointed out, was acceptable etiquette in the then-nascent Internet. However, the ready availability of those resources or even the implicit etiquette codes shared among online users does not meet the significantly higher standards for informed consent required in human subjects research. One counter-argument to the concern, however, is that participants can protect their privacy through participating only in forums that require registration and protect user posts from reading by those outside the known group members through the use of user names and passwords.

While most online groups would be best classified as peer-support forums, there have been some randomized control trials of clinical interventions delivered in a digital format. Wagner, Knaevelsrud, and Maercker (2006, 2007) reported promising results for an 18-month longitudinal study of 25 bereaved individuals who completed an email-based cognitive behavioral intervention for complicated grief compared to 25 assigned to a matched "waiting group" (control). When comparing the treatment group to the nontreatment control group, the researchers noted significantly greater reduction in psychological symptoms of complicated grief such as intrusion and avoidance as well as in levels of depression and anxiety among the treatment group individuals. The participants in the treatment group expressed positive feelings about the online setting. Citing the work of Rochlen, Zack, and Speyer (2004), this study's authors hypothesized that self-disclosure seemed to have been enabled by a phenomenon of "telepresence," the feeling (or perhaps illusion) of experiencing the therapist's presence even though the therapist is not sharing physical space with the therapy group member.

Online support groups have also been found to be beneficial to participants who are depressed. Houston, Cooper, and Ford (2002) found that 53.4% of their 103 online support group participants accessed the support group more than five hours in the previous two weeks. This finding was significant because their cohort reported very low levels of social support, implying that the online support group provided a beneficial supplement to their face-to-face interventions. Contrary to the researchers' fears, online participants did not jettison their in-person support but rather used the online support group as an adjunctive treatment. A significant majority (95.1%) reported their use of the online support group helped their depressive symptoms.

The plethora of online resources for bereaved individuals is not limited to support group forums and libraries of psychoeducational materials; online memorialization sites also abound. Personal obituary sites abound on the Internet, providing a unique kind of support for bereaved individuals. There can be a sense of catharsis in developing the site, writing the text for the obituary, reflecting on stories from the deceased individual's life, and selecting photographs to include. The dialogue that develops in shared comments between mourners take on elements of supportive dialogue in face-to-face support groups, with the exception that generally the mourners on any one site tend to be linked together by some relationship with a single deceased individual. In her analysis of the creation of web-based memorials, Roberts (2004) noted the frequency of messages addressed directly to the deceased. In one letter, an adult sibling wrote,

> I do not know why you committed suicide, A_____, you took the answer to that question to the grave. . . . I often go down to the beach

> where you said goodbye to the world. Its (sic) a peaceful spot. Mum and Dad miss you very much, C___ and S___ don't understand that you won't be coming home, they wait for you at the window. Where ever (sic) you are think of me like I think of you. (cited in Roberts, 2004, p. 59)

In a touching "postscript" to the research report, Roberts recounted her own experience creating a memorial webpage for a friend who died suddenly. Without intending it to be a support group, it quickly became one, as friends, formerly unknown to one another, joined the project, contributed pictures and stories, and offered encouragement to one another through the website. While not specifically intended, the incidental development of social support for this group has apparently been helpful to this collection of bereaved friends. In summary, the researcher wrote about this very personal experience of a close friend's death and the memorialization that followed it:

> In short, the connections that were fostered by discussion of and work on the Web page have blossomed and our bonds with our deceased friend have been well supported. We are getting along about as well as any group could, given the extent of our loss. Would we feel the same today if we had not created our Web memorial? Perhaps, but as our research participants have told us, it would have been harder to get here. (Roberts, 2004, pp. 73–74)

In her review of the history of online grief support communities, Cendra Lynn, founder of GriefNet, recounted the first attempts at online support through the exchanging of emails between a few bereaved individuals in the earliest days of Internet use. Referring to her work with Edward Vielmetti, whom she calls a pioneer in Internet development, she wrote, "Ed created a discussion group using a program called Majordomo, whereby we could all talk with each other. We called it grief-chat, and it became the first e-mail-based grief group on the internet in May 1994" (Lynn & Rath, 2012, p. 88).

Lynn and Rath (2012) pointed out several disadvantages of bereavement support through the invisible Internet. The kind of "intimacy" that develops among people on website chat rooms is devoid of such important elements of face-to-face intimacy like nonverbal communication clues through facial expression and body language. Real intimacy is difficult to develop, the authors asserted, in the absence of knowing anything about a person's cultural background, education, accent, or gender. Moreover, the anonymity of the Internet "provides both freedom and danger" (p. 92). Assumptions about what users write and how users reply can lead to misunderstandings and increasingly to vitriolic communication and heightened disinhibition, a feature of the anonymity of online support groups also noted by van der Houwen, Stroebe, Stroebe, Schut, and van den Bout (2010); Walter, Hourizi, Moncur, and Pitsillides (2011–2012); and Döveling (2015). Lynn and Rath (2012) recount an episode during the year-end holidays of 1996 when several bereaved parents used their own Christian beliefs to describe the hopefulness they experienced in the midst of their loss. Some parents who did not share their faith perspectives objected, and the hurt and anger grew. "The messages grew angrier and angrier," Lynn and Rath wrote, "until they were out-and-out flames (personal attacks), and finally, almost the entire group unsubscribed and departed hurt and very angry" (p. 93).

Although the GriefNet staff debated the issue internally, the organization eventually decided to forbid religious discussion on the site in the quest to provide an emotionally safe place for all. The organization's website explains its current position about religious discussion:

> Please do not discuss religion or spiritual beliefs. Our membership is composed of people from all over the world who embrace a variety of faiths and religious beliefs. What comforts one person may greatly offend another. Discussion or mention of mediums in any way is expressly forbidden. We do have two groups for discussion of religious or spiritual beliefs, which you may join by sending a request. (GriefNet.org, n.d.)

In their analysis of Internet bereavement groups, van der Houwen et al. (2010) found both advantages and disadvantages of Internet support groups for bereaved individuals but also raised two fundamental reasons for research into these groups' efficacy. First, they suggested, research should help answer questions about whether online support groups actually harm bereaved individuals. Second, research can provide evidence to answer the question of whether bereaved individuals' investment of time seeking support online can reasonably be expected to help them. In their study of 253 bereaved individuals from multiple nations, the researchers found that when compared with bereaved individuals who had never participated in online bereavement support, those who were currently participating or had at one point tended to be of a younger age and nonparticipatory in organized religious communities and included more bereaved parents than the control group. Living in a rural location without ready access to services, a commonly mentioned advantage for online versus face-to-face support groups, was not in evidence in the study. Respondents averaged more than one hour per day in online bereavement support, a number that could be deduced to be substantially higher than bereaved individuals who attend one 90–120 minute group per week. In this study, the use of online mutual bereavement support did not predict changes in mental health over time in measures of grief, depressive symptoms, emotional loneliness, or positive mood.

In a similar study, Feigelman, Gorman, Chastain Beal, and Jordan (2008) examined the support experiences of 403 bereaved parents after the death of a child by suicide, including 104 who had participated in an online support group and 297 who had participated in a face-to-face group. Eleven of those participating in a face-to-face group had also participated in online support, although not during the preceding year. Feigelman and colleagues also pointed out that individuals bereaved by suicide often prefer peer-led groups, in part because many feel they were "failed" by a mental health system that did not prevent the suicide in the first place.

Of the bereaved parents participating in online groups, there were several reasons cited for their involvement. More than 80% indicated the online bereavement support they received helped them because it offered help to cope with the pain and sadness of loss, provided a "safe place" to discuss taboo topics such as suicide, and provided a forum for sharing information and experiences (Feigelman et al., 2008, p. 226). Other items mentioned by more than half of respondents included in their descriptions that online support provided an opportunity to memorialize the loved one, help for facing holidays, and availability of a source of help when survivor problems arose. Sixty-three percent of respondents reported benefitting from their online participation, in part because they were able to help others in their loss experiences.

When Dominick et al. (2009–2010) began their research, they reported finding no research about online self-help interventions for individuals with relatively uncomplicated grief, so they set out to develop and test a psycho-educational resource. After developing a grief education module they titled *Making Sense of Grief*, they used a well-designed randomized control trial with 33 individuals in their treatment group and 34 in their control group. In reporting their results, they wrote, "Treatment participants had large gains compared to control participants with the greatest benefit coming in comparisons of attitude/knowledge, self-efficacy, and state anxiety." Acknowledging the short time interval between baseline evaluation and posttest, the researchers noted the need for longitudinal testing of their intervention to evaluate if benefits were maintained over longer period. However, they concluded, the "significant and substantive effects were obtained on all three of the outcome measures providing support for the efficacy of the intervention" (p. 83).

In an important mixed-methods study, Döveling (2015) analyzed 2,127 Internet postings from 318 users on three large German online bereavement platforms, including one used primarily by older children and teens. Based on previous research, Döveling hypothesized that some individuals use online platforms to express their grief because they sense a lack of social support in their "offline" world. In her analysis, she found a statistically significant 12.4% of all users identified their lack of support outside the online platform as a factor that drew them to this means of support; 15.6% of users on the predominantly youth platform ("Young Wings") identified lack of social support as an important reason for using the online platform. Additionally, one-third of participants in these three online communities displayed a memorializing pattern of writing messages addressed specifically to the deceased. Citing the work of Klass and Walter (2001), Döveling (2015) wrote, "bereaved people often preserve a bond with those loved ones who have died. Continuing such a bond in shared online memorialization does not interfere with bereavement, nor is it unresolved grief, but is understood as an integral part within the grieving process, an attachment that is not associated with measures of poor adjustment" (p. 116). The freedom users feel in sharing their continuing bonds with the deceased, Döveling noted, is in part because of the anonymity provided in online bereavement platforms.

Any individual who has written an email and then delayed sending it knows the potential conflicts and misunderstandings that have been averted versus those who phone immediately to settle a conflict. Internet sites often refer to themselves with terms such as "discussion boards." In everyday speech, "discussion" is usually assumed to be a verbal conversation between two or more individuals, but in the sense of Internet forums, these discussions are comprised of written prose exchanged between two or more people. Written communication differs from oral communication in several significant ways. With written text, writers have the ability to edit, delete, and rewrite their text before "posting" it for others to see, an advantage not readily apparent in oral communication. How this editable text affects what parts of the story the bereaved individual shares with others is an important question that may have an effect on the level of "transparency" apparent in a group. Moreover, in the absence of facial expressions and other body language, readers have a difficult task in deciphering inflection and vocal "tone" in online postings, increasing the risk of miscommunication and potentially hurtful misunderstandings.

The written nature of the text also means that conversations or individual postings on the Internet survive for a very long time, possibly in perpetuity. Reading postings of other participants' early loss experiences can become emotionally overwhelming, especially for the newly bereaved. In other words, the ready accessibility to postings made years ago may be a positive experience for the newly bereaved or a significantly painful one, a distinction Aho, Paavilainen, and Kaunonen (2012) noted in their analysis of 631 Internet postings from bereaved mothers. Though the study involved a very small number of participants, the almost journal-like data from the participants provides a rich picture of grief's evolution over time; the analysis included postings over a six-year period.

These researchers observed three main themes emerging about the support these mothers provided for each other. The postings demonstrated *emotional support* (including such items as providing positive feedback, sharing "oppressive feelings" such as fear, anger, or guilt, and showing compassion to each other). Additionally, postings demonstrated bereaved mothers' reliance on the group for *informational support* including referral to face-to-face groups and professional counselors as well as notification about upcoming events of interest and printed materials. The third theme the researchers noted was what they labeled *support through community*, whereby participants welcomed one another to the group, derived help from and provided help to others related to hearing the story of the child's death, and provided a place where others would understand the shared term of "angel baby."

With the well-documented importance of meaning reconstruction or spiritual sense-making in the bereavement process (Hoy, 2015; Neimeyer & Sands, 2011; Worden, 2009), it is of little surprise that 51% of respondents indicated they gained spiritual comfort or support from their online group experience. With larger numbers of online support group users being unaffiliated with organized religious communities, it is possible that the online bereavement group becomes the "spiritual community" for many bereaved individuals.

A recent study of 148 bereaved parents using an online forum found similar exploration of religious and/or spiritual issues. In their survey of online postings from parents after stillbirth and neonatal loss, Bakker and

Paris (2013) found 37.2% expressing what the researchers categorized as a theme of "religious disorientation" (p. 662) and 20.9% expressing what the researchers described as eventual "religious reorientation" (p. 664). In taking the findings of these studies with varied people groups and types of loss together, online forum administrators should carefully evaluate policies that forbid spiritual sharing in online forums, perhaps enacting rules that call for mutual courtesy in all areas of experience rather than expressly excluding the religious and spiritual dimension of grief from discussion.

One respondent in the LEAP study provided an extensive orientation to the Facebook® support group used in the organization with which the research participant works. While there is no easy way to quantify member activity on the site, the current group membership approaches 300; group membership is limited to bereaved individuals whose loved one was in the care of the sponsoring organization or one of its affiliates. Four different professional staff members (all master's degree trained in behavioral health fields) alternate monitoring the group, and one staff member acts as group administrator, responsible for overseeing the group registration process. On the staff member's "days on," he or she posts an item of interest or a question to encourage discussion among group members, checking back on the site throughout the day and evening to interact. In the rare case that a group member posts something inappropriate or that raises a clinical concern, the administrator can remove the post and the bereavement professional can follow up with the group member by email or phone.

Just as digital technology has revolutionized communication, travel, education, and commerce, it will continue to play an important role in the provision of bereavement support. While there are organizations that exist only "virtually" in an online format, among the LEAP study respondents, organizations hosting online forums rely on face-to-face groups as their primary group intervention.

TERMINATION: WHEN GROUPS COME TO AN END

As the adage reminds with clarity: "All good things come to an end," termination of a group experience perplexes leaders and participants alike. Time-limited groups come to the end of their advertised duration, and providing a good ending is as important as providing a good beginning. LEAP study participants discussed making sure that participants have access to referral sources or the resources of the sponsoring organization. One study participant said, "I want to make sure people don't feel adrift in a small boat on the ocean. They need to know that just because the group is over doesn't mean we think their grief should be."

In a time-limited group, termination begins at the first group meeting. In a time-limited group I observed several years ago, the facilitator talked candidly about the group's duration in her first-meeting introduction.

> By saying our group runs seven weeks, we are not suggesting your grief should be over by the end of the group. In fact, it might be the opposite; you might discover new parts of your relationship to work on, and that means your grief might seem worse. But what I hope we will discover together in this seven weeks are some tools that really help in walking this pathway. You will learn some new coping strategies from the discussions we have. You will make some new friends, and I hope some of those relationships last a long time. I hope you will learn how to "breathe" in your grief.

"Drop-in" groups that meet indefinitely also struggle with termination, especially as members leave the group and as facilitators change. While several of the LEAP study participants indicated they expect leaders to make at least a one-year commitment to lead a group, there is a strong possibility that a leader will be finishing his or her commitment around the same time that a new participant joins the group. Getting used to a new style of leadership and a new personality—just as the participant begins sensing rapport with the original facilitator—can be difficult. By their nature, open-ended groups have a consistent "come and go" feel to them. Often, members will disappear without saying goodbye. One LEAP study participant explained that group leaders in that organization are taught not to pursue group members who quit attending; "We want leaders to trust the instincts and process of their group participants," this respondent reported. One concern, however, is that the disappearance from a group changes the dynamics of the group, occasioning yet another loss.

These losses can be profound. Individuals attending a bereavement group have already experienced one of the most significant losses in life, whether that is a parent, partner, or child. Even when predicted and contracted from the beginning, the ending of the formal gathering of this group of "friends" occasions another loss for an already potentially fragile individual. Yalom (1995) suggests that in a successful group, participants hate to let it die and may attempt to pretend that the group is going to continue through reunions or informal social gatherings. Nevertheless, once the group officially ends, this group of people will no longer assemble in this place at this time with this leader.

Termination must be faced squarely. From the beginning of the group's life, the leader is wise to talk about a future for participants that does not include participation in this group. Among those respondents in the Bereavement LEAP Study, they overwhelmingly endorsed the concept of not negotiating for a few extra weeks at the end of a time-limited group. A practical reason for ending a time-limited group on the day published is because some individuals will only commit to a group because they know it runs for six weeks or eight weeks. In fact, it is the ending day itself that helps some of these individuals contain their anxiety. For group members to negotiate for more days tacked on to the end puts those individuals who signed up for a time-limited group in a very difficult place. They may not say they are annoyed by the practice, but that might just be because they do not feel they have a voice against the majority who want to continue. A group needs to end when it says it will end—and not one day or one hour later.

From Yalom's (1995) perspective, members of traditional psychotherapy groups should be discouraged from further contact after a group ends, but the same rule does not apply with bereavement support groups. In fact, in such cases, he writes, the group leader may want to help in the transition to a future "leaderless" format by attending a few meetings as a "consultant" but with less and less frequency. "In my experience," he writes, "it is particularly desirable to make such arrangements when the group is primarily a support group and constitutes an important part of the members' social life—for example, groups of the elderly who, through the death of friends and acquaintances, are isolated" (p. 367). He concludes that he has heard reports of successful launching of leaderless groups for the bereaved.

QUESTIONS FOR REFLECTION AND DISCUSSION

- What is one creative art activity you have seen effectively used with bereaved adults? What do you think contributed to that activity's effectiveness?
- Of the "group themes" (such as "recovery," continuing bonds, physical well-being, etc.) described in this chapter, about which do you feel best equipped to lead a discussion? About which would you need to do some additional reading and thinking?
- What are some themes or topics you think need to be addressed with bereavement groups that are not described here? Why do you think they are important?

- What do you think about the growth of online bereavement support groups? What do you see as the biggest advantages and disadvantages of them?
- How do you envision terminating groups? Do you agree with the author's assumption that when a time-limited group reaches the last day of its published duration, it needs to end? Why?

CHAPTER 5

Meeting Challenges in Support Groups

A new widow at age 34, Maria was now parenting four children alone after her husband's unexpected death from a cerebral aneurism just nine weeks earlier. When she had taken her seat at the table, she had at least two things in common with the other six adults in the conference room of the bereavement center. First, she was grieving deeply, hardly able to speak without dissolving into sobs. Second, she attended on the first night of a 10-week group mostly because the bereavement center coordinator had strongly recommended she join the parents group while her children were participating in grief groups with others their own ages.

Now five weeks into the group, she had kept coming because there was a strange sense of warmth about these people. They were all hurting deeply, she realized, but there seemed to be an overarching feeling of hopefulness. The facilitator asked questions that made Maria stop and think, but she had said little in the group, in part because she was not confident of her ability to speak English. "What if I say the wrong word?" she asked herself. She knew that at work she was not always successful *saying* in English what she was *thinking* in her native Spanish. More than once, coworkers had laughed at the imprecision of her translation. The group facilitators had given Maria opportunity to speak, but she had quietly declined.

This night had been different for Maria. During the group meeting, the facilitators had led the adults to make "memory boxes" from simple fiberboard containers. For a couple of weeks, the facilitators had reminded participants to bring photos, memorabilia, and other items to use in creating their boxes. Maria knew that her children would also be making boxes during the evening, and they had excitedly collected items all week to bring with them. She was also secretly relieved when at the first group meeting, the leaders explained that a donor had given boxes and art supplies to the program; there was certainly no extra money in her meager family budget to buy art supplies for Maria and the children to participate in the group project.

As the parents in Maria's group began telling the stories behind the boxes they had decorated, Maria found her voice for the first time. She was still weepy as she described the music notes decorating the box that memorialized her husband's love of the guitar he played after dinner every night. She spoke clearly about his influence on their family, how much she missed him, and how at the beginning of the group, she had wondered how she could ever go on without him.

However, she also told the others in the group, the people she now described as *mi familia* (my family), how they had supported her when she felt unable to talk. As she talked that night, Maria explained that making the memory box rekindled a love of creative art she had known as a child. Making the box had provided a way to express what she was thinking and feeling—using photos and symbols instead of words. Now with the box in her hand as a "stage prop," she told her friends in the group about how the box had become a miniature *ofrenda*, the family shrine set up in memory of a loved one at the annual *Dia de Muertos* (Day of the Dead) observance in the village where she grew up. Her box provided a dignified holder for some of the dried orange petals from the *cempasuchil* (marigold) flowers that had graced her husband's casket.

Like most bereavement group leaders, the facilitators who led the group in which Maria participated had understood there could be many reasons to explain a participant's quiet demeanor. They remained alert to the possibility that a monopolizing group participant made it hard for others to speak. They were always on watch for group participants who disenfranchise the experiences of others, implying that some were not grieving "correctly." The two of them worked hard to engage quiet members of their group but remained convinced that bereaved individuals speak when they are ready to talk—and not before. Most of all, they understood from their training and their experience leading other groups that some individuals express the meaning of their loss much better through art, music, or games than they ever will through words. Just as Maria discovered, sometimes the impetus for talking is the product of a creative activity in one's hands.

DIFFICULT GROUP PARTICIPANTS

Virtually every bereavement support group includes participants who cause leaders to wince. While it is not likely the goal of these individuals to make life difficult for group leaders, their presence in the group can become problematic. The following paragraphs provide some of the more common among this difficult "cast of characters." Whether it is their attitude, their behavior, or the complex underlying issues they bring to the group, they can become nemeses or allies in developing a vibrant bereavement support group.

Unsolicited Helpfulness

Helpful individuals frequently attend groups with ideas in mind about how every other group member should experience loss. Group participants who easily offer unsolicited helpfulness frequently express opinions about the right way to get through grief, advice about business decisions, referrals to household repair technicians, and "proven methods" for dealing with relatives. Unfortunately, the advice giving is rarely requested by other group members. Sometimes, the advice has limited applicability; at other times, the advice is just wrong.

Group leaders who plan ahead can often avert unsolicited advice from well-meaning group members. Talking at the beginning of group sessions about why unsolicited advice may not be useful is one strategy to cause some group participants to rethink their advice. LEAP study participants using techniques such as reminding all group participants that individuals in grief need a place to "safely" share their story without others constantly trying to "problem-solve" might also help these unsolicited helpers from proffering their advice. One respondent recalled telling group members that advice giving often stops the bereaved person's story in midsentence and frequently creates in the mind of a newly bereaved person the notion that he/she is "not doing this right."

If these reminders to the entire group are not enough to discourage unsolicited advice-giving, a group facilitator may need to take the offending group member aside at the end of the meeting to tactfully—but firmly—explain that the behavior must stop.

Monopolizing

Groups with nondirective leaders create fertile ground for participants to "take charge." Typically, group participants who monopolize the group meeting will take far longer than anyone else in describing the loss situation and will give in to the tendency to make a comment after everyone else's remarks—often with words of advice the other group members did not request.

Individuals who attempt to monopolize group meetings must be dealt with firmly. If attempts to redirect the conversation during the group meeting do not work, a facilitator will need to take the individual aside after the group meeting and share observations. One LEAP study participant said that a simple suggestion might be all that is required to help the monopolizing individual see the problem and correct it. This leader reported taking a monopolizing person aside after the meeting with words such as these:

> John, I need your help. You know how important it is for all the group members to be able to share their story. You might notice that I rarely make comments after the stories of others because I have realized that often "shuts down" the conversation. Will you help our group by refraining from offering additional perspectives until everybody else gets a chance?

During group meetings, individuals with a tendency to monopolize the conversation can sometimes be redirected with a simple comment such as, "Let us hear from some of you who have not had a chance to talk yet."

Perceived Goal Incompatibility

Yalom (1995) discussed how perceived goal incompatibility can lead to frustration for group members and leaders alike, especially early in the life of a group. While he was addressing psychotherapy groups, bereavement support groups can encounter the same problem, as group participants all need something different from the group; I have found this to be an especially acute issue in open-ended groups where new participants regularly join and older participants depart. Sometimes, group participants grow frustrated at their own goals (feeling better) and the goals group facilitators cherish (helping group members sense congruence and community). Facilitators inevitably struggle with their own insecurities as we work to make sure everyone in the group is happy and getting what he or she came to get, an often untenable goal.

Quiet Participants

Every group includes individuals who seem content to sit and absorb rather than participate in the discussion. Many newcomers to bereavement groups say very little during the first or second meeting they attend, but the hope is they will eventually begin to offer their perspectives in the group meetings. Sometimes there is a concern on the participant's part about language skills; the group participant may sense his or her ability to speak the common language of the group is simply not enough. Quiet participants sometimes remain quiet because they do not sense they have the opportunity to talk. Frequently, quiet participants remain quiet in groups where loud, monopolizing group participants seem to have unfettered opportunity to speak. Larger group sizes (more than 10 or 12) often produce several quiet participants, as well.

After a quiet participant has attended several group meetings without saying much, I have simply worked to draw out the member: "Michael, we've not heard much from you; how about a penny for your thoughts . . ." or "Michael, what do you think about this issue?" Group leaders always walk a fine line with quiet members. Groups work because no one is forced to say anything, and leaders will want to affirm this value. Perhaps a group member feels she has nothing valuable to add to the group discussion, so your encouragement might be all it will take for her to talk more openly. With a little encouragement, your Quiet Quentin might begin to share ideas that reflect the depth of thought and emotion characteristic of people who talk less.

Raw Emotion

Most LEAP study respondents reported encouraging newly bereaved individuals to wait a few weeks after the death before attending a group. In writing about adolescent grief and support groups, however, Tedeschi (1996) suggested this may not be as important as it might seem. Many teens have been involved in school-based support groups in the days immediately after a classmate dies. I have led many of these groups myself and can attest to their seeming effectiveness in helping teens sort out the complexity of emotions and cognitions that follow a contemporary's unexpected death.

The conventional thinking about delaying the beginning of support group participation for several weeks is that in early grief, emotions are often raw and the individual's emotional equilibrium is tenuous; hearing the stories of others can often just be too much to bear (Gamino & Ritter, 2009). The unfettered emotional expression (wailing, unremitting sobbing, screaming) that sometimes accompanies early grief would be counterproductive in a group setting.

Especially after an unexpected death, well-meaning friends, family members, and even professionals seem to think "immediate counseling" is in order, especially for children; see Chapter Six for more depth in this perspective. In addition to helping bereaved people find the "emotional equilibrium" to which Gamino and Ritter (2009) referred, a delay of a few weeks might have the added benefit of allowing bereaved individuals to discover just how good their internal resources and coping strategies really are.

Underlying Mental Health Issues

For this group participant, bereavement is just another problem in a litany of life's challenges. This individual was apparently raised by abusive parents, had an alcoholic mate, possesses a long list of failed relationships, and has never had employment success. While our family and community relationships have a direct influence on how a person processes loss, people with underlying mental health issues need the guidance of a mental health professional to deal with the string of family and personality issues present in life.

Frequently, this person begins to monopolize the conversation because the grief group has become a place to share all these problems with empathetic listeners. Even with clinical training and experience, this individual poses a challenge in groups that facilitators cannot effectively manage. The group leader's focus eventually becomes fixed on managing the behaviors of the person with underlying mental health issues and, more and more, a positive group dynamic is lost. Helping these individuals connect with a family therapist or clinical psychologist is not only helpful for the participant, but it will also provide a needed refocusing of the group's attention.

Effective bereavement group leaders take on a role of "protector." For a group to become a safe community, leaders must assume a leadership role that assures everyone of an opportunity to tell his or her story without being subjected to unwanted advice, rude behavior, and a host of other problems that disrupt the group experience. Paying attention and addressing these difficult characters will go a long way to making support groups more effective for everyone attending.

All of these problems share similarity in how they are addressed. Problem behaviors often disappear as participants are reminded of the "group rules" that participants agreed to uphold when the bereavement group began. Kindness and compassion help create an essential tone for communication with difficult group participants.

OUTSIDE INTERACTION BETWEEN GROUP MEMBERS

In the experiences of program leaders and group members interviewed in the LEAP study, most bereavement groups permit—and even encourage—the interaction of group members with each other outside of the group meeting times. Even though discouraged in many psychotherapy groups, this behavior is common in "12-step" or recovery groups. Rogers (1970) saw this outside interaction as pivotal to the group process as group members talked, shared problems, worked toward common understanding, and supported each other in problem-solving.

> When I see two individuals going for a walk together, or conversing in a quiet corner, or hear that they stayed up talking until 3:00 a.m. I feel it is quite probable that at some later time in the group we will hear that one was gaining strength and help from the other and that the second person was making available his understanding, his support, his experience, his caring—making himself *available* to the other. (p. 32)

Yalom (1995) even encouraged outside contact among group members between regularly scheduled meetings of a hypothetical conventional psychotherapy group for suicidal persons, suggesting, "perhaps even mandating a certain number of phone calls from patients to therapists and between patients each week" (p. 453).

In a group for bereaved parents I facilitated a decade ago, moms began getting together for lunch on a regular basis. Whoever was free to join the "lunch bunch" was welcome, and the reports I heard caused me to conclude that as much helpful interaction occurred in those informal lunch time gatherings as occurred in our planned group meeting times. I have seen group members cluster in twos, threes, and fours to attend movies, visit museums, and travel together on day trips or weekend excursions.

Outside interaction has become a problem for a few of the respondents interviewed in the LEAP study. After one particularly difficult group experience, one of the facilitators began adding to the instructions when the group begins that while outside socializing is encouraged, "pairing off" is not. While the respondent indicated no real way to enforce the rule, at least the group members hear the suggestion at the beginning of the group that dating each other is not a good practice. This respondent indicated she usually explains the downsides of jumping into new relationships too quickly, especially after the death of a spouse. In explaining her views on the topic, the facilitator pointed out that individuals who are in need of a bereavement support group are not ready to be dating, although she conceded some participants clearly join a support group *because* they see it as a place to meet a romantic partner.

MAINTAINING CONFIDENTIALITY IN THE BEREAVEMENT SUPPORT GROUP

A perennial concern of bereavement support group facilitators and program leaders is the maintenance of confidentiality between members of a group and with outside individuals. A common theme for LEAP study respondents was that grief groups provide a "safe place" or a "haven" for grieving individuals. If group participants do not believe what they say is held in strictest confidence, these respondents indicated, this sense of emotional safety will be quickly lost. On the surface, maintaining a confidential environment may seem easy by implementing and reminding group participants of a basic ground rule: What is said in the group stays in the group. However, this goal may be easier stated than accomplished. In their landmark volume on the intersection of grief counseling and ethics, Gamino and Ritter (2009) devoted an entire chapter to confidentiality. There, they wrote,

> Confidentiality is a *sine qua non* of grief counseling . . . a sacred trust upon which the counselor-client relationship rests. Indeed, confidentiality is one of the fundamental reasons clients consult counselors, along with seeking the benefit of a counselor's expert knowledge and opinions. Clients trust that whatever information they convey in the counseling context will not be revealed to any other party. . . . In short, confidentiality is a core aspect of the ethical principle of fidelity. (p. 71)

Two primary concerns about confidentiality surfaced in interviews with respondents to the LEAP study: the need to protect the anonymity and/or personal information of support group participants and the importance of assuring the confidentiality of communication within the group.

Because bereavement support groups are frequently sponsored by hospices, bereavement support agencies, and faith communities, some record of participation is expected; most agencies need to be able to count numbers of individuals involved in programs to evaluate whether the program is achieving its programmatic objectives. Moreover, organizations receiving grant money from governmental organizations and nonprofit foundations often must report ethnicity and income data on individuals participating. While this data is usually aggregated to prevent the release of sensitive personal information, some level of disclosure is usually required by participants in groups sponsored by these organizations. Most often, participants disclose name, address, and contact information through a simple registration process. Some respondents indicated their agency asks participants to provide their relationship to the person who died and time since the death. Depending on what kinds of demographic information is needed to report to financial grantors, agencies might also ask participants to reveal age, gender, ethnicity, and family income level.

Purely peer-led groups developed on the 12-step model popularized by Alcoholics Anonymous (AA) usually operate with different expectations. The decision by AA founders in 1935 to protect the anonymity of fellowship members grew out of the social stigma that accompanied alcoholism in the first third of the 20th century. AA fellowship members are reminded that the stories of those who participate are their stories to tell. As a result, members are instructed to not disclose content from their meetings or even to provide the names of others who attend. Though members only introduce themselves at AA meetings with their first names, pre-existing relationships with members often exist, potentially jeopardizing the "anonymity" so dearly prized in the organization. Alcoholics Anonymous leadership considers even the publishing of a member's own photograph or name in connection with disclosure he or she is a member of AA to be a violation of the organization's expectation of anonymity (Alcoholics Anonymous, 2011).

Several LEAP study respondents indicated they collect no data on group participants. One leader of a group sponsored by a faith community has worked with congregational leadership to assure no other events occur on the campus during the time the grief group meets, providing what this group leader believes is an additional and needed level of anonymity to attendees. This respondent also reported that several of the attendees to the group over the years have come from other faith communities, in part, the respondent believed, because individuals did not feel "anonymous enough" attending a group sponsored by their own congregation.

Keeping personal information private was one intention of the U.S. Health Insurance Portability and Accountability Act of 1996 ("HIPAA"). While support groups per se may not be subject to statutes about protecting personal information, the provisions of the law provide a good framework for leaders of support groups. Organizations engaged professionally in health care services for which government health plans are billed (such as hospitals and hospices) are held to a higher standard than other organizations. Therefore, the sponsoring agency will want to consult legal counsel on what part of support group record-keeping may be within the scope of HIPAA regulations (U.S. Department of Health and Human Services, n.d.).

Two questions are preeminent in considering the gathering of personal information from group participants: What is the purpose of gathering the information, and how will the organization keep it secure? Knowing information about participants can help program leadership make decisions about how to expend resources and how to advertise programs. For example, it can be very helpful to know how many men attend groups or how the ethnic outreach of a program is impacting participation. In practice, however, much data that is collected is not ever analyzed or used in program planning. Collecting the information in such cases is ethically questionable.

Program leaders will also want to consider how the information will be stored and safeguarded. One problem with collecting information is that it must then be protected so that it is not inadvertently discovered by an unauthorized person. In recent years, I have seen personal information kept in an unlocked desk drawer, a binder on a program staff person's desk, and on a home computer; these storage devices do not provide the level of safeguarding individuals have a right to expect from group leadership. An often-overlooked concern on this matter is how information will be discarded when it is no longer needed. Shredding paper documents is one easy remedy, but electronic storage is not erased so readily. Since many computer hard disc drives maintain information indefinitely, this concern has ramifications for how organizations dispose of outdated computer equipment (Hoffman, 2014).

Helping group participants understand and apply rules of confidentiality is another issue of concern for group facilitators. In a survey of Canadian organizations providing support groups for persons living with HIV/AIDS, Olivier (2009) found nearly all respondents discuss confidentiality in the first session of a group, when new members join a group, and from time to time in open-ended groups. Some of the respondents reported providing specific examples of content that could or could not be shared within the bounds of confidentiality, and 44.2% of respondents indicated they required group members to sign a confidentiality agreement. LEAP study participants spoke clearly about efforts to remind group members that matters shared in the group were to remain in the group, but several conceded difficulty with group participant compliance. The perspective of including these instructions in the group's "ground rules" and reminding group participants about the importance of keeping the rules is corroborated by several authors who have written about bereavement support group development (Gamino & Ritter, 2009; Hoy, 2007; Worden, 2009).

The risk to confidentiality potentially becomes greater in groups that are part of close-knit, intimate communities. In his perspective on maintaining confidentiality in rural communities, Townsend (2009) explains a phenomenon that may seem quite foreign to urban dwellers:

> In rural communities, maintaining confidentiality is challenging, simply because residents are privy to each other's activities and lives. There continue to be some communities where local radio stations update listeners about current hospitalizations, and clergy offer public prayers to help guide a named physician in the diagnosis of a certain patient. This may seem quaint to an urban audience, but it is part of normal networking in some small communities. (p. 132)

The intimacy of close-knit communities implies that individuals know one another on many levels. Often, multiple generations and branches of a family (a clan) live in close proximity, participating in a single faith community, receiving health care services from one provider, and with children attending the same schools. The individual who acts as receptionist at the local hospice may be a neighbor and fellow-congregant with a patient and his or her family, while their children and grandchildren may all play on the same sports teams. The typical sharing of information that defines community life in such contexts often makes it very difficult to maintain confidentiality.

Whether group participants likely participate in common social circles or not, leaders will want to regularly explain the importance of keeping personal information private. Acknowledging the benefit of community sharing while also insisting on confidentiality can be helpful. These words to a group provide one way to help participants know how to respond when asked about others in the group:

> One of the great things about living here is that we all know what is going on in each other's lives; that is what makes it possible to care deeply for each other. But if our group is going to work, it will only be as we agree with one another that what is said here stays here. Give your fellow group members a chance to tell their own story to their family and friends; don't rob them of that chance. If a friend asks you, "Oh, so I know so-and-so goes to that group you're in; how is she doing?" just politely smile and say, "You know, grief is really hard. I bet she would really appreciate a note or a call from you to check in on her."

Like other professional associations in the human services, the Association for Death Education and Counseling has incorporated an entire section on confidentiality and privacy (Section VIII) into its code of ethics and expects its members to uphold that standard: The association's Code of Ethics specifically requires that client welfare be held uppermost in the work of members, that members inform clients about limits to confidentiality (such as in mandated reporting of child abuse), and that written records are protected to maintain confidences (Association for Death Education and Counseling, 2004, n.p.).

THE CHALLENGES OF EVALUATING EFFECTIVENESS

Evaluation is an important part of support group leadership, but it is not always easy to know the best ways to assess quality. In a master of social work thesis, Nieves (2014) conducted a small qualitative study to ascertain the value of a bereavement support group intervention in a Connecticut hospice. The researcher acknowledged in the literature review that little empirical research exists to demonstrate the efficacy of these types of interventions. Though the study interviewed only three respondents, the researcher discovered how difficult it is to ascertain quality of the intervention and to clarify just how long-lived changes might be.

Assessment of the effectiveness of bereavement support group interventions is one of the "thorny issues" in bereavement research and practice; questions of the value of group interventions helped propel the discussion several years ago about whether grief counseling helps, provides no effect, or actually harms participants. As explained earlier in this volume, there is little to support the notion that intervention is harmful generally, and bereavement group involvement specifically, is harmful to participants. Nevertheless, the empirical study of bereavement support group effectiveness has lagged significantly behind other fields of inquiry. At least two issues arise when contemplating how to effectively evaluate program offerings: the *research abilities* of program leaders to conduct scientifically useful research and the *time constraints* already felt by program practitioners, who rightly wonder how they will add one more potentially time-consuming activity to their overcrowded schedules.

While not a scientifically derived sample, the participants in the LEAP study may be representative of group facilitators and program leaders currently using support groups to assist bereaved people. With few exceptions, the participants in that study had difficulty articulating specific evaluation measures in place to ascertain the value of group participation for those attending. A few individuals responded to assessment/evaluation questions with phrases such as, "I'll know people are not getting helped when they quit coming" and "People keep coming back;

I suppose it is working," often preceded or followed by a chuckle. In one interview, a facilitator and program leader responded,

> Well we've operated by a 'No news is good news' model around here, but I know that just is not good enough. If I am honest, though, I have to say that our administration wants to know our numbers (of people being helped) are growing every year. If that is happening, I don't get any trouble. If that doesn't happen, I don't really think it will make a lot of difference what scientific evidence I have for how people grow in their grief.

While not specifically stated by group facilitators interviewed, program administrators interviewed were more direct in the role of evaluation evidence.

> Obviously, I want to know who and how many are in our groups; that's important internally. But grantors are a lot more picky about what they will and won't fund. If I want money from big foundations and little ones alike, I better be able to put my money where my mouth is. I better have data that shows our people are better off. So far, we've done that by pointing to studies of how bereaved children have been helped in Arizona (Family Bereavement Program, Sandler et al., 2010) and how their academics, their family interactions, all of that improve. But I don't think that is going to always work in the future. The foundations I look to for our funds want to know how *our* program works. I think we'll have to do that with pre-tests and post-tests of grief levels, although frankly, I'm a little scared of what those results will show. I think we'll also interview some parents about six months after their family has been in our program and ask, "How is it going now? What differences are you seeing in your kids?"—stuff like that. (LEAP study anonymous participant)

Another LEAP study respondent indicated an intense interest in the results research would provide and affirmed the importance of a more rigorous testing of bereavement interventions. This respondent even indicated interest in pursuing a PhD and said that research into the effectiveness of the participant's program would be a major thrust of inquiry if that goal were ever to be realized. But the participant also admitted, "I am a clinician, and I just don't have the training now to conduct a real research project to look at what we're doing and how we're doing it. I also don't have money to hire somebody who does know research procedures."

Other respondents echoed the sentiment that lack of training in research methodology was part of what prevented empirical study of bereavement support group effectiveness, and some added that program budgets had no room for research money, either. One wonders, however, if some grantors would be interested in funding a qualified researcher to spend a year or two in an agency studying the effectiveness of interventions.

Though the variations are legion, scientific research generally follows a sequence of problem articulation, literature review, hypothesis casting, experimentation/inquiry, analysis of results, and conclusion drawing. While graduate students learn research methodology, their early practices tend to be related to the first two steps: defining the problem and conducting a thorough review of the literature. In many graduate professional programs (social work, counseling, and practical theology, for example), students often gain very little experience in designing and conducting actual research. One dominant field producing bereavement support practitioners is social work; its standards for accreditation place a high priority on applied practice but make rather sparse mention of student abilities in actually conducting research (Council on Social Work Education, 2015).

Thorough and ongoing literature review is an important, though frequently overlooked, first step for creating evidence-based practices. As one LEAP study respondent implied, depending on research of similar bereavement support programs (the Arizona Family Bereavement Program, in that respondent's case), is far better than hoping one's assumptions are correct and that one's interventions are sound. One LEAP study participant described how attending the annual conference of the Association for Death Education and Counseling had dramatically and positively impacted program decisions but quickly added that agency cost reductions had made conference attendance a financial impossibility. Because of budget reductions preventing conference attendance, one experienced group leader discussed the value of online journal access included with Association for Death Education and Counseling membership:

> I signed up to receive the table of contents from ADEC when each of those three journals (*Death Studies, Omega: Journal of Death and Dying,* and *Grief Matters: The Australian Journal of Grief and Bereavement*) publishes a new issue. I make it a practice to review them when they come and set aside an hour or so each week to read the articles. Access to those journals makes ADEC membership a great value, even when I cannot go to the meetings.

Effective evaluation of bereavement support groups contains at least three components. First, program leadership needs to assess whether a group is reaching its objectives in a way that justifies the investment of resources (financial, staff, volunteer, etc.) Secondly, program coordinators need to evaluate the abilities, skills, and effectiveness of group leadership to assure their constituents that the program is delivery excellence in care. Thirdly, program leaders will want to evaluate how group participants are either helped or harmed by participation in the group. None of these are particularly easy assessments to make and fit into an ongoing process.

Even though the sponsoring bereavement center does not ask for documentation of group attendance, one LEAP Study respondent reported providing a sign-in sheet after each monthly meeting. The form provides basic information on program attendees to the community-based organization's grantors and other major contributors. The information collected includes the cities where the group members live, their ages, and their gender. Though the organization invests few resources in the support group, the facilitator indicated she believes this is one way to maintain a relationship and to communicate with the sponsoring organization about the success of its efforts.

Participant evaluations of support groups can be particularly useful. Some LEAP study respondents reported collecting anecdotal data by periodically asking an evaluation question as part of the group discussion. Much like the concept of a "focus group" utilized in marketing research, these study respondents indicated that they use between 10 and 20 minutes periodically during groups to assess how group participants perceive the group is helping and how it could be more useful. Questions for these guided discussions could be drawn from the suggested items for surveys listed below. One group leader reported regularly asking group participants to tell about one change they have observed in someone else in the group. The leader noted readiness to offer a perspective about all group participants in the event one or more group members are not selected by another member. The leader reported that this is rarely necessary, because group members are sensitive to including everyone.

Respondents in the LEAP study offered a diversity of ways they assess the quality of the groups they lead. One respondent suggested, perhaps somewhat tongue in cheek, that it was easy enough to tell if people were getting help; "When they stop getting help," she said, "they stop coming." In the LEAP study, most respondents indicated they did utilize various forms of participant (quality assurance) surveys, most frequently at the end of a closed-ended group. A review of the published bereavement group literature revealed many examples of such participant evaluation measures, usually mixed-method type studies that included quantitative Likert scales ("On a scale of one to five, how helpful did you find . . .?") and qualitative comment sections ("Tell us about the three most important changes you have seen in your family since participating in our program . . ."). Finucane and McGuinness (2011) reported positive feedback from participants in a pilot study using creative arts in a bereavement program and promised forthcoming results from a randomized control trial.

In the quest for evidence-based practice, some program leaders and funders have increasingly called for randomized control trials and similarly rigorous empirical evidence of the benefit to group participants. However, in their quest to improve the "patient centeredness" of pharmaceutical development, the U.S. Food and Drug Administration (FDA), European Medicines Agency, and British National Health Service (NHS) have increasingly approved the use of patient-reported outcomes to evaluate subjective "quality of life" improvements, acknowledging the validity of assessing how patients feel subjectively along with objective data about treatment for illness (McClimans & Browne, 2011; Weldring & Smith, 2013). For organizations providing bereavement interventions such as support groups, asking individuals to report their experiences potentially provides useful ways to measure nuances in the ways individuals interact with the organization, its staff, and its programs. Developing survey measures (patient-reported outcome measures or PROMs) based on a standardized list of patient-reported outcomes is a promising way to collect this data (Weldring & Smith, 2013).

Traditionally, measures of efficacy have depended on satisfaction measures of individuals participating in bereavement support interventions. The LEAP study revealed that in many programs, there has been no tool used to measure "satisfaction" with the group other than whether individuals kept attending. Several respondents in the study reminded the interviewer that their organization was small and unable to engage in detailed research. Nevertheless, a quality assurance survey that allows group participants to evaluate logistical details, group leadership, and changes in self can be part of a comprehensive evaluation. The following items can be evaluated on a Likert scale (0–5, with 0 meaning "strongly disagree" and 5 meaning "strongly agree," for example), with opportunity with each item for comments. Present tense language is appropriate for periodic assessments in ongoing groups but can be changed to past tense language for end-of-group evaluations (i.e., "Group facilitator[s] begins and ends the meetings on time" becomes "Group facilitator[s] began and ended meetings on time").

Changes in Myself

- I am learning to deal with expectations of others about my grief.
- I am discovering how to cope with overwhelming emotion.
- I am enhancing my own coping skills through this group.
- I am developing new friendships within the group.
- I am gaining hope for a positive future in my life.
- I am finding new ways to positively remember my loved one.
- I am discovering resources in my community I did not know about.

Group Leadership

- Group facilitator(s) helps group participants share appropriately.
- Group facilitator(s) shows respect for all group participants.
- Group facilitator(s) effectively keeps the group "on track."
- Group facilitator(s) begins and ends the meetings on time.
- Group facilitator(s) encourages me to participate.

Meeting Logistics

- Day and time for the meeting makes it easy to participate.
- Meeting room is conducive to our group conversation (place, temperature, etc.).
- It was easy to get needed information about registering for the group.
- This group provides an emotionally safe place to talk about my experiences.

Including a space below each item for comments can provide group participants an opportunity to clarify or expand their responses if desired. Participants who want to complete the survey quickly can respond to a 10- to 15-item evaluation without comments in about five minutes. Providing a combination of scaled items and open-answer items lets group participants choose how to evaluate the group. Open response items might include:

- What are the one or two ways you have changed most because of this group?
- Which group session "stands out" as most important for you?

- What is the hardest part of participating in this group for you?
- How could this group be improved?

Third-party payers such as the Center for Medicare Services in the United States increasingly rely on patient-reported experience measures to determine reimbursement for care rendered by hospitals. At this writing, one of the arguments in the American health care system questions this formula, since patient satisfaction can sometimes be, but is not always, a reliable indicator of clinical quality, as is the case in surgical care (Lyu, Wick, Housman, Freischlag, & Makary, 2013). Since bereavement groups are not specifically reimbursed by Medicare or private insurance, program administrators need not be concerned about that issue. However, measures of efficacy are of interest to philanthropic foundations, who often provide funding support for programs.

CONTINUAL LITERATURE REVIEW

Not all relevant studies must be conducted in the local setting. While specific empirical studies of various group interventions compared to nontreatment control groups are important in bereavement work, few programs will have the funding or the knowledge base to create such studies. Nevertheless, what is readily accessible for program leaders and group facilitators alike is a vast array of literature in the field. Every year, the dominant journals in bereavement publish dozens of studies, accompanied by hundreds of other articles on virtually every aspect of end-of-life care, bereavement assessment, and intervention.

In the introduction to her book, Aveyard (2010) explained the value of literature review in evidence-based practice and then overviewed the importance of reading one perspective in the context of other studies on a particular topic. She then suggested, "the literature review is regarded as increasingly important in health and social care and the method for undertaking a literature review has become an important research methodology in its own right" (p. 2). Ridley (2012) echoed and expanded Aveyard's concepts by suggesting that literature reviews serve multiple purposes, including providing historical background, contemporary context, and theoretical underpinnings of the topic being investigated.

Systematic literature review is likely in the skill set of every master's-trained practitioner and many who do not possess advanced degrees. A growing number of colleges and universities expect undergraduate students to develop skills in critical literature review, especially if the students participate in academic honors programs. Aveyard (2010) provided a simple template for conducting a thorough literature review, including the development of a research question, making decisions about what and how to access literature for potential review, synthesizing findings, using findings in program development, and communicating findings to others. The "six steps to success" envisioned by Machi and McElvoy (2012) in their literature review methodology emphasizes the "back and forth" interplay between selecting and refining topics and arguments while simultaneously overviewing, surveying, and eventually critiquing the literature. They conclude their book with the sixth step: write the review. Besides the brevity of the 174-page text, their volume understands the usefulness of literature review in clinical practice, so it is written not only with students in view but also of practitioners.

One respondent in the LEAP study indicated that she expects college interns in her program to write a literature review as part of their work in the organization. Through a local college, this program obtains an intern for placement either in one-semester or two-semester blocks. The supervisor's perspective is that the literature review about a topic of interest in bereavement always expands the knowledge base of the student, making him or her into a better-equipped practitioner, and the literature review and discussions of it throughout the semester often contributes needed theoretical perspective to the program leader's knowledge, as well.

In bereavement organizations that utilize undergraduate or graduate interns, there could be great value in those interns being assigned the responsibility of summarizing and critiquing the literature on some specific aspect of the agency's program. With supervisors who are attuned to needs for analysis and student interns who need to practice integrating research into direct clinical service, this seems to be a promising possibility, indeed.

QUESTIONS FOR REFLECTION AND DISCUSSION

- What group member behaviors do you find most challenging to manage? What do your colleagues say about how they respond to those behaviors?
- How do you envision discussing matters of confidentiality with groups? How do you think this will be especially difficult in close-knit communities? Do you think there is an inherent danger of breach of confidentiality in groups where participants have a pre-existing relationship?
- In the absence of empirical research about the effectiveness of groups in your program, what value could literature review provide to understanding the basics of group efficacy?

CHAPTER 6

Supporting Children and Teens Through Grief Groups

Jasmine telephoned the bereavement center on the advice of the counselor at the intermediate school her two youngest grandchildren attended. In many ways, Jasmine had been the girls' guardian since they were born to Jasmine's 20-year-old daughter, a woman addicted to alcohol, marijuana, and crack cocaine. Now, 11 years later, the twins' mother had died, and Jasmine faced the reality of parenting these two precocious pre-teens on her own.

In some ways, she told the bereavement counselor, it would be easier now. For the last 15 years—well before the twins were born—her daughter had been in and out of the house and in and out of drugs. "I thought early on we should have just given them up for adoption," the young grandmother explained. "Now, I can't imagine my life without them." Always good students, the girls had both seemed distant and disengaged in the eight weeks since their mother died. Jasmine explained to the bereavement counselor, "I don't really get it. Her death sort of made things normal again. I'm not sure what there is these girls have to grieve about."

As is frequently the case, however, Jasmine was also dealing with conflict of her own about her daughter's death. In the bereavement group for parents and guardians she began attending while the girls were in their own group, Jasmine told the others, "I sometimes wonder if there wasn't something more to do. I tried everything I knew . . ." and her voice trailed off. "But I guess it just wasn't enough." Fortunately for Jasmine and her 11-year-old twin "daughters," they had found a bereavement center that understood that a child's loss was really a family's grief.

Long before data began emerging about the efficacy of the Family Bereavement Program pioneered at Arizona State University (Sandler,

Ayers, et al., 2010; Sandler, Ma, et al., 2010; Schoenfelder, Tein, Wolchk, & Sandler, 2015), Shapiro (2001) asserted, "The research findings overall suggest that useful family interventions can help explore and expand family communication, cohesion, and shared narratives of the loss and its implications. Therapeutic group interventions can be especially useful to bereaved children, especially when paired with interventions that enhance the parent's responsiveness"(p. 319). These data and observations echoed the findings of the even earlier Harvard Child Bereavement Study, which concluded that bereaved caregiver mental/emotional well-being was a clear predictor of child and adolescent well-being (Silverman & Worden, 1992; Worden, 1996). Worden (1996) wrote, "The functioning level of the surviving parent is the most powerful predictor of a child's adjustment to the death of a parent. Children with a less well-functioning parent will show more anxiety and depression, and sleep and health problems" (p. 95).

In the last few decades, interest has increased in understanding how best to support bereaved children. Whether the child's experience with grief was occasioned by the death of a parent, sibling, grandparent, teacher, or friend, bereavement specialists have become acutely aware that these younger bereaved are often "forgotten mourners" (Smith, 1999). Child grief was "on the radar" early. When public television *Sesame Street's* Mr. Hooper (played by Actor Will Lee) died in 1983 at the age of 74, the producers used the opportunity to talk with children about death. The Sesame Street Workshop's commitment to bereaved children continues through the widely available *When Families Grieve* kit for families, which has been provided to hundreds of hospices, funeral homes, hospitals, and other organizations (Mullen, Lynn, & Knell, 2010).

Though grief support groups for children have become ubiquitous to "insiders" in the bereavement support community, it was not always so. When the Dougy Center began in 1982, it was the first in the United States and probably the world, founded on a simple concept of providing peer support to bereaved children, teens, and their families. Named for 13-year-old Dougy Turno, the Dougy Center is widely considered one of the premier programs in the world, not only serving hundreds of bereaved families every year but also training hundreds of professionals and volunteers to provide supportive care to bereaved children. Since its beginning in 1982, this Portland, Oregon-based center reports it has served more than 30,000 children, teens, and family members (www.dougy.org).

Bo's Place in Houston, Texas, offers nine-week LIGHT (Looking Inward Grieving Healing Together) Family Groups, gatherings of children ages 5 to 18 with their families after experiencing the sudden or unexpected death of a child or parent. When families complete the LIGHT group, they are welcomed to join an ongoing family group that meets twice monthly. There is no time limit on how long families may participate in those groups. The twice-monthly family groups are available immediately to families after an expected death without first completing the LIGHT group. In addition to family groups and groups for children and teens, like many bereavement centers, Bo's Place offers groups for young adults, adults, pregnancy loss, and "little friends" (children ages 3–4 with their guardian).

Like most bereavement programs for children, Bo's Place began as a small nonprofit with a vision to help bereaved children and point their families to resources in the Houston metropolitan area. Their services are provided free of charge, and their vision and organizational belief is "that it is helpful and healing for grieving children and adults to share their stories, memories, experiences, thoughts, and feelings with other grieving children and adults." The operating philosophy of the organization is that: 1) grief is a natural reaction to the death of a loved one; 2) the duration and intensity of grief are unique for each individual; 3) in a safe and supportive environment, people have a natural capacity to heal; 4) moving through the grief journey is not about letting go; it is about finding ways to incorporate memories of the deceased and their legacy into one's life so that, over time, the loss is less painful; and 5) essential to the work of Bo's Place is a guiding belief that the support group environment can be a source of empathy, understanding and encouragement to grieving children, adults, and their families during a very difficult time in their lives (www.bosplace.org).

Bereavement programs for children and teens exist around the globe, including the Raymee Grief Center in Dubai, United Arab Emirates, "a pro-bono initiative that provides education and free grief support groups to the children, teens, and adults of the UAE" (www.lighthousearabia.com/grief-support). In similar ways, Khululeka Grief Support in Cape Town, South Africa, envisions

> a South Africa where all grieving children and adolescents have access to support and opportunities for healing . . . (where the) mission is to build the resilience of children, adolescents and their caregivers by equipping them with tools to process their experiences of loss and death . . . [t]hrough a holistic approach. (www.khululeka.org)

Like many other programs around the world, Cruse Bereavement Care in the United Kingdom is a volunteer-driven organization. Its innovative website designed specifically for teens and older children provides opportunity to post reflections and stories and connect with volunteers by telephone and email and offers links to one-to-one and in-person grief counseling groups. The colorful interactive website is "Hope Again: Young People Living After Loss" (www.hopeagain.org.uk).

Child bereavement programs range from grassroots organizations with volunteer staff and borrowed or rented facilities to multi-million dollar organizations. Several of the aforementioned organizations enjoy annual revenues of $1 million to $3 million, employing large clinical staffs and occupying thousands of square feet of state-of-the-art facilities. One respondent in the LEAP study said, "Children's grief is an important issue, and I am grateful we have generous donors. These generous people really believe in what we do. Don't get me wrong; We can always do more, but at least I don't have to think about laying off staff every other month." Significant support for child bereavement programs in recent years has come through the New York Life Foundation's Grief Reach program. In a recent year, the foundation awarded $750,000 to 22 child grief programs across the United States.

COGNITIVE DEVELOPMENT AND THE BEREAVED YOUNG PERSON

Developmental psychologist Jean Piaget first articulated four sensorimotor stages of development, postulating that toddlerhood to early childhood (about age 7) was characterized by "preoperational" thought. Beginning at around age 7, children begin thinking in a "concrete operational" pattern, which began to give way to a "formal operational" pattern around the onset of puberty. The preoperational stage, Piaget suggested, was characterized by symbolic thought with increasing language ability, memory, and imagination. Of most significance to bereavement support staff, perhaps, is the notion that children during this stage of development are thought to develop an ability to differentiate between past and future. During this phase of development, Piaget believed, children make decisions largely on intuition rather than through logic and have difficulty connecting such mature concepts as cause and effect (Beilin, 1992).

Piaget's cognitive development theory is by no means universally accepted. Most theorists now assume that cognitive development is a process without rigid boundaries between thinking styles. Moreover, cognitive development includes important factors such as enculturation, family customs, learning abilities, and personal neural development.

Whatever else is known, however, it is assumed that death is a vaguely grasped concept for younger children. The death of a primary caregiver or a person with whom the child interacts daily will greatly impact a young child, while the death of a neighbor or distant relative can be expected to have little impact. A child's concept of death changes rapidly throughout the maturation process.

Speece and Brent (1996) articulated five components of a mature death concept, suggesting that as children mature, they begin to develop a more adultlike death concept. The five components of a mature death concept include death's universality (all living things die), irreversibility (death is physically not reversible), and nonfunctionality (after death, there are no more humanlike movements). Unlike the concept of death held by young children, a mature understanding includes causality (the body's systems cease working, caused by disease or injury) and noncorporeal continuation (there is the possibility of continued existence outside of the physical body after death). While the youngest children cannot be expected to hold these mature views, the development of death concept is a process and does not proceed according to neat predictable stages or on within any predetermined age cohort.

Changes in the family, especially related to caregiving responsibilities, are likely the greatest issue for infants and toddlers after a loved one's death. Since children sense these changes whether accompanied by an adult explanation or not, a child who is not told the truth may conclude that the tears and chaos in the home are his or her own fault.

The early school years provide opportunities for children to discover the nature of the life cycle, and as early as grade two, children often learn about the reality of death in the plant and animal kingdom. As children mature, they learn that living things die and that dead things stay dead. They also may struggle with causality and often bring the notion of "My dad's death was my fault" to the bereavement support group with them.

> Like many 9-year olds, Brandon got in trouble for talking in the classroom and had been repeatedly warned by his teacher. When the behavior persisted, his teacher called home to report the problem to Brandon's parents. The next morning, shortly after arriving

> at work, Brandon's dad died of a massive heart attack. In the days and weeks that followed, all Brandon could think of was that his behavior and the teacher's call to his dad had caused the heart attack, consuming him with guilt. (Hoy, 2007)

Children in the "middle years" of 8 to 11 are sometimes enamored with details about the death. Group leaders must be prepared for discussions that border on the macabre as youngsters describe details and swap stories. Unfortunately, sometimes the details children share with friends or in groups are based on their own fantasies, a fictional account they imagine because the adults in their lives were not forthcoming with the true story. Children in this age group might desire to know more about the condition of the body, for example, than some family members have been willing to discuss.

While adolescence is a period filled with transition, death concepts for teens are usually similar to adults. Adolescents typically understand that death is universal and irreversible, though they are often struggling with causality. Even though developmental psychologists assume "magical thinking" begins to dissipate in the middle years of childhood, adolescents sometimes act as if they are still captivated by it. For many adolescents, actions communicate they believe they are invincible. "Death might come to others," they seem to think, "but it won't touch me." Adolescence is also the period where young people are learning to individuate from their parents and their authority. As a result, this period can be filled with boundary-testing as adolescents try out their emerging independence. This can also be a period characterized by significant upheaval in belief systems as teens endeavor to make sense of faith, philosophy, and the worldviews that have been passed on to them by parents and teachers.

Honest, forthright language and details are important for children and teens alike. Several respondents in the LEAP study who work with young grievers pointed out the difficulties poured onto bereavement programs and their leadership by parents and caregivers who have masked the real cause of death or have, in the case of what they told young children, not discussed death directly at all. Citing Linda Mahon's earlier work on dealing with youngsters after a sibling's death, Jones, Deane, and Keegan (2015) wrote,

> Clear and unambiguous language and accurate factual information about the circumstances of the death is important for children in their understanding. Using words like "death" and "dies" rather

than "gone (to) sleep" helps the child to understand the different elements described above. (p. 45)

COMPETENCIES FOR PERSONS WORKING WITH BEREAVED YOUNG PEOPLE

The characteristics that LEAP study participants described that inform their search for facilitators in bereavement groups in general certainly apply to persons who want to work with bereaved children and teens. Reliability, authenticity, a collaborative style, flexibility, and emotional stability are absolutely essential qualifications for individuals who plan to work with bereaved young people. Out of my work with bereaved children and teens, I find special resonance with the qualities of reliability, collaborative style, and flexibility.

Death in the life of a child or teen is usually a chaos-producing experience. Being able to "count on" the bereavement support group and its facilitator can be extraordinarily important. Facilitators who arrive late for groups or who do not arrive at all engenders another loss for these young people—the loss of confidence that adults in their lives will do what they say they will do.

Children and teens who participate in bereavement support groups do not likely want to sense they are in school. One bereavement professional with whom I worked had been congregational education coordinator in a faith community before joining the bereavement center staff. This individual insisted on using the word "classes" to designate bereavement support groups and typically described the strategy for an evening's bereavement group session as a "lesson plan." The group environment had an old-school feel to it with very clear lines of authority drawn between the "teachers" (group leaders) and the "students" (group participants). Unfortunately, this reinforces the notion of the leader as grief "expert," with grieving children and teens in the role of "grief learner." I have always thought this particular notion got that exactly backwards; it is we who lead who are the learners and those who are bereaved who are our best teachers. Bereavement groups—whether for adults or for young people—must be places of collaboration.

Facilitators of child and teen bereavement groups must also exhibit significant levels of flexibility. American comedian Art Linkletter was perhaps best known for his 1957 book, *Kids Say the Darndest Things*, based on his interviews with youngsters who were far less filtered in what they said than the grown-ups in their lives might have liked. When working with children and teens, leaders must raise flexibility to an art form. In the words of one LEAP study respondent who works with children, "You never know what will come out of a kid's mouth. It might be funny, it could be sweet, or it could be really traumatizing to everybody in the room. You are dead in the water if you don't know how to just roll with the punches."

Professional and volunteer caregivers who work with bereaved young people make up the Irish Childhood Bereavement Network (ICBN). Established in 2012 in response to a research study of bereavement services available for children, the network has become a place for disparate professionals, disciplines, and organizations to work together with a shared sense of purpose. Recently, the ICBN set out a set of "competencies," suggesting they should become the standards for both professionals and volunteers who work with bereaved young people:

> - All practitioners providing support to children who experience a loss should have a basic understanding and knowledge of the potential impact of bereavement on children;
> - Practitioners need an understanding of children and young people's evolving needs and changing understanding of death as they progress through the developmental stages, paying due reference to their relevance to social and cultural context;
> - Any support, counselling or therapeutic intervention with bereaved children should acknowledge the context of the child's family/support system and should acknowledge and support the ability of that family/support system to care for and support the child in their bereavement taking into account their material circumstances and other family events that might impact on their child's history and everyday life;
> - Appropriate competencies to work with bereaved children and young people are developed through a combination of academic learning and practice wisdom gained working directly with bereaved children and young people within the context of regular supervision and mentoring;
> - Everyone working in this area should work within their competencies.
>
> (Jones et al., 2015, p. 48)

While there seemed to be some latitude in what LEAP study respondents expected from group leaders who work with adults, there was far more rigidity in expectations about those who would work with children. This expectation may have grown out of more rigid legal requirements for individuals who work with minors. Increasingly in the West, agencies expect staff and volunteers who work with minors to pass criminal background checks. Judicial convictions for sexual misbehavior or abuse of children would be considered in most organizations to be disqualification from working with minors.

This insistence on high standards for volunteers and staff has been the reputation of the Dougy Center in Portland, Oregon. Since the Dougy Center seems to be an influential force in the training of leaders for child bereavement groups and programs, it is not surprising to see these standards expected in other child-focused bereavement programs, as well. In their analysis of training and supervision of grief workers in one program, Baugher et al. (2012) noted, "The concerns expressed by European scholars regarding the use of volunteers in bereavement services is, therefore, somewhat ironic since volunteers facilitating children's bereavement groups in the United States appear to be more highly supervised than both their lay counterparts in other fields and professional workers in the field of bereavement" (p. 277).

ACTIVITIES TO ENGAGE GRIEVING CHILDREN AND TEENS

In interviews for the LEAP study, it became clear that respondents who work with bereaved children and teens use a vast array of activities to help young people express their experiences with grief and to derive support from one another. An important focus among the respondents is that grief programs for young people focus on teaching positive coping skills. While the number of activities to be used with bereaved young people is legion, a few are included here for reference.

Facilitators who lead bereavement groups and agency staff members who coordinate programs focused on bereaved children and teens will want to consult the very fine published manuals for specific ideas about leading groups. In my judgment, there are none better than Linda Goldman's (2014) guide for facilitating children's groups and Mary Kelly Perschy's (2004) manual for leading teen groups. Included here are ideas I have used with bereaved children or that have been suggested by respondents in the LEAP study.

Dead Plant

In advance of the group, leaders gather two plants of the same species—one live and one dead. During the group, leaders show children the two plants and invite them to discuss how they are different. The leaders help children discuss the changes that occur in living things when they die, noting that no amount of water or fertilizer will cause the plant to live again. This activity helps children articulate who in their lives has died, as well. In the transition to a discussion of grief, facilitators can ask questions such as, "Has anything or anyone in your family ever died? Tell us about it. How did you find out it/he/she died? What was that like/How did you feel about it?"

Gingerbread Emotions

Using cookie cutters, leaders help children trace a gingerbread person and agree on a color code for emotions (like red for anger and blue for sadness.) While children are coloring their gingerbread person, the facilitator can lead a discussion about the various colors (emotions) children are selecting. This activity allows the group leaders to affirm the value of all emotions, including those that may be considered "negative" in some families. Pictures that do not seem age-appropriate or that possibly demonstrate exaggerated grief (scribbling angrily on the page) as well as young people who consistently seem disengaged from the entire process may indicate that the child would benefit from individual intervention.

Drawing

When children create pictures, they unlock a part of the brain that simply cannot be accessed with words alone. Almost any theme can provide an opportunity for children to draw, but here are a few examples of "invitations to draw" that children in a bereavement support group can utilize:

- Draw a picture of a favorite memory you have with the person who died.
- Draw a picture of anger, guilt, fear, or some other emotion.
- Draw a picture of how your family looks now.
- Draw a picture of your favorite place to go together.
- Draw a picture of your favorite holiday.

When the children have finished drawing their pictures, leaders will want to invite the youngsters to tell the group about what they have drawn. Facilitators can improve the impromptu expression of grief with the children by inviting more information. When a child says, for example, that Halloween was his favorite holiday with his grandfather, a leader can ask the child to elaborate. Inviting the child to "Tell us more" or asking, "What did you most like about spending Halloween with your grandpa?" will likely engage the child in conversation.

Art therapy is a specialized field with its own training systems, modalities, and certifications. LEAP study respondents were united in their preference that volunteers and professionals without specialized training not attempt to interpret drawings or see "deeper meanings" in them. Instead, support groups for children seem to work best when they create a climate for free expression of the experiences of grief (Goldman, 2014; Perschy, 2004).

Games

In an earlier support group manual (Hoy, 2007), I discussed the value of using common games with teens and children. For many years, my preference has been toward games that could be purchased in a discount store. *Chutes and Ladders* for younger children helps them see the inevitability of making great progress, only to "slide" nearly back to the beginning, a good picture of the grief process for many individuals.

Jenga is especially useful for older children and teens as the youngsters take turns removing wood blocks while trying to prevent the tower from falling. With *Jenga*, I like to invite young people to share something about their loved one—a special memory, a favorite holiday, or a gift they treasure given by the person who died.

GRIEF CAMPS AND THEIR ROLE IN SUPPORTING BEREAVED YOUNG PEOPLE

In their review of the literature on grief camps, McClatchey and Wimmer (2014) reported that brief weekend grief camps have been available for bereaved children and teens since the early 1990s. Through numerous quality surveys, it seems beyond doubt that children and their parents/guardians generally consider the camps to have been helpful, to have increased the likelihood of conversation within families, and to have improved the child's outlook on life (McClatchey & Wimmer, 2014). There are many models for grief camps, but one common expression of the model is a Friday night to Sunday afternoon camp experience at a nearby camp used for summer overnight camp experiences. Most often, two LEAP study participants explained, grief camps are held on weekends during the part of the year when camp facilities would be available to be rented inexpensively. Closely akin to grief camps are wilderness experiences for grieving adolescents.

Outward Bound, an organization that uses wilderness experiences to teach life skills, is one such program. The grief work that is "woven into every aspect of the curriculum helps young people to connect, build relationships, and share in a relevant healing experience with real-world outcomes" (Outward Bound, 2015, n.p.). Weaving together the learning of wilderness "survival" skills with the learning of new grief coping skills, the metaphor resonates with many in the child/teen grief support community. Wilderness experiences include backpacking, coastal sailing, and white water rafting. Key components of white water rafting trips include:

> hands-on, progressive training in a variety of expedition and personal skills. . . . As they learn to cook, sleep, stay warm, navigate and select routes together, students also join in nightly discussion circles, acknowledge shared losses, and take part in grief rituals together. (Outward Bound, 2015, n.p.)

LEAP study participants with experience in weekend bereavement camps described complex operations requiring many volunteers. Two respondents indicated the number of volunteers exceeds the number of campers since the campers are assigned a "buddy" for the weekend. Additionally, program and administrative staff oversee the entire operation.

While there have been many studies documenting camper experiences and offering opportunities for children and guardians to evaluate change, controlled outcome studies have been largely absent from the literature. One earlier study by McClatchey, Vonk, and Palardy (2009) explored the effects of a 48-hour grief camp experience for 100 children age 6 to 16. The children were divided into two groups, and researchers administered a battery of instruments to all children. The first group participated immediately in the camp and the second group was waitlisted for two weeks.

Results of a post-test showed the individuals who participated in the camp experienced reduced traumatic grief and posttraumatic stress disorder (PTSD) symptoms. While these results clearly show statistically significant improvement in trauma-related symptoms for the group participating in the first camp, the comparison group received no intervention. Trauma symptom improvement is not the same as grief symptom improvement, so we must be careful in generalizing these results. Like other studies, this study shows clear improvement for young people who receive some intervention instead of no intervention. What it does not demonstrate is whether young people would have been helped as much by some other kind of group intervention, such as a weekly support group in their community.

This last question is the one that perplexes program leaders, researchers, and philanthropic funders alike. The issue is not whether or not grief camps are beneficial; they subjectively are, and these results are regularly reported by campers, parents, and camp staff. The question revolves around whether grief camps are as effective as or more effective than other grief interventions. When one considers the "human capital" required for a weekend camp, many program leaders would want to see results that exceed those of grief groups within the community. These indirect costs of volunteer recruitment, training, and time investment, of course, do not include direct costs for camp rental, food, transportation, and other supplies. Clearly, grief camps need to be studied more thoroughly, including randomized control trials with children who receive grief camp interventions and standard community-based grief group interventions. Results such as these will help inform program planners and philanthropists where to best invest resources.

Many of the principles that inform bereavement group work with adults provide guidance for group work with children and teens. Substantial empirical research has demonstrated the value of grief work with children and has generally pointed in the direction of group work to accomplish those goals. Longitudinal studies examining the effectiveness of the Family Bereavement Program piloted at Arizona State University has demonstrated value in the kinds of activities being used with child and teen grief groups around the world. In the years ahead, hopefully we will come to understand more effectively why particular programs are effective and to whom they may deliver the most assistance.

QUESTIONS FOR REFLECTION AND DISCUSSION

- If it is true that child and teen bereavement programs enjoy high revenues, what do you suppose accounts for individuals' reasons for giving to them?
- Explore the website of the National Alliance for Grieving Children, an agency on its "find a program" link or the website of one of the programs featured in this chapter. What do you see as similar and different between the programs you examined?
- What do you think about the author's rather "tepid" acceptance of grief camps? Why do you suspect his perspective seems so "guarded"?

CHAPTER 7

Dealing With Complicated Grief in the Support Group

Since their only child's sophomore year in high school, Jeff and Carol had become accustomed to late night phone calls from Sam or from the police—reporting that he had been arrested or that he was too drunk to drive home. His early descent into a world of drugs and alcohol had cost their son and them dearly. Sam was expelled from high school in his senior year for having drugs on campus and had never gotten his diploma. He had drifted from one low-paying job and poor living situation to another. Jeff had lost count of how many times he and Carol had dipped into savings and retirement funds to pay for bail bonds, lawyers, and rehabilitation programs. No amount of rehabilitation or incarceration had made a lasting difference.

Jeff was just making the morning coffee when the knock came at their patio door shortly after dawn that Saturday morning. Standing in the doorway was Bob Patterson, their small city's chief of police and a high school and church friend of Jeff's and Carol's. One look at Bob's face and Jeff knew the news was not good. As Carol appeared in the kitchen, the three sat down at the breakfast table and Bob began to tell the story.

A little after midnight, two of Bob's officers answered a domestic disturbance call at the apartment where Sam and his off-again, on-again girlfriend were living. When the officers arrived, they found Sam, almost certainly under the influence of alcohol or drugs, holding a gun to the head of his girlfriend and her 4-year- old daughter. When the officers told him to put down the gun, he aimed it at the two of them and fired. Though the bullet only grazed one officer's shoulder, the second returned fire, killing 26-year-old Sam instantly.

In the days and months after the shooting, Jeff and Carol learned more about the story. David Kelley, the officer who fired the fatal shot, was a high school classmate of Sam's. The lives of their families had been intertwined with Officer Kelley and his wife and children as well as his parents, who all attended the same congregation as Jeff and Carol. David and Sam had been close friends in elementary and junior high school. A four-year veteran of the small 27-officer police department, this was the first time David had used his service revolver in the line of duty.

When Jeff and Carol walked into a bereaved parents' support group meeting about two months after Sam's death, they had just received the final autopsy report. The seven-page report showed Sam had died of a single gunshot wound to the upper torso; the death certificate reported the interval between "injury" and "death" as "seconds." Toxicology reports showed Sam had moderate levels of heroin, marijuana, and alcohol in his blood. As they told their story at that first support group meeting, Carol confessed that she wished they had done more to help their son. In a restrained but angry voice, Jeff retorted, "I don't know what else we could have done. He spent 10 years doing everything he could to destroy our lives—and now it looks like he has finally succeeded."

Though faces and details are different, Jeff and Carol's story is not unique. In a multinational, cross-cultural review of the relationship between substance use and homicide, Darke (2010), summarized a well-documented international trend:

> One of the most robust features of the literature in recent years has been a strong correlation between national alcohol sales and homicide rates, a finding that has been reported across a range of nations and cultures. Thus, in periods when total volume alcohol sales increase, so do homicide rates. Conversely, when there are declines in sales, homicide rates typically decline. . . . There is also tentative data suggesting a similar relationship for illicit drugs. (p. 204)

Darke (2010) further concluded,

> Psychoactive substances are strongly associated with homicide, and the data make it abundantly clear that this is true of both offender and victims. . . . One of the major societal benefits that can be derived from active attempts to reduce alcohol and other drug use is that we might reduce the global rates of homicide, as well the death rates of substance users from such violence. (p. 211)

While drug-related deaths are a small percentage of all bereavements, the circumstances surrounding these deaths dramatically raise the risk of survivors developing what has been broadly defined as complicated grief. Several participants in the LEAP study indicated they have observed an increase in drug-related deaths reported by the bereaved individuals their groups serve. One program coordinator estimated between one-third and one-half of all families served report that the loved one's death was related to alcohol or narcotics, adding, "This is not 1950s grief anymore."

Known by many different names—pathological grief, traumatic grief, prolonged grief, and the perennial, if generic, favorite, complicated grief—few bereavement professionals would debate that sometimes the experience of grief really does go awry. In the introduction to their research anthology on the topic, Stroebe, Schut, and van den Bout (2013) wrote, "In general terms, complicated grief (CG) can be understood as something like a 'derailing' of the normal, usually painful process of adapting to the loss of a significant person" (p. 4). What far fewer professionals in the field agree about is exactly what does and does not characterize this phenomenon of complicated grief that almost every experienced grief worker knows when he or she sees it.

While randomized control trials of the phenomenon and consensus labeling of a psychopathological condition are recent innovations in the construct, the notion of complicated grief has been part of the grief literature for most of the last century (Parkes, 1964). Prior to World War II, Helene Deutsch (1937) discussed ways grief could go awry, likely becoming the first to label a specific complicated grief manifestation of "absent grief."

Eric Lindemann (1944), arguably the father of contemporary bereavement theory and practice, observed complicated grief in his clinical practice. His classic paper differentiated what he called "normal grief reactions" from "morbid grief reactions" (p. 144). Considering the horribly traumatic circumstances that exposed many of his patients to the loss that brought them into his care, it could hardly be otherwise. As explained in Chapter One, Lindemann developed his clinical understanding of grief using as many of his subjects victims from Boston's famous Cocoanut Grove fire, some of the most traumatized bereaved individuals one could imagine.

Herein lies an important concern about the morbid grief Lindemann observed. Many of the cases he reported in "Symptomatology and Management of Acute Grief" would not be considered merely "grief reactions" by 21st century definitions. In our contemporary nomenclature, we would refer to these as cases of trauma, with many of these individuals exhibiting not symptoms of loss but rather of posttraumatic stress disorder (PTSD). In fact, Lindemann only made passing reference to "trauma," the term so frequently used by contemporary clinicians. In his first paragraph, he seems to have subsumed all loss under the vague expression "traumatic experiences." Lindemann wrote:

> The duration of a grief reaction seems to depend upon the success with which a person does the *grief work,* namely, emancipation from the bondage to the deceased, readjustment to the environment in which the deceased is missing, and the formation of new relationships. One of the big obstacles to this work seems to be the fact that many patients try to avoid the intense distress connected with the grief experience and to avoid the expression of emotion necessary for it. (p. 143)

Then, to what would surely be seen with surprise by most bereavement-related professionals today, Lindemann concluded that eight to 10 sessions over a period of a month to six weeks was all that was required to help these victims adapt to their losses. He wrote, "this was the case in all but one of the 13 Cocoanut Grove fire victims" (p. 144). Was Lindemann considering "settled grief" in some way very different from 21st century clinicians? Could it be that in the midst of World War II, individuals were simply "more prepared" for horrific death? Were midcentury Boston-area residents more resilient then than the typically traumatized bereaved individuals seen by most bereavement professionals today?

Whatever the answers to these questions, bereavement group leaders face an array of vexing concerns when working with individuals whose loss experiences can be exceedingly complicated. Jeff and Carol, the couple whose story began this chapter, present many of these challenges: their son, a young man, died a violent "out of time" death. Moreover, their grief was almost certainly made more complicated by the fact that in the course of his job of protecting self and innocent victims, a friend of the family had fired the shot that had killed their son. As in many families two months (or two years) after the death, Jeff and Carol clearly were struggling with different interpretations of their own culpability and what more could or could not have been done.

Assuming that the group in which Jeff and Carol participated was one facilitated by a peer volunteer without professional training, these problems could be difficult to manage in a group setting, especially if their conflict surfaced in a more demonstrable way. Though in the

LEAP study I did not pose this scenario to respondents, based on their explanations of prescreening requirements, many respondents would have wanted to work first with Jeff and Carol as a couple before introducing them to a support group experience. This was, however, not the unanimous perspective, even among professional respondents; some indicated they do not prescreen group participants and would not even suppose to "know what a grieving person needs." In any case, individuals like Jeff and Carol show up regularly in bereavement support groups.

COMMON COMPLICATIONS

When thinking of complicated grief, much of the literature assumes that either an individual does or does not meet the condition, with little "gray area" in between. This is not surprising, since for the purposes of research, a condition of study must be either present or not present; in the same way that a person is either pregnant or she is not, the research literature concerning complicated grief implies either one meets the conditions of the emerging disorder or the individual does not. As many readers of this volume undoubtedly know, however, the clinical reality of complicated grief is far more complex, with levels of complication existing along a spectrum of complexity and severity.

Whether peer volunteer or professional, a group leader must be able to appreciate the intersection between complicated grief and the bereavement support group. Leaders must know the boundaries of their own competence. Formal education notwithstanding, participating in clinical supervision, gaining additional training, and developing experience with increasingly complex grief experiences has caused my competence to grow, along with my confidence that I know what I am doing. After three decades of supporting and counseling bereaved individuals, I simply refer some to more specialized care. In practice, this has most often been because the mission of the center where I practiced did not have a practical way to provide for grief complicated by serious underlying mental health conditions. Sometimes, however, I referred cases to others simply because I knew that to treat the patient in question, I would be clearly out of my depth. I believe maturity in practice means we refer individuals for whom we do not have the expertise or simply do not have the time and energy to treat.

Likewise, group leaders must know the boundaries of their own abilities and be ready to refer group participants to additional resources. Interestingly, LEAP study respondents with the least formal training and the most likelihood of being unsupported by a competent counseling professional were also the least likely to possess an extensive list of resources in the community. Conversely, counseling professionals in the LEAP study were most likely to be able to list several specialized resources available, especially in areas related to pre-existing mental health disorders and grief complicated by extreme trauma responses. Certainly part of this disparity exists because counseling professionals will have the most connections with people like them, while peer volunteers would not typically interact informally with these professionals in local and regional associations. Establishing relationships with more experienced professionals, nevertheless, is essential for leaders, whether lay or professional.

Several LEAP study respondents who lead bereavement support programs in faith communities indicated they would refer individuals who are "in trouble in their grief" (the term I used in the interviews) to their pastor. Perhaps these pastors have the skill to assess psychological complication and routinely refer individuals to competent counseling care when indicated, and I am personally committed to the faith community's potential role in helping bereaved individuals. However, my experience indicates that many clergy do not have the training or expertise to address these kinds of issues with congregants.

Volunteers and program staff who lead or oversee bereavement support groups in voluntary organizations such as faith communities must assure there is a competent and willing group of professionals to whom individuals with complicated grief can be referred. Preferably, these professionals need to not only be trained in mental health counseling, but they also need to be thoroughly acquainted with current diagnostic and treatment protocols for complicated grief. Certification from the Association for Death Education and Counseling (www.adec.org) is one such certification.

In recent decades, a plethora of programs has arisen, theoretically to provide both training and "certification" to individuals who want to provide support to bereaved individuals. Konigsberg (2011) was unfairly critical in her assessment of the motives for the establishment of some of these programs, but she is correct that some were developed by individuals with dubious credentials. Popular models include one- to four-day seminars through which peer volunteers and counseling professionals alike can become "certified" to provide support to bereaved individuals. In my opinion, when a professional already possess a broad background in counseling, the best of these programs can provide a quick overview of the field so that professionals can update their skills and knowledge.

When used by persons with no foundational knowledge of counseling principles and practices, such "certification" may imply a level of expertise unlikely to be gained in such an eclipsed fashion. Unfortunately, my review of several of these programs has led to the conclusion that some of the most expensive of these programs evidence no connection to current thinking about the bereavement process.

In addition to their own competence, leaders must also understand the kinds of individuals who will likely derail a bereavement support group, jeopardizing the experience for all participants. Individuals exhibiting significant borderline, histrionic, or narcissistic personality disorder symptoms, for example, will likely have difficulty connecting with others in the group in mutually supportive ways.

There is good evidence that the right kind of group can be highly beneficial for individuals suffering from some forms of what might be clinically labeled as complicated grief. Indeed, as one clinical group leader in the LEAP study put it, "We wouldn't have groups at (name of agency) if we didn't take people with complicated grief. That's about all we see."

In his definitive text on grief counseling and therapy, Worden (2009) devoted an entire chapter to developing what he called seven "mediators of mourning." Any counselor with experience working with bereaved people knows that grief is a highly individual experience. Worden suggested that one way to understand this phenomenon is by considering how his four tasks of mourning are "mediated" by various factors, including the age of the deceased and his or her relationship to the bereaved; how the person died; the bereaved person's prior experiences with loss; personality variables; social variables; and concurrent stresses. Understanding these factors, Worden suggested, are "especially important when one is working with complicated mourning" (p. 57).

As a way to more effectively view complicated grief, my own evolving understanding of the phenomenon labels three somewhat overlapping domains of complicated grief: *situation, support*, and *selfhood*. The domain of *situation* considers the circumstances of the death, the level of "expectedness" of the death, age of the deceased, and the level of comorbid trauma present in the loss experience.

The *support* domain considers the level and helpfulness of social support the bereaved individual perceives is available, the durability and helpfulness of his or her belief system, the potential disenfranchisement of the loss, and the bereaved individual's participation in ceremonies and rituals that provide support in the experience.

Selfhood factors include such things as pre-existing mental health concerns (such as ongoing treatment for depression or anxiety), functionality of the attachment bond with the deceased, substance use and abuse, the level of ambivalence in the relationship with the deceased, the age of the bereaved person, and coping strategies developed in prior life experiences.

Clearly, there are areas of overlap between these domains. For example, individuals with the pre-existing psychopathological condition of borderline personality disorder, a component factor of the *selfhood* domain, most likely do not benefit from strong social *support* among relatives and friends, since BPD behaviors often cripple or destroy supportive relationships. However, the inability to connect supportively with others that is "textbook" in BPD likely counteracts the positive effects that could be derived from participation in a bereavement support group. Moreover, significant borderline tendencies in one participant in the group can greatly reduce the helpfulness of the group process for other participants, as well. In the sections that follow, I explain how clinical experience and research evidence inform specific factors from these domains as they are most likely seen in bereavement support groups.

DEATH OF A CHILD

While it is unfortunate to put loss on a "pecking order," suggesting one kind of death is dramatically worse than others, there does seem to be wide consensus among bereaved individuals that the death of a child is an unimaginably difficult loss. Perhaps unintentionally, scholars often contribute to the "grading" of grief with statements such as, "For parents, no loss is as devastating and painful as the death of their child" (Toller, 2008, p. 306). Nevertheless, I have worked with individuals who, having been both widowed and parentally bereaved, indicated the death of their *mate* was the more difficult loss to manage. Moreover, the notion of a child's death as "life's greatest tragedy" (Brown, 1989 cited in DeVries, Lana, & Falck, 1994, p. 48) is a construct of both Western and recent invention.

The Luo people of the Nyakach Plateau in rural western Kenya, for example, seem rarely to share the "child death tragedy" motif, perhaps in part because the death of a child is a frequent occurrence. Deaths of young children are sad, but parents and community understand the likelihood of such a loss, which perhaps lessens its impact (H. Ogola, personal communication, 25 May 2015). In a recent study on the intersection of spiritual meanings with health care decisions in that close-knit community, Dillon Stull, an undergraduate researcher at Baylor University, discovered strikingly common perspectives among middle-aged adults in that community, most of whom had suffered the death of a child. He concluded,

> My interviewees demonstrated significantly less grief for the losses of their children than I might have expected. I think it no stretch to call the death of a child a 'frequent occurrence' in Luoland. Several even told inspiring stories of faith in God specifically during times of mourning for the deaths of their children. (D.C. Stull, personal communication, 25 August 2015)

Stull later wrote,

> Death is ubiquitous in Luoland, even among the young and 'healthy.' Many in the 1980s and 1990s died in the HIV/AIDS epidemic. Many young men also died in the inter-tribal fighting in the years following Kenya's 2007 presidential election. Many continue to die from motor vehicle accidents, cattle thieves, sicknesses, etc. Thus, the death of even an older child is not uncommon. (D.C. Stull, personal communication, 1 September 2015)

Citing similar observations, medical anthropologist Nancy Scheper-Hughes reflected on her extensive work in shantytowns of rural northeastern Brazil. Over three generations, Scheper-Hughes (2013) observed the average woman has nine pregnancies, 8.5 live births and 3.5 infant deaths. However, what she observed was that these women rarely grieved the deaths of these children in any way approximating "normal" by Western standards, preferring instead to refer to these deceased infants as "angelbabies." She noted that high expectation of infant death and normalization of that experience actually mediated maternal bonding with the young infant. When Scheper-Hughes inquired into what someone meant when they expressed surprising levels of comfort with the infant death during a community meeting, one woman from the community posited that the children were taken by God to spare their mothers' suffering, while another remarked, "God knows the future better than us. It could happen that if the baby were to live he could turn out a thief, or a murderer, or a good for nothing. There are many reasons to rejoice at the death of an angelbaby!" (Scheper-Hughes, 2013).

These observations about the meaning of a child's death in the context of the family serve as an important reminder that cultural customs, family history, and religious beliefs can dramatically impact the ways bereaved parents memorialize and continue bonds with their deceased children. While parents whose belief system has produced these kinds of meaning constructions (Neimeyer & Sands, 2011) would not likely consider themselves in need of a grief support group, some may attend support groups at the behest of well-meaning family, friends, and professionals who see the parents' responses to loss as pathological. Practices that may seem unusual or even unhealthy may be completely within the expected range of "normal" behaviors. In their small study of Mexican-American families following the death of a child, for example, Doran and Hansen (2007) found that most individuals "cherished objects that were used by the deceased" (p. 206). They observed one mother who regularly unpacked, washed, and repacked a child's clothes, and another mother often used her son's special blanket and told of her wish to be buried with it at her death.

Nevertheless, most "first world" (Sauvy, 1952) parents whose children are living have a hard time imagining what it would be like to have a child die. LEAP study respondents confirmed my own experiences leading bereavement support groups of widowed individuals when a bereaved parent joins the group. More often than not, many of those dealing with their own conjugal loss turn their focus to the bereaved parent, using phrases such as "what an unimaginably difficult loss that must be" and "I don't think I could ever get through that."

Often embedded in the death of a child, adolescent, or young adult is the parents' perspective of "unfulfilled dreams" (DeVries et al., 1994; Toller, 2008). Even older adults confront these difficulties, as articulated by Mahgoub and Lantz (2006): "By the time a child has reached adulthood, the parents have made an extensive emotional and financial investment in this individual, and death of their adult child provokes an intense feeling of unfulfilled dreams" (p. 878). In some cases, the "unfulfilled dreams" motif of "first world" parents is supplanted by a sense in the developing world of a "gap" in the family, making it far more difficult to provide adequate shelter, food, and protection when an older child has died (D.C. Stull, personal communication, 1 September 2015). Bereavement support leaders in the industrialized West must be especially alert to these themes with bereaved parents, especially among those who may have immigrated from rural or close-knit communities in the southern or eastern hemispheres in the last generation.

Frequently, unfulfilled dreams are mixed with anger over choices a child made that perhaps contributed to his death. In a stirring interview recollection of their grief, Ameche family members told of how the car crash death of their son and brother, 22-year-old Paul, had impacted individuals similarly and differently. Family members deftly mix their sadness and anger together, matter-of-factly stating that the young man died after driving his car through a stop sign after participating in a party. Yvonne Ameche, Paul's grieving mother, tearfully explained to interviewers,

> I know people ask me if I am angry at God and I'm really not angry at God and I tell them God wasn't driving the car; Paul was. And I find myself sometimes angry at Paul, and I think this life that I held so dear, that I feel is so precious and was so precious, and all his goodness and all he had to offer, and what a good husband and father he would have made and what a good citizen and just a fine human being, and he wasn't careful, he just wasn't careful. (Group Two Productions, 1987)

When bereaved parents attend bereavement support groups that include individuals with a diversity of losses, facilitators must be vigilant to protect these parents from the potential disenfranchisement of individuals with other losses. In my experience, group participants whose spouse or sibling has died, for example, may unintentionally minimize the pondering of these parents about unfulfilled dreams by glibly offering the "cheap comfort" of words such as, "Well it sounds like he packed a lot of living into his 19 years."

Adding to the existential issues present in the deaths of young people, these are most frequently violent and unexpected deaths, as well. Of the 29,667 Americans ages 15–24 years who died in one recent year, 12,330 (41.6%) died in accidents, 4,822 (16.3%) died by suicide, and 4,554 (15.4%) died by homicide; mortality statistics reveal similarly high incidence of traumatic deaths among children younger than 15, as well (U.S. Centers for Disease Control, 2014, Table 10). Parris (2011) reported that an average of six people die each day on British roads, with an estimated 3,900 road deaths per day worldwide and that traumatic injury is the most common form of death for those younger than 15 (p. 140). An additional way to interpret mortality data from the United States is that of the 35,303 motor vehicle accident deaths in 2011, slightly more than 40% were to individuals under the age of 35, most of whom could be assumed to have parents surviving (U.S. Centers for Disease Control, 2014, Table 10).

In Rubin's (1989–1990) study of parents following an adult son's death in Israeli military service, he found that one complicating factor was the plethora of conflicting messages in the loss. Along with the parent's experience of profound loss and the need to grieve the many dimensions to the emotional experience and history with that child, parents also had to deal with issues of patriotism, "belief in the national quest," and perhaps conflicts about the morality of war. Rubin wrote, "In addition to the psychological aspects, the social mores of war bereavement in Israel may exert a powerful influence on the ways in which parents enter and exit the mourning process" (p. 335). Anecdotal reports from colleagues who work with families of both American and Canadian military personnel killed in action, as well as emerging research data about this subset of mourners, indicate similar complication is present for these parents, as well.

While not all bereaved parents will meet the emerging clinical criteria for persistent complex bereavement disorder, most bereaved parents experience grief that is significantly complicated by the circumstances of the death and the age of the child. "No parent should have to bury his child," one bereaved father said. Bereavement support group leaders making a "place at the table" for bereaved parents must be patient, aware that this work is often of very long duration.

VIOLENT DEATH AND PTSD[1]

Jeff and Carol, the couple whose story began this chapter, not only faced grief following the death of their only child but also had to grapple with the *manner* in which he died. Violent deaths potentially pose challenges for bereaved individuals for several reasons, and these are often expressed in support groups.

Violent deaths are most often unexpected, leading to significant shock and numbing. Human biology seems to accommodate overwhelming emotional experiences through temporary emotional anesthesia, much like the numbing effect that occurs with many minor surgical procedures. Unfortunately, this numbness can persist throughout the early period of grief, allowing bereaved individuals to experience memorial activities with no memory of having participated. One benefit to seeing a crowd of caring individuals at a loved one's funeral, for example, seems to be the embedded message that bereaved individuals are cared for by others (Hoy, 2013). Most likely, an individual reeling from the shock of the death will be emotionally unable to receive the full supportive benefits such rituals could otherwise provide.

Bereavement support group leaders must be alert to the presence of posttraumatic stress disorder (PTSD) since it frequently accompanies experiences of grief following violent death. Though a thorough review of PTSD symptomatology is beyond the scope of this book and beyond the work of most bereavement support groups, understanding the phenomenon is important. The disorder can be diagnosed by a mental health professional when the traumatized individual experiences ongoing, clinically significant disturbance in functioning lasting for more than one month. PTSD is characterized by troubling intrusive recollections of the traumatic event, deliberate avoidance of stimuli related to the event, negative cognitions (resigned to injustice, inability to trust, or sensing that the experience will never end), and altered arousal (such as angry outbursts without provocation, sleep disturbances, or hypervigilance) (American Psychiatric Association, 2013). When program leaders suspect a group participant or potential participant is exhibiting these characteristics, a professional consultation is warranted.

Violent deaths also carry with them what J. William Worden has described as the "torment of trauma." Bereaved individuals wonder about whether their loved ones suffered during the dying experience, a common refrain heard from bereaved parents such as Yvonne Ameche (Group Two Productions, 1987). In a provocative examination of the role of viewing the body after traumatic deaths, Canadian social workers Harrington and Sprowl (2011–2012) recorded the tormented musings of one bereaved mother who was prevented by authorities from approaching the scene after her son's fatal car crash: "They said Henry died instantly. Maybe he was still there inside, for two hours later he was waiting for me, for his mother to come by and hold him. And I wasn't there. I feel like I let him down somehow" (p. 76).

While much research has pointed to the helpfulness of viewing the body after a traumatic death (most often at the hospital or funeral home) (Harrington & Sprowl, 2011–2012; Hoy, 2013; Singh & Raphael, 1981), some evidence indicates that actually finding the body can complicate the grief experience (Burke & Neimeyer, 2013). Family members sometimes discover their loved ones hours or days after a fatal collapse, as was the case of a participant in a support group I led; this woman had discovered her mother several hours after the mother had apparently died in her sleep. Though the bereaved woman's religious beliefs did not accommodate viewing the body, she told our group: "I just had to see her in her casket, you know, at peace. Otherwise, I just couldn't get the scene out of my mind."

Finding the body seems to be especially problematic after deaths by suicide. In one study of 540 bereaved parents, Feigelman, Jordan, and Gorman (2008–2009) found significantly higher levels of grief-related distress among suicide survivors who found the body as compared to those who did not see the body prior to the funeral. Like many studies in bereavement, their sample was overwhelmingly high socioeconomic status (SES), white, American, and female. In view of apparent preferences for viewing of the body among some ethnic minorities (Hoy, 2013; Hoy & Na, 2015), it would be interesting to know how these results might have been different among a more ethnically diverse, multicultural sample.

Apparently, a much larger number of newly bereaved individuals are notified of a loved one's death by law enforcement or medical personnel than actually find the body. In their phenomenological study of next of kin after learning of an unexpected death, Harrington and Sprowl (2011–2012) reviewed the literature relating to the role, purpose, and potential benefit or harm done by viewing soon after the death, pointing out that family members often request to see the body immediately upon notification of death. Out of their experience as hospital-based medical social workers, they offered helpful guidelines for viewing, including the importance of explaining post-death changes to family members and covering large injuries. They indicated that unlimited time with the body and the opportunity to touch are invaluable, noting that generally, it is health care professionals' discomfort with emotionality that drives the need not to offer these opportunities (pp. 67–68). In light of their results, bereavement support group leaders will likely want to explore participants' experiences with death notification and viewings at the scene or hospital and the participants' reactions to those opportunities.

The unexpected nature of most violent deaths raises the likelihood that bereaved individuals have "unfinished business" with the deceased. One support group participant explained that for him, "Time just stopped" when his son died, "almost as if my grief were locked in time like the 'freeze-frame' function in watching a movie." Several respondents in the LEAP study noted the emotional struggles of individuals in their groups who had difficulty balancing the last words or the final fight with a now-deceased loved one. In my experience, bereaved individuals talk openly in groups about "what I wish I would have said/done" in group discussions focused around guilt and regrets. The empathetic listening by group members and leader alike seem to make these experiences easier to bear for some group participants. However, leaders must be attentive to other group members, who may try to minimize their own discomfort by prematurely offering reassuring words such as, "You did all you could," "I think she must have known you loved her," and "He would have known you didn't really mean that."

Because violent deaths are not the result of "natural causes," there is an "agent" who can be held responsible for the loss. Highway safety experts seem to believe that motor vehicle crash fatalities are often caused by such "human error" factors such as not wearing safety belts, cell phone use, influence of alcohol or drugs, and general carelessness in driving. Family members and friends of individuals who die by suicide often struggle with issues of blame (toward self and others) as well as intense anger. Bereaved individuals blaming themselves for the suicide death when there have been prior attempts also appears to be a common theme. Feigelman and colleagues (2008–2009) found that prior suicide attempts placed bereaved parents at an elevated risk of intensified grief after the completed suicide of children.

Some level of guilt and regret is common to bereaved individuals, especially in light of a death that is viewed by survivors as preventable. Often, the sharing of those regrets in the supportive context of a bereavement group, along with normalization of those feelings by leader and other group members, is enough for bereaved individuals to be reassured in their grief and for this guilt to not become a defining characteristic of their experience. However, guilt is also one manifestation of exaggerated grief examined by both Worden (2009) and Rando (1993, 2013) discussed below. Feelings of guilt that become such a defining characteristic or that persistently damage the self-esteem of the bereaved individual are not likely to be resolved in the context of a support group, regardless of how supportive the participants and leader are. Individuals struggling with persistent guilt should be referred to a competent professional for individual counseling.

UNDERLYING MENTAL HEALTH ISSUES

After hearing one caller's story about the death in his family and the need for support from our agency's family group, our receptionist, with tongue in cheek, remarked to me, "Grief is number nine on this family's list." The phrase became somewhat of a mantra in our office as we encountered with increasing frequency families with significant mental health issues and unhealthy functioning in the family system.

The World Health Organization (2013), for example, estimates that depression affects 350 million people worldwide, a major contributor to the global burden of disease and a major cause of disability. One global survey placed the one-year prevalence of depression at approximately 5%. Approximately 10.8% of Americans over the age of 12 use antidepressant medication, though antidepressants are prescribed for a variety of conditions, including major depression, anxiety disorders, and symptoms of menopause (Pratt, Brody, & Gu, 2011). In its annual survey of mental health, the U.S. Substance Abuse and Mental Health Services Administration (2014) estimated that 18.5% of all American adults have some diagnosable mental illness, 17.5% of whom also meet the criteria of a substance use disorder; substance use disorders and developmental disorders are excluded from SAMHSA's definition of mental illness. According to the agency's estimates, nearly 4% of adults in the United States had serious thoughts of suicide in the most recent year. Since a serious relationship loss tends to exacerbate mental health conditions such as depression, anxiety, and suicidal ideation, clinical experience indicates these conditions and disorders would be no less prevalent among bereaved individuals seeking the help of a support group or other intervention.

Individuals with depression and anxiety disorders attend bereavement support groups. Whether the disorders are in addition to bereavement or caused by their bereavement, the real issue for group leaders is how these individuals connect and function in a bereavement group. In my experience and among most of the respondents in the LEAP study who assess for clinical disorders, persons who want to participate in the group are welcome to participate. In the words of one LEAP study participant, "We address bad behavior in the group for what it is: bad behavior. It doesn't really matter to me what the diagnostic label or condition is. If a person can participate in the group and feels she or he is getting help, I'm fine with them coming."

In addition to mood and anxiety disorders, bereavement group leaders will want to consider the attachment bonds of potential participants. One of Worden's (2009) mourning "mediators" is the functionality of the attachment bond between survivor and deceased. In my experience, the narratives of individuals suffering from anxious attachments, for example, often include words signifying abandonment. Upon first meeting one potential group member, I did not readily understand that her husband had died because she persisted in saying how lost she had felt "since he left me." I may have unknowingly reinforced the disordered attachment by asking as a follow up question, "Will you tell me a little about how and when he left?" It took several interchanges like that for me to realize that her husband had died and that, as a result, she felt abandoned.

In their helpful clinical guide, Kosminsky and Jordan (2016) pointed out that disordered attachment in childhood can lie at the root of poor social support for adults. These individuals, they suggested, may go "through life convinced that other people cannot be trusted, (looking) for the insult in every comment directed their way" (p. 122). Learning through therapy to understand the source of such perspectives and to reappraise the intentions of others become important in helping bereaved individuals to reduce interpersonal conflict, thereby potentially improving their level of social support. While Kosminsky and Jordan intended this work for individual therapy, helping participants to reframe insults can be important work for support groups. For example, when a group participant complains about the "stupid" advice and hurtful comments offered by friends and family members, a support group facilitator can ask the group: "So it sounds like Mary found these comments hurtful. What might be the reasons people say such hurtful things?"

A discussion such as this might more clearly reveal whether the group member is suffering from a disordered attachment or simply responding to hurtful comments. In this kind of discussion, group members may evaluate unhelpful comments with words like, "people just want to help, even though they are misguided," or "well, my friends say dumb things because they haven't experienced this kind of loss and they don't know better." After just such a discussion, one group member concluded, "Over the last few weeks, I've begun to realize that people don't say this because they want to hurt me; they say it, stupid as it is, because they care and want to help. If they didn't care, I guess they would just say nothing at all."

If group participants persist in attributing negative motives to the misguided helpfulness of others, group facilitators would want to consider referral of the group member to competent professional support to work on possible attachment issues. In my experience and that of my colleague Bill Worden, issues of disordered attachment will not likely be resolved in the context of a support group, requiring instead some level of individual professional support (J. W. Worden, personal communication, 18 August 2015).

LACK OF SOCIAL SUPPORT

Perhaps the most common reason individuals give for wanting to join a bereavement support group is that they feel alone or perceive they have less social support available to them than they would like. Often, bereavement support group participants acknowledge that they believe family members want to be helpful but that they do not know how to assist the bereaved appropriately.

An equally large number of participants in my experience articulate a fear of "wearing out" or "burning out" their social support system. One bereaved individual described such concerns to the group in which she was participating: "After a while, you realize your family is just tired of hearing about it, of you moping around all the time, of not being your old self. They don't know that I won't be my old self ever again." Moreover, even the presence of a large extended family in no way guarantees the bereaved individual will sense an adequate level of support. In their study of 94 bereaved individuals whose spouse or child had died in a car crash, Lehman, Ellard, and Wortman (1986) found that unhelpful social support most often came from family members and close friends. This counterintuitive finding might be in part because of these support persons' own grief experiences or because of their own desire to see the bereaved parent or spouse "recover" (p. 443).

While many groups evaluate social support on the basis of the quality of the support and the perception of availability, this cannot be considered a culturally universal construct. Over my years of practice, I have met many individuals who calculated the supportiveness of their network on the basis of how many people attended the funeral, the number of sympathy cards received, and the number of floral offerings sent to the funeral home.

One Canadian study of 61 psychiatric outpatients with complicated grief examined how perceived social support might influence the course of bereavement. This study built on an earlier project that demonstrated that pre-therapy social support from friends was predictive of favorable outcomes in bereavement-related therapy, while the results were mixed for perceived social support from family members or a significant person (Ogrodniczuk, Piper, Joyce, McCallum, & Rosie, 2002). Though they conceded the results should be interpreted cautiously, Ogrodniczuk, Joyce, and Piper (2003) found that the patients' perception of supportive significant person, family members, and friends increased in the six months following participation in a 12-week psychotherapy group for complicated grief and that this increased perception of support was positively correlated with a reduction in depressive symptoms.

Possible explanations abound for the reported change in perceived social support for these patients. The researchers suggested that either as a result of therapy or the lessening of symptoms, perhaps patients behaved in more socially desirable ways, thereby encouraging more support from their natural support systems. Of course it is also possible that the improvement in perceived levels of support actually facilitated improvement in symptoms. These researchers reached one clinical conclusion of significant importance for those who seek to support individuals with complicated bereavement. They found that while the support of a special person, family, and friends produced positive change, "perceived support from family was not significantly associated with changes in symptoms. Thus, [therapists might best] facilitat[e] improvements in social support and depressive symptoms by focusing on social relationships that involve friends and a close person" (Ogrodniczuk et al., 2003, p. 530).

SPIRITUAL CONFLICT

Spiritual resources and beliefs seem to provide an important cornerstone for the coping strategies of many bereaved people. In her interviews of 30 middle-aged African-American women following the deaths of their mothers, Smith (2002) found belief in an afterlife and hope for heavenly reunion was seen as important in the subjects' ability to cope with loss.

These findings were corroborated in a recent PhD dissertation. Spreadbury (2011) found that when religious ritual was seen as highly important for older spousally bereaved adults, this belief predicted lower levels of measured grief and depression. Daily spiritual practices (Bible reading, prayer, etc.) predicted lower levels of anxiety. A Taiwanese study of the role of religious beliefs in bereavement among older widowed women also indicated that those with intrinsic spiritual beliefs and practices exhibited better overall coping than those with extrinsic religious beliefs or no religious belief (Shih, Turale, Shih, & Tsai, 2010). Taken together, these findings echo the preponderance of studies in the last two decades that point to the generally positive role of spirituality in overall health, mental health, and daily functioning (Koenig, 2013).

While, on the whole, spiritual beliefs do act as a buffer to some complicated grief experiences, participants in groups sometimes detail the hurtful comments made by individuals whom the bereaved had hoped would be supportive. One individual attending a support group I led told how her pastor had "scolded" her about 12 weeks after her husband's death for "not having enough faith." Moreover, when she attended a dinner meeting of the congregation's group for seniors, another woman asked, "Well, have you come here to steal one of our husbands?" My group participant indicated she hoped the latter comment had simply been a careless joke but, upon reflection, indicated that she was not sure since she had not felt particularly welcome in the group. In any case, the plaintive tone with which she shared the story made it clear the comment had been deeply hurtful, whether uttered in jest or not.

Many times in my career, individuals have found their way into one of the groups in our nonreligious hospice and bereavement center in part because it was *not* part of their faith community. Some individuals are deeply distressed to share the depth of their pain with people whom they perceive might look on them with spiritual disdain. While bereavement groups in some faith communities take important steps to decrease this disenfranchisement, some individuals seem to feel more comfortable joining a support group outside their congregation. My experiences were echoed by several respondents in the LEAP study, as well.

Pargament, Smith, Koenig, and Perez (1998) and Pargament, Koenig, and Perez (2000) suggested that some individuals use religious coping strategies the researchers classified as either positive or negative. On the positive side, individuals conceive of a sense of spirituality, a secure relationship with God, a sense of spiritual connectedness to others, and a belief that there is meaning to be found in life. Negative religious coping, on the other hand, included such factors as an insecure relationship with God, a tentative and threatening view of the world, spiritual struggle, and spiritual discontent.

In a study of 46 homicidally-bereaved African Americans, Burke, Neimeyer, McDevitt-Murphy, Ippolito, and Roberts (2011) found that survivors used both positive and negative religious coping strategies. While the use of negative religious coping has consistently predicted complicated grief, researchers have found mixed results about the use of positive religious coping strategies. Burke and Neimeyer (2012) found that religious beliefs appeared to be associated with better decision-making practices, altruistic behaviors, and health-inducing behaviors. Taken together, these researchers have suggested that clinicians work together with congregational clergy to watch for evidence of complicated grief, since their data unequivocally pointed to increased incidence of complicated grief when bereaved individuals expressed significant spiritual struggles in the loss.

Unlike the Internet-based organization described in Chapter Four that does not permit spiritual content on its discussion boards, respondents in the LEAP study who discussed the matter unanimously endorsed encouraging discussions of spiritual disappointments and spiritual support in their groups. While several specifically indicated that they intervene if group participants use the group time as a forum for proselytizing, these LEAP study respondents explained that they believe spiritual support and spiritual searching are important parts of the grief process.

One caution, however, bears mention. Faith communities and religious sponsors of bereavement support groups must walk a particularly fine line in this regard. Most of these groups seem to be open to the entire community, including individuals who would not subscribe to the prevalent beliefs of the sponsoring organization, and even members of the sponsoring organizations may be struggling significantly with beliefs as a consequence of their loss. For example, bereaved individuals frequently disclose anger at God, the faith community, and the clergy. The loss experience of these individuals can be further disenfranchised if some group participants are made to feel their views are "unacceptable" beliefs within the support group.

As in any bereavement support group, participants are likely to share ideas that are not in line with the sponsor's (or leader's) personal perspective. One way group leaders can provide "equal time" for dissenting voices is by saying, "John clearly has strong opinions about this that grow out of his experiences. What do some of the rest of you think? What could be another way to look at this?"

The challenge with "belief sharing" in support groups is that not all (or even more than one) of the group participants share the perspective. A hospice bereavement coordinator leading a support group may feel very uncomfortable when a support group participant says, "I believe hospice overdosed my father on painkillers and he died sooner than he should have" or "The hospice nurses just wouldn't help us enough." While these perspectives do not represent common occurrences, or even, in most cases, medically accurate observations, they are the opinions of group members, and they must be respected.

COMPLICATED GRIEF AND EVIDENCE-BASED PRACTICES

In their review of the then-extant research literature, Jacobs and Prigerson (2000) called for the development of a new psychiatric disorder they referred to as "traumatic grief" (p. 479). This review followed by several years an earlier paper articulating the need to codify a diagnostic category for such complex experiences with grief (Prigerson et al., 1997). Over the next several years, Prigerson and her colleagues began referring to the phenomenon as "Prolonged Grief Disorder," developing proposed criteria for the then soon-to-be-updated *Diagnostic and Statistical Manual of Mental Disorders* (Prigerson et al., 2009).

Complicated grief, the umbrella term that has become part of the bereavement caregiving lexicon in the last few decades, has led to a great deal of research and is a much-discussed topic in the literature. A 2015 search of the term "complicated grief" in the U.S. National Library of Medicine's database (http://www.ncbi.nlm.nih.gov/pubmed), for example, yielded 487 articles published since 2000, including reports on 37 clinical trials. The studies designed to test the effectiveness of various intervention strategies for individuals with complicated grief show overall positive results. Since 2005, Katherine Shear and her colleagues have been developing and refining a treatment protocol for complicated grief that has been tested with both individuals and groups. Its promise is most compelling because of the randomized "controls" utilized in several of the resulting studies, leading to conclusions about what differences the intervention really makes when compared to the experiences of bereavement of those who receive no intervention or who receive help in some other form.

The scientific contributions of O'Connor (2005); O'Connor, Irwin, and Wellisch (2009); and O'Connor and Sussman (2014) have also been important in better understanding the nuances of complicated grief. In addition to research specifically on the role of yearning in loss (O'Connor & Sussman, 2014), O'Connor's work using functional magnetic resonance imaging (fMRI) with bereaved individuals has yielded important understandings in how grief may be "seen" in neuroimaging (O'Connor, 2013; O'Connor et al., 2009). In one study, 23 individuals participated in a clinical interview (Prigerson & Jacobs, 2001) using items drawn from the Inventory of Complicated Grief (Prigerson et al., 1995). The participants were all females whose mother or sister had died from breast cancer in the previous five years. Using data from the clinical interviews, the participants were divided into a group of 11 meeting the criteria for complicated grief and 12 with noncomplicated grief. The participants were then each shown a slide-show including photos of the participant's deceased loved one combined with photos of strangers, along with images showing grief-related words (e.g., collapse, funeral, lost) and neutral words (e.g., announce, ceiling, list). When shown the reminders of their loved one and grief-related concepts while undergoing fMRI, the group labeled as meeting the criteria for complicated grief showed greater neural activation than those with non-CG in a subcortical area of the brain called the nucleus accumbens (O'Connor, 2013; O'Connor et al., 2008).

Shear et al. (2005) explained their treatment for complicated grief as a three-phase (introductory, middle, and termination) process of psychotherapy. Through approximately 16 sessions, trained therapists worked with patients using, as a framework, Stroebe and Schut's (1999, 2010) dual process model of grief. To make application to the dual process model (as explained in Chapter One of this volume), the introductory phase of treatment not only focused on the telling of the loss story (loss orientation) but also on the client's personal life goals and plans (restoration orientation). The treatment protocol addressed relationship quality, prior or concurrent stresses, and attachment issues between griever and deceased. When issues of trauma around the death arose, the treatment protocol focused on retelling the story through an imaginal process the researchers labeled as "revisiting" (p. 2604).

In their initial trial, Shear et al. (2005) found that individuals participating in the targeted therapy for complicated grief improved more than those receiving conventional interpersonal psychotherapy. Specifically, 51% of those participating in complicated grief therapy showed improvement on follow-up assessment, while 28% of those participating in interpersonal psychotherapy showed improvement. As a first step, these results were widely seen as encouraging. Complicated grief therapy (CGT), as the protocol eventually became known, has been used in multiple studies since its introduction. Cruz et al. (2007) compared the effects of the treatment between white and African-American participants finding no significant difference in outcomes. Shear et al. (2014) examined the treatment protocol with elderly persons and found significant benefit to CGT over conventional interpersonal therapy, with the improvement remaining when participants were assessed again in six months.

Similarly, Supiano and Luptak (2014) found that the older adults in their study improved more with the use of protocols of complicated grief therapy than older adult participants in the standard "treatment as usual" group that had been in use in the bereavement center where the research was conducted. While published studies of complicated grief therapy (CGT) generally report on interventions through individual psychotherapy, Supiano and Luptak examined outcomes with the protocol delivered in a group context. Though peer-led or self-help model bereavement support groups do not include the clinically trained leadership utilized in this study (all facilitators were master's-level, licensed mental health professionals), the findings of their study likely are transferable and applicable to bereavement support group contexts. In their discussion of their results, the researchers reported, "Although participants in both groups showed improvement in measures of Complicated Grief, participants in the Complicated Grief Group Therapy group realized significantly greater improvement" (p. 852).

One randomized control trial for individuals with complicated grief was delivered in a digital (online) format. Wagner et al. (2006, 2007) reported promising results for an 18-month longitudinal study of 25 bereaved individuals who completed an email-based cognitive behavioral intervention for complicated grief, comparing them to 25 assigned to a matched "waiting group" (control). Exclusion criteria included such things as severe depression, substance abuse, suicidal intention, dissociative tendency, and current participation in treatment. Since the intervention was delivered in German, participants also had to report fluency in the language.

Most participants (61%) were grieving the death of a child, and the time elapsed since loss ranged from 14 months to 29 years. All participants showed high levels of complicated grief, defined as intrusion and avoidance (Horowitz et al., 1997) measured through the Impact of Events Scale (Horowitz, Wilner, & Alvarez, 1979). Additionally, participants scored high on a measure labeled as "failure to adapt," defined as trouble sleeping, feeling worthless, altered sense of the future, and feeling lonely or empty, characteristics measured through an instrument developed by Langner and Maercker (2005). Participants in the treatment group completed two 45-minute writing assignments each week for five weeks, with the therapist and patients communicating only through email. A psychoeducational component began each of the three phases (exposure to bereavement cues, cognitive reappraisal, and integration and restoration). On comparison, the treatment group to the nontreatment control group, the researchers noted significantly greater reduction in the cluster of psychological symptoms of complicated grief (intrusion, avoidance, and failure to adapt) as well as in levels of depression and anxiety among the treatment group individuals.

When the long-awaited fifth edition of the *Diagnostic and Statistical Manual of Mental Disorders* (*DSM-5*) was released in May 2013, clinicians "held a collective breath" to see how bereavement, and especially complicated bereavement, would be addressed. Among the "Conditions for Further Study" near the end of the volume appeared proposed criteria for persistent complex bereavement disorder (American Psychiatric Association, 2013, pp. 789–792). To the relief of many, the proposed criteria require at least 12 months to have elapsed since the death. Intense longing for the deceased, intense sorrow and emotional pain, and preoccupation with the deceased person or preoccupation with the circumstances of the death coupled with at least six symptoms from a list of 12 criteria would be required to diagnose an individual with the condition. Since this diagnosis is not yet available for clinical use, its inclusion in the *DSM-5* was primarily viewed as a way to systematize criteria for research. One of the frustrations articulated by clinicians about the emerging diagnosis has been that symptom lists have continued to "morph" through the years, making it very difficult to compare research reports or proposed intervention strategies.

In spite of herculean efforts to systematize a criteria set for diagnosing complicated grief and very promising results from the clinical trials to test various intervention strategies, some clinical scholars object to the narrow definition of complicated grief in current use. In her summary of complicated mourning, Therese Rando (1993, 2013) described eight complicated grief syndromes: absent grief, delayed grief, inhibited grief, distorted grief (extremely angry or guilty), conflicted grief, and the previously mentioned prolonged grief disorder. Rando (2013) noted that definitions and descriptions of complicated grief have been surprisingly nonspecific, leading to confusion in interpreting the data included in the literature. In early work, Rando (1993) explained the concept of complicated grief:

> In all forms of complicated mourning, the mourner attempts to do two things: (a) deny, repress, or avoid aspects of the loss, its pain, and the full realization of its implications for the mourner and (b) hold on to and avoid relinquishing the lost loved one. These attempts, or some variation thereof, are what underlie and cause complications in the "R" processes of mourning. (p. 149)

Preferring the term "complicated mourning," Worden (2009) wrote that the phenomenon actually encompasses four different kinds of reaction. What he described as *chronic* grief is closest to complicated grief as the term is currently used. But in addition to this chronic, unremitting kind of sorrow, Worden has suggested there are three other diagnostic categories that, together with chronic grief, make up the dimensions of complicated mourning: delayed grief, exaggerated grief, and masked grief.

Though sometimes dismissed by other scholars (Bonanno et al., 2002), Worden maintained that *delayed* grief was a real phenomenon affecting 4–8% of bereaved individuals. Not to be confused with Deutsch's (1937) "absent grief," Worden wrote that in his clinical experience:

> grief was not absent around the time of the loss, but for some reason, usually the absence of social support, the person didn't process it adequately, and it reappeared much later, often in the form of deep sorrow and excessive crying related to a lesser loss. (Worden, 2009, p. 141)

Individuals undergoing *exaggerated* grief reactions, according to Worden, experience an unusual intensification of normal bereavement behaviors to the point the bereaved individual feels overwhelmed, often acting out in maladaptive ways. Intense anger or rage, clinical depression, anxiety, phobias, and substance abuse are a few of the most common ways mourning gets exaggerated, according to this schema. According to Worden, these symptoms are similar to normal grief but exaggerated to the point of dysfunction and often warrant a *DSM* diagnosis. A therapist would treat the exaggeration in the same way the therapist would address the diagnosis if it were unrelated to grief. However, the therapist would, in this case, also explore the conflict of the separation that seems to underlie the extreme behavior.

Finally, *masked* grief reactions, according to Worden's description, exist when the bereaved individual does not recognize symptoms that are related to the loss. In a recent conversation, he told me of frequently having physicians refer patients to him with supposed somatoform disorders (referred to as somatic symptom disorders in *DSM-5)*. The symptoms typically look like physical illnesses (i.e., pain in the stomach, radiating pain in the arm, etc.), which is what generally presages the call to the physician in the first place. These patients often complain of specific or nonspecific illnesses and their symptoms causing real distress. Many times, Worden reported, interviews with the patients revealed that their loved one had died from an illness similar to the somatic symptoms they were reporting. In clinical interviews with the patients, the unnoticed connection often became clear, and the bereaved individual saw decided improvement in the symptoms (J. W. Worden, personal communication, 18 August 2015).

For obvious reasons, bereavement support group leaders will not see evidence of masked grief in their groups since, by definition, the relationship between the symptom and the root cause (grief) is invisible to the grieving person. However, exaggerated grief reactions and delayed grief reactions, in my experience, are in ready supply in bereavement support groups. When individuals present themselves to the group after a delayed grief reaction, group members are generally both surprised and supportive. However, it is helpful to explain to the group how lack of social support sometimes causes grief to "go underground," resulting in a need to find support once the connection becomes clear. Even if 20 years have passed since the loss, individuals whose long-delayed grief has been "triggered" by some new experience need the support the group can provide. In my experience, these individuals are often dealing with the loss in ways very similar to any other newly bereaved individual, including wild fluctuations in emotion, unremitting fatigue, loss of appetite, and inability to concentrate.

I worked with a woman early in my career whose husband had died quite suddenly. She reported that through the funeral period, she remained "stoic, calm, and collected." Throughout the first couple of years of grief, she said she rarely cried while she went about the tasks of settling the estate, selling her home, and moving to the retirement community she and her husband had long discussed. Nearly three years after his death, however, the car he had bought for her a few years before his death was destroyed when another driver hit the unoccupied vehicle. Unable to stop crying, she longed for the car he had given her—and for him, as well. Meanwhile, her well-meaning friends and family members could not understand how this event was anything but a good thing. She was not hurt, and the other driver's insurance policy would pay to replace her car. Moreover, friends and family members did not understand why the loss of her car evoked more tears than the loss of her husband. According to her report, her family and friends thought, "I am off of my rocker."

Leading a group when one or more participants display evidence of exaggerated grief requires tact, patience, and, sometimes, willingness to deal with conflict. Group members who display intense rage can be disarming to other group members and leaders alike. One respondent in the LEAP study recalled a time when law enforcement had to be called to remove a group participant who the leader thought was "about to go off." Fortunately, such experiences are extremely rare, but leaders should have a thought-out plan for responding to a group member who exhibits extreme rage or attends a group while under the influence of alcohol or drugs. One LEAP study respondent indicated that in group leader training, "We throw everything we can at them in role-play. I want them to know how to handle the worst situation you can imagine."

CHALLENGES TO THE SCIENCE OF COMPLICATED GRIEF

Perhaps there has been no more ardent critic of *DSM-5*'s classification of disordered bereavement than New York University social work professor Jerome Wakefield. His work detailing the over-diagnosis of bereavement pathology (and many other psychological conditions) dates back at least to 2007, when he and Rutgers sociologist Allan Horwitz published *The Loss of Sadness: How Psychiatry Transformed Normal Sorrow Into Depressive Disorder*. In that volume, the two of them explain how vital context is, for example, in differentiating major depressive disorder from common bereavement. Horwitz and Wakefield (2007) seemed to have sound reason for their concern; one study in the United States, for example, showed antidepressant use had increased 400% between 1988 and 2008 (Pratt et al., 2011).

Wakefield has published extensively on the medicalization of bereavement (Wakefield, 2011, 2012, 2013; Wakefield & First, 2012; Wakefield &

Schmitz, 2014), calling into question the scientific interpretation of the data on the need to pathologize complicated grief. Although they are certainly preeminent voices in the debate, Wakefield and colleagues are not the only ones. Australian psychiatrist Gordon Parker (2013) has called for a wider classification of grief than the simple dichotomous view of depression or grief, seeing them simply as "normal" or as disordered.

Wakefield (2013) concludes that primary medical care professionals have an important role. By viewing uncomplicated depression as a problem with solutions more effective than medication, primary care professionals can direct patients to such resources as psychotherapy and support. "The empirical findings should be of particular interest to primary care physicians, who often are the ones to see stress-related depressive cases in the community and who might be encouraged to refer uncomplicated cases to nonmedical professionals rather than prescribing medication" (p. 842). In light of Wakefield's conclusions, bereavement support group leaders and program administrators should expect some level of mild reactive depressive symptoms among group participants. Moreover, program leaders may want to make certain that primary medical care professionals such as internists, family doctors, and pediatricians are aware of the availability of groups. Anecdotal evidence suggests many physicians mislabel bereavement as depression, evidenced by the large number of potential group members who report having had antidepressant medication prescribed in the first few weeks of bereavement.

In one Danish study of the role education has on treatment practices of general health care practitioners (GPs), researchers discovered that after providing informational pamphlets and clinical tools for diagnosing complicated grief, scores on patient bereavement measures improved as practitioners referred more to mental health professionals, educational resources, and supportive services. Practitioners in the nonintervention control group tended to more frequently prescribe psychotropic medication to bereaved patients. Though the patient improvements did not reach statistical significance, the results demonstrated the possibilities for further education of primary care providers (Guldin, Vedsted, Jensen, Olesen, & Zachariae, 2013).

One additional "hook" in the continuing education of primary health care providers is the demonstrated compromise to health as a potential consequence of untreated complicated bereavement. Stroebe et al. (2007) reported significant risk to physical health of those who have been bereaved, a finding reaffirmed recently by Boyle, Feng, and Raab (2011). Widowhood, for example, has been associated with increased mortality from cancer, infection, and cardiovascular disease (Elwert & Christakis, 2008), declines in memory (Aartsen, Van Tilburg, Smits, Comijs, & Knipscheer, 2005), and elevated risks of suicide among some groups (Luoma & Pearson, 2002). Acknowledging that researchers do not know the exact mechanism for the relationship between bereavement and physical health, O'Connor (2013) affirmed that complicated grief is linked to hypertension (high blood pressure).

One oversight in much of the "over-pathologizing of bereavement" argument is that the individuals using *DSM-5* for diagnostic coding (i.e., clinical psychologists, social workers, clinical counselors, and marriage and family therapists) are not the individuals who generally have authority to prescribe antidepressant and anxiolytic medication. According to one study by the U.S. Centers for Disease Control & Prevention (CDC), 60% of patients had been taking antidepressants longer than two years, but only 29.3% of antidepressant users had seen a mental health professional in the previous year (Pratt et al., 2011, p. 4).

ASSESSING FOR COMPLICATED GRIEF

Among respondents to the LEAP study, approximately 60% reported that they or their agency had a means in place for the assessment and/or screening of participants before the group began. Like many aspects of grief intervention, study participants shared a diversity of opinions about such measures, including those who said they did not believe in limiting group participation to those who "meet our artificial criteria" as well as those who indicated they would not consider running a group without prescreening participants. The reasons for not screening included peer volunteers who indicated they do not have the skill to accurately assess individuals who want to attend a group. Another participant reported a "hard-and-fast rule" that no one attend the group earlier than two months after the loved one's death.

Among those who reported assessing or prescreening participants, respondents offered several ways to do so. One respondent reported using a telephone interview to elicit basic demographic information, the decedent's cause of death, and the potential group participant's "hopes" for attending the group. Based on responses to these questions, the group leader reported asking subsequent questions about the potential group member's support system, self-assessment about health and well-being, and prior experience with groups and counseling. The respondent indicated that the question about prior group and counseling involvement often reveals pre-existing mental health issues such as depression, anxiety, and PTSD. This respondent reported several experiences of discovering would-be participants who met the criteria or had been diagnosed with such mental health conditions as borderline personality disorder and histrionic personality disorder, diagnoses that the respondent noted "could ruin a group faster than anything."

One clinician who responded to the LEAP study indicated that she had led groups including individuals with borderline personality disorder who participated appropriately. "It really all depends on how—and if—the individual is being treated. When the conditions are well-managed by a combination of medication and psychotherapy, I think they can participate very well," the respondent explained. The respondent then added, "I would much rather have a person in my group who is being treated for a mental illness than somebody who has a mental illness they aren't being treated for."

Another respondent in the LEAP study indicated, however, that telephone and even face-to-face screening rarely yields enough information to be particularly helpful. Having practiced a policy of interviewing all participants before they come to the first group meeting, I can concur with that evaluation of the process; I have missed serious psychopathology among potential participants more often than I care to admit, only to have those issues surface in a group meeting.

Instead of prescreening, this agency invites all potential group participants to an orientation evening, at which time leadership announces "group rules." If needed, the agency reserves the right to remove individuals whose behavior becomes counterproductive to the group. Various kinds of conduct disorders among children would be the most likely problems to interfere with the group process, this respondent pointed out, and the agency has almost never needed to remove either adult or child participants because of their behavior. One sound reason for utilizing a co-facilitator model is so that one facilitator is free to accompany a child or adult with a behavior problem to another room. This study participant noted that even some individuals with diagnosed issues that would seem theoretically to prohibit them from full participation in a group are actually able to participate in a 90-minute group session without incident, staying focused and behaviorally appropriate throughout the experience.

One popular area for assessment of complicated grief has been the patient/client's level of psychosocial functioning. When the *Diagnostic and Statistical Manual* (American Psychiatric Association, 2013) was last updated, the Global Assessment of Functioning was replaced by several assessment instruments, the focus of which is the level of symptomatology and the level of functioning exhibited by the patient. A LEAP study participant noted that if a person is able to get dressed and to the group, in all probability, the individual's participation will be appropriate. "Predictions don't always turn out correct," the respondent said. "A lot of people just surprise me." Rubin (1999) pointed out that at least when addressing experiences of bereaved parents, "it is necessary to look beyond the level of functioning following death as we attempt to further our understanding and our ability to intervene following loss and mourning" (p. 697), though he added a page later that "after the lapse of a significant amount of time (often measured in years), the bereaved will achieve a new level of organization in his or her life" (p. 698). Only in that context, he concluded, was it possible to expect balance between psychosocial functioning and relationship to the deceased.

In his paper overviewing the two-track model, Rubin (1999) presented two cases from his own practice to help better explain the clinical application of this framework for understanding bereavement. Forty-four-year-old "Tanya" had taken care of her mother, by her account, because she was the only child left; her 15-year-old sister had died many years earlier, as it turned out, in an automobile crash. She sought psychotherapy not because of the loss but because she was having difficulty functioning in day-to-day activities because of sleeplessness, anxiety, and abdominal upset; Rubin's presentation indicated that Tanya did not see a connection between her symptoms and her loss. It is quite likely this individual would have been experiencing what Worden (2009) called "masked grief," and, as such, she would not likely have ever made her way to a bereavement support group. "After all," she would likely have concluded, "grief is not the root of my problem."

Though 36-year-old "Nan" talked openly about the death of her older brother/mentor/father figure in her teen years, what became evident in the early therapeutic discussions was that her parents had also suffered the death of another child in toddlerhood, about the time Nan was 4 years old. In any case, because Nan saw loss as an important element in her symptoms, it is quite likely she would have wanted to attend a bereavement support group, especially if a well-meaning friend or a professional (such as her family physician) had referred her to the group. Because the loss was so far in the past, some group members might inadvertently disenfranchise Nan's loss, reckoning it to be too far in the past for the group to have been helpful. Nan seems to have suffered from what Worden (2009) called delayed grief, especially in light of Rubin's assessment that she had functioned well in the early aftermath of her brother's death. Her inability to create a lasting and satisfying relationship with a man was a significant element that initially brought Nan to therapy.

Whether either of Rubin's patients would have received help from participation in a bereavement support group is difficult to predict. However, in the words of the LEAP study respondent who indicated prescreening rarely reveals enough information to be useful, "Who am I to say whose grief is right for a group and whose is not?" Another respondent offered a similar perspective on prescreening: "I don't have a crystal ball. When I try predicting who will and will not be a good candidate for a group, I get it wrong about as often as I get it right. This is just too complex an issue, this 'who'll fit and who won't' business; people's needs are really diverse." The perspectives of these respondents were similar to those shared by other LEAP study participants who do not generally prescreen participants.

CULTURAL CONCERNS IN COMPLICATED GRIEF

What is considered "normal" for bereavement must always be evaluated in light of the bereaved individual's cultural context (American Psychiatric Association, 2013; Rosenblatt, 2013). Rosenblatt (2013), for example, began his very helpful paper on the role of culture in complicated grief by writing, "Psychiatric diagnostic categories and psychiatric standards for what is normal and health and what is not are saturated with the standards of Western culture" (p. 27). The American Psychiatric Association's *DSM-5* website provides several downloadable assessment tools to help clinicians assess the role of cultural customs, spiritual beliefs, and religious practices in the mental health history of clients. Even though the assessment questions are not bereavement-focused, clinicians will find the questions to be well-formulated for use in interviewing, and bereavement support group leaders will find the questions to be useful for beginning the discussion around diverse cultural customs in the group. Using the "Cultural Formation Interview" questions with bereaved individuals allows them to reflect on how family and community make sense of the experience, how the individual's beliefs might influence their perspective of causation (death due to a "curse," for example), and how cultural or spiritual beliefs provide support in the loss.[2]

Rosenblatt (2013) suggested that several cultural assumptions are implicit in most of the theory, research, and practice related to complicated grief. One is that there is an optimal time-limited duration to an individual's experience with grief, and this time limit may be far shorter or far longer than current psychiatric diagnostic thinking might permit as "normal." The Maisin of Papua New Guinea, for example, traditionally believed that protracted mourning over years was normal, although more recently embraced Christian standards call for a shorter course to mourning behavior. On the other hand, bereaved individuals in Bali are often teased by family members and friends, told that they must be cheerful and happy; it is commonly believed that protracted grieving leaves a bereaved individual susceptible to sorcery. Rosenblatt (2013) also suggested there is an assumption implicit in much talk about complicated grief that grieving in all cultures is "rather the same," ignoring the substantial evidence that individuals "deal with and talk about losses quite differently from one culture to another" (p. 30).

Though he does not specifically label the phenomenon as "individualism," Rosenblatt (2013) suggested that many researchers, theorists, and clinicians writing about complicated grief consider bereavement from a worldview that assumes it is the individual in need of "healing." He then related a compelling hypothetical case of a Guatemalan widow whose husband was assassinated for his criticism of injustices. Caregivers from outside the culture would likely make efforts to help her manage her loss experience so that it carries less intensity and is less dominating of her life. Looking at her individual psychology, however, ignores the very important role a "collectivist" worldview plays in the society of which she is a part.

Seeing some cultural challenges is easy because skin colors and language are different. However, as researchers and providers focus on understanding individuals with varied cultural customs, bereavement support groups and their leaders will hopefully become less likely to view practices as "strange" or even, in some cases, unhealthy. In their interviews of Mexican Americans after a child's death, Doran and Hansen (2007) found that their study respondents continued their bond with the deceased in ways that might be viewed as problematic in the dominant culture. In 300 pages of transcripts, they noted, there was no mention of "closure" or "moving on" (p. 206), and more than half of their interviewees reported vivid dreams about the deceased. The families all reported a continuing "sense of presence" of the deceased in their lives.

However, when cultural challenges are because of differing physical abilities, sexual identity, or religious convictions, such cultural challenges might be much harder to identify. In any case, group facilitators and program leaders must always ask themselves in what ways they may be stereotyping segments of the population, assuming for example that "Latin

American" people or "Indigenous Australian" people comprise a single cultural group with similar language, values, customs, and beliefs.

Rosenblatt (2013) acknowledged that the construct of complicated grief is well supported by evidence. However, he suggested that "the evidence and its interpretation are culturally saturated" because there is, in his opinion, "no psychological research method that is not saturated with the assumptions, ways of thinking, beliefs, and values of a specific culture" (p. 33). In spite of the importance of considering culture in group planning, it is important to remember that some evidence indicates that individuals who participate in an intervention may respond similarly, regardless of ethnic background or cultural heritage. For example, a small study compared the treatment outcomes of African Americans and Caucasian Americans who participated in individual sessions focused on complicated grief, although the study's small size (19 African Americans and 19 Caucasian Americans) as well as several other confounding variables limit how generalizable the results were (Cruz et al., 2007). Nevertheless, the results may be well transferred to or applied in other settings (Ghesquiere, 2013; Seale, 1999).

Complicated grief can pose serious challenges in support groups, not just because of the change in group dynamics that it can create but because bereaved individuals may find that their experience with loss is too complex to receive significant help in a group context. Whether peer volunteers, interns, or seasoned professionals, group leaders may feel overwhelmed by the presentation of deep grief in the group settings rather than first encountering these deeply felt expressions of bereavement in individual conversations. Moreover, other group participants may be overwhelmed at the complexity of the loss and even traumatized by hearing the details of a group member's recollections from a violent death.

Expressions of complicated grief exist on a continuum, often defying efforts to categorize by a set of specific symptoms and criteria. Learning when to refer a bereaved individual to more specialized care is a matter of facilitator training, experience, and confidence. Equally important when an individual with complicated grief shows up in a support group, however, is how that person's presence contributes to or distracts from the overall experience of group support for all participants. The welfare of the entire group must be of supreme interest to the facilitator. When all criteria are considered, this may very well be the most important concern for a bereavement support group leader.

QUESTIONS FOR REFLECTION AND DISCUSSION

- What complications in the social support system do you see in Jeff and Carol?
- What do you think about the notion of assessing or prescreening potential group members? What factors have led you to that discussion? Are you drawn more to the side of the debate that requires prescreening or to the side that suggests it is unnecessary?
- If you have experience leading groups, what have been kinds of losses you have found most difficulty in groups? If you are new to the process, what do you expect will be hardest?
- In light of the information presented in this chapter, to whom would you refer? What do you look for in a program or colleague to whom you refer a bereaved individual?

NOTES

1. This section is largely excerpted from the author's article, "Violent Death, Grief, and PTSD," originally published in *Grief Perspectives* (August, 2015). Used by permission of Grief-Connect, Inc. (www.griefconnect.com/Our_Newsletter.html).
2. The American Psychiatric Association publishes a collection of forms and protocols for the Cultural Formation Interview. At this printing, they can be accessed at no cost from http://www.psychiatry.org/psychiatrists/practice/dsm/dsm-5/online-assessment-measures. Cultural resources are under the menu expansion "Early Development and Home Background."

EPILOGUE

The Future of Grief Groups

For more than 22 years, I have taught college students. For all but the last few of those years, I served as an adjunct or part-time professor, teaching students in the evening while carrying on a clinical practice during the day. As a veteran of the collegiate classroom, I learned to help students constantly ask questions and to accept little as incontrovertible fact. Recently, I have suggested to students to keep a "Yes, but . . ." page in at the end of their notes for the class. On those pages, I suggest, students should write their musings about the "other side" of the story, the corrective to the clear pronouncements we so frequently make in academe. In spite of working in this volume to cover the bases on the state of the art in bereavement support group leadership, I sense there still needs to be a "Yes, but . . ." We still do not have answers to a vast array of issues about groups. The field demands an ongoing dialogue and a robust research agenda to discover the nuances of how, when, and why bereavement support groups actually provide solace to grieving people. Here are the arenas I believe we, as a bereavement support community, need to invest resources and energy in to better understand the work we do.

ONGOING EMPIRICAL RESEARCH

Randomized control trials, surveys, quality assurance measures, meta-analyses, and interviews all provide important contributions to better understanding what bereaved individuals need in the way of social support after a loved one's death. As we continue learning from bereaved individuals, discovering the nuances of their loss experiences, presenting at conferences for colleagues to reaffirm and challenge, and publishing the fruits of these discoveries, we will continue to make strides in better support for bereaved people.

The Association for Death Education and Counseling has made an important contribution by reducing membership dues and conference fees for students and new professionals just starting out their careers. As we who are "seasoned" professionals mentor and guide those who follow us, we will make an important and lasting contribution to our field by helping the next generation.

ASSESSMENT

One thing that became evident to me in conducting the LEAP study is that we still do not know what the best methods and tools are to prescreen group participants, assuring we get the right people in groups. More importantly, we need to continue developing instruments and assessment questions to assure that those who have unusually complicated loss experiences get the individualized psychotherapeutic assistance they need rather than attending a bereavement support group. I am increasingly concerned that organizations that provide only bereavement support groups without enduring connection to competent clinical assistance on an individual basis may be acting like the old American farming axiom: "If the only tool you have is a hammer, everything looks like a nail." There must be ongoing dialogue about assessment procedures to make sure right people are in groups.

ROLE OF THE FAITH COMMUNITY IN ETHNIC SUPPORT

During the summer I was completing this manuscript, my professional community, the Association for Death Education and Counseling, said goodbye to one of our luminaries. Renowned for his understanding of African-American bereavement issues, the late Ronald Barrett said in a 2001 interview that clinicians must recognize and respect the role spirituality plays among many African Americans. In referencing the interview, Burke et al. (2010) suggested,

> Pointing Black homicide survivors toward church or faith-based counseling and grief support groups would likely affirm aspects of their culture that can aid them in the grieving process.
>
> As clinicians gain knowledge about how African-American homicide grievers traverse bereavement, they, in turn, are in a position to share that knowledge with those in the faith community. (p. 20)

Ron did a fine job of reminding us of the importance of connecting faith community to bereavement, especially in cases where groups clearly prefer and trust that venue for receiving the help they need. We can go far in honoring Ron's memory by heeding his instruction to discover the ways we can create better collaborations between congregation, school, health care, and mental health organization.

NEEDS FOR CROSS-CULTURAL INTERVENTION

Engaging people from people groups other than the dominant cultural group has been an ongoing challenge in bereavement interventions. Perhaps people of immigrant/newcomer communities as well as people of other nondominant social groups (gay parents or differently-abled individuals) have some built-in sense of community support, making community bereavement support groups irrelevant. Nevertheless, we must discover what the truth is about those different hypotheses. For way too long, we have depended on stereotypes ("Hispanics just don't join grief groups") and rationalizations to justify our own lazy thinking at trying to understand why, at least in North America, bereavement support groups do not in any way represent the diversity of bereaved individuals.

As stated throughout this volume, it is possible that many ethnic communities have far better ways to support bereaved individuals than the "artificial" communities created by bereavement support groups. If that is the case, we must redouble our efforts to sit at the feet of those who "get" community and learn from their wisdom.

GROWING INFLUENCE OF ONLINE SUPPORT INTERVENTIONS

I believe it is now safe to say: The Internet is not going away. For years, I resisted the allure of buying books on Amazon.com, thinking it was just a fad. "Just because they can sell all that stuff," I smugly said, "doesn't mean they can make enough money to stay in business." I am wrong about a lot of things, and judging by the amount I have spent in the last year or two on Amazon, I'm happy I was.

In the arena of bereavement support groups, online resources are going to continue to morph and grow in the years ahead. New technologies will emerge and bereavement caregivers will laud—or laugh—at them. There is undoubtedly a segment of bereaved individuals who either cannot or will not access face-to-face support of any kind. What some of them will do, however, is access resources for their grief via the web. What we must do in the coming years is seek to understand in what ways those strategies are helpful and in what ways they are not. In any case, we must learn how to help individuals build real support communities—in towns, clubhouses, schools, senior centers, faith communities, and online.

Bereavement support groups are a real and enduring part of the grief landscape. Not every service can be evaluated just on the basis of whether people keep using them. When it comes to bereavement groups, however, use them they do. Perhaps grieving individuals are just like mythical lemmings, following each other blindly along hoping to find something of benefit. After three decades in this work, however, I do not think this is the case. Rather, something extraordinary, almost mystical, happens in many bereavement support groups. Individuals become friends, and in spite of the naturally self-focused process of bereavement, become interested in supporting others in their loss. That is the vision of bereavement support groups, and it appears, on the whole, that this vision is realized in the lives of bereaved individuals every day.

REFERENCES

Aartsen, M. J., Van Tilburg, T., Smits, C.H.M., Comijs, S.H.C., & Knipscheer, K. C. (2005). Does widowhood affect memory performance of older persons? *Psychological Medicine*, *35*(2), 217–226. doi:10.1017/S0033291704002831

Aho, A. L., Paavilainen, E., & Kaunonen, M. (2012). Mothers' experiences of peer support via an Internet discussion forum after the death of a child. *Scandinavian Journal of Caring Sciences*, 26(3), 417–426. doi:10.1111/j.1471-6712.2011.00929.x

Alcoholics Anonymous. (2011). *Understanding anonymity*. New York, NY: Alcoholics Anonymous World Services.

American Psychiatric Association. (2013). *Diagnostic and statistical manual of mental disorders* (5th ed.). Washington, DC: APA Press.

American Psychological Association. (2012). *Recognition of psychotherapy effectiveness*. Retrieved from http://www.apa.org/about/policy/resolution-psychotherapy.aspx

Andrew, S., & Halcomb, E. J. (2011). From 'should we be?' to 'how are we?': Moving forward with mixed methods health research. *International Journal of Multiple Research Approaches*, *5*(1), 139–143.

Appiah, K. A. (2007). *Cosmopolitanism: Ethics in a world of strangers*. New York, NY: W. W. Norton.

Association for Death Education and Counseling. (2004). *ADEC code of ethics*. Retrieved from http://www.adec.org

Aveline, M. O. (1993). Principles of leadership in brief training groups for mental health professionals. *International Journal of Group Psychotherapy*, *43*(1), 107–129.

Aveyard, H. (2010). *Doing a literature review in health and social care: A practical guide* (2nd ed.). Berkshire, UK: Open University/McGraw-Hill.

Axelsson, P., Sköld, P., Ziker, J. P., & Anderson, D. G. (2011). Epilogue: From indigenous demographics to an indigenous demography. In P. Axelsson & P. Sköld (Eds.), *Indigenous peoples and demography: The complex relation between identity and statistics* (pp. 295–308). New York, NY: Berghahn Books.

Bailey, G., & Peoples, J. (2014). *Essentials of cultural anthropology* (3rd ed.). Belmont, CA: Wadsworth/Cengage.

Bakker, J. K., & Paris, J. (2013). Bereavement and religion online: Stillbirth, neonatal loss, and parental religiosity. *Journal for the Scientific Study of Religion*, *52*(4), 657–674. doi:10.1111/jssr.12066

Balk, D. (1995). Bereavement research using control groups: Ethical obligations and questions. *Death Studies*, *19*(2), 123–138.

Baugher, J. E., McIntyre, M., House, C., Mawhinney, M., O'Brien, B., & Reagan, A. J. (2012). When grieving adults support grieving children: Tensions in a peer support bereavement group programme. *Mortality*, *17*(3), 276–299.

Beck, U., Bonss, W., & Lau, C. (2003). The theory of reflexive modernization: Problematic, hypotheses and research programme. *Theory, Culture & Society*, *20*(2), 1–33. doi:10.1177/0263276403020002001

Beckett, C., & Dykeman, C. (2015). Preservice counselors' initial perceptions of client grief style: An analogue study. *Omega: Journal of Death & Dying*, *71*(3), 219–232. doi:10.1177/0030222815575501

Beilin, H. (1992). Piaget's enduring contribution to developmental psychology. *Developmental Psychology*, *28*(2), 191–204. doi:10.1037/0012-1649.28.2.191

Bender, T., Karagülle, Z., Bálint, G. P., Gutenbrunner, C., Bálint, P. V., & Sukenik, S. (2005). Hydrotherapy, balneotherapy, and spa treatment in pain management. *Rheumatology International*, *25*(3), 220–224. doi:10.1007/s00296-004-0487-4

Benkel, I., Wijk, H., & Molander, U. (2009). Managing grief and relationship roles influence which forms of social support the bereaved needs. *American Journal of Hospice and Palliative Medicine*, *26*(4), 241–245.

Best, S., & Kellner, D. (1997). *The postmodern turn*. New York, NY: Guilford.

Billig, M. (2013). *Learn to write badly: How to succeed in the social sciences*. New York, NY: Cambridge University Press.

Bliss, C. (1904). *The world's best poetry: Sorrow and consolation, Volume 3*. Philadelphia, PA: Morris.

Bonanno, G. A. (2004). Loss, trauma, and human resilience: Have we underestimated the human capacity to thrive after extremely aversive events? *American Psychologist*, *59*(1), 20–28. doi:10.1037/0003-066X.59.1.20

Bonanno, G. A. (2009). *The other side of sadness*. New York, NY: Basic Books.

Bonanno, G. A. (2012). Uses and abuses of the resilience construct: Loss, trauma, and health-related adversities. *Social Science & Medicine*, *74*(5), 753–756. doi:10.1016/j.socscimed.2011.11.022

Bonanno, G. A., & Keltner, D. (1997). Facial expressions of emotion and the course of conjugal bereavement. *Journal of Abnormal Psychology*, *106*(1), 126–137. doi:10.1037/0021-843X.106.1.126

Bonanno, G. A., Keltner, D., Holen, A., & Horowitz, M. J. (1995). When avoiding unpleasant emotions might not be such a bad thing: Verbal autonomic response dissociation and midlife conjugal bereavement. *Journal of Personality and Social Psychology*, *69*(5), 975–989. doi:10.1037//0022-3514.69.5.975

Bonanno, G. A., Wortman, C. B., Lehman, D. R., Tweed, R. G., Haring, M., Sonnega, J., . . . Nesse, R. M. (2002). Resilience to loss and chronic grief: A prospective study from preloss to 18-months postloss. *Journal of Personality and Social Psychology*, *83*(5), 1150–1164. doi:10.1037//0022-3514.83.5.1150

Bowlby, J. (1969). *Attachment and loss: Volume 1. Attachment*. San Francisco, CA: Basic Books.

Boyle, P. J., Feng, Z., & Raab, G. M. (2011). Does widowhood increase mortality risk? Testing for selection effects by comparing causes of spousal death. *Epidemiology* *22*(1), 1–5.

Bradner, J. H. (1995). Recruitment, orientation, and retention. In T. D. Connors (Ed.), *The volunteer management handbook* (pp. 61–82). New York, NY: John Wiley & Sons.

Bretherton, I. (1992). The origins of attachment theory: John Bowlby and Mary Ainsworth. *Developmental Psychology*, *28*(5), 759–775. doi:10.1037/0012-1649.28.5.759

Brown, F. H. (1989). The impact of death and serious illness on the family life cycle. In E. A. Carter & M. McGoldrick (Eds.), *The changing family life cycle: A framework for family therapy* (2nd ed.) (pp. 457–482). Boston, MA: Allen & Bacon.

Bryant, R. A., Kenny, L., Joscelyne, A., Rawson, N., Maccallum, F., Cahill, C., . . . Nickerson, A. (2014). Treating prolonged grief disorder: A randomized clinical trial. *JAMA Psychiatry*, *71*(12), 1332–1339. doi:10.1001/jamapsychaitry.2014.1600

Burke, L. A., & Neimeyer, R. A. (2012). Meaning making in bereavement. In M. Cobb, C. Puchalski, & B. Rumbold (Eds.), *The textbook on spirituality in healthcare* (pp. 127–133). Oxford, UK: Oxford University Press.

Burke, L. A., & Neimeyer, R. A. (2013). Prospective risk factors for complicated grief. In M. Stroebe, H. Schut, & J. van den Bout (Eds.), *Complicated grief: Scientific foundations for health care professionals* (pp. 145–161). New York, NY: Routledge.

Burke, L. A., Neimeyer, R. A., & McDevitt-Murphy, M. E. (2010). African American homicide bereavement: Aspects of social support that predict complicated grief, PTSD, and depression. *Omega: Journal of Death & Dying*, *61*(1), 1–24.

Burke, L. A., Neimeyer, R. A., McDevitt-Murphy, M. E., Ippolito, M. R., & Roberts, J. M. (2011). Faith in the wake of homicide: Religious coping and bereavement distress in an African American sample. *International Journal for the Psychology of Religion*, *21*(4), 289–307. doi:10.1080/10508619.2011.607416

Butler, C. (2002). *Postmodernism: A very short introduction*. New York, NY: Oxford University Press.

Cameron, W. B. (1963). *Informal sociology: A casual introduction to sociological thinking* (5th ed.). New York, NY: Random House.

Caramanica, K., Brackbill, R. M., Liao, T., & Stellman, S. D. (2014). Comorbidity of 9/11-Related PTSD and depression in the world trade center health registry 10–11 years postdisaster. *Journal of Traumatic Stress*, *27*(6), 680–688. doi:10.1002/jts.21972

Carr, D. S. (2004). Black/White differences in psychological adjustment to spousal loss among older adults. *Research on Aging*, *26*(6), 591–622.

Chaturvedi, M., & Chander, R. (2010). Development of emotional stability scale. *Industrial Psychiatry Journal*, *19*(1), 37–40. doi:10.4103/0972-6748.77634

Chiu, S., Niles, J. K., Webber, M. P., Zeig-Owens, R., Gustave, J., Lee, R., . . . Prezant, D. J. (2011). Evaluating risk factors and possible mediation effects in posttraumatic depression and posttraumatic stress disorder comorbidity. *Public Health Reports*, *126*(2), 201–209.

Christ, C. T. (1995). Browning's corpses. *Victorian Poetry*, *33*(3/4), 391–401.

Church Initiative. (2015). *How GriefShare works*. Retrieved from http://www.griefshare.org

Clift, S. (2012). Creative arts as a public health resource: Moving from practice-based research to evidence-based practice. *Perspectives in Public Health*, *132*(3), 120–127.

Cobb, S., & Lindemann, E. (1943). Neuropsychiatric observations. *Annals of Surgery*, *117*(6), 814–824.

Compassionate Friends. (2015). *About us*. Retrieved from http://www.compassionatefriends.org

Council on Social Work Education. (2015). *Educational policy and accreditation standards*. Alexandria, VA: CSWE. Retrieved from http://www.cswe.org/Accreditation/EPASRevision.aspx

Covey, S. R. (1989). *The seven habits of highly effective people*. New York, NY: Fireside.

Cowman, S. E., Ferrari, J. R., & Liao-Troth, M. (2004). Mediating effects of social support on firefighters' sense of community and perceptions of care. *Journal of Community Psychology*, *32*(2), 121–126. doi:10.1002/jcop.10089

Cruz, M., Scott, J., Houck, P., Reynolds, C. F., Frank, E., & Shear, M. K. (2007). Clinical presentation and treatment outcomes of African Americans with complicated grief. *Psychiatric Services*, *58*(5), 700–702. doi:10.1176/appi.ps.58.5.700

Dageid, W. (2014). Support groups for HIV-positive people in South Africa: Who joins, who does not, and why? *African Journal of AIDS Research*, *13*(1), 1–6.

Dansby-Giles, G., Giles, F., Haralson, A., & Johnson, I. (2014). African Americans and bereavement. *National Association of African American Studies, Conference Proceedings* (pp. 247–262). ProQuest document 1692817406. Retrieved from http://www.proquest.com

Darke, S. (2010). The toxicology of homicide offenders and victims: A review. *Drug and Alcohol Review*, *29*(2), 202–215. doi:10.1111/j.1465-3362.2009.00099.x

Deans, G., Bennett-Emslie, G. B., Weir, J., Smith, D. C., & Kaye, S. B. (1988). Cancer support groups: Who joins and why? *British Journal of Cancer*, *58*(5), 670–674. doi:10.1038/bjc.1988.284

Deutsch, H. (1937). Absence of grief. *Psychoanalytic Quarterly*, *6*, 12–22.

DeVries, B., Lana, R. D., & Falck, V. T. (1994). Parental bereavement over the life course: A theoretical intersection and empirical review. *Omega: Journal of Death & Dying*, *29*(1), 47–69.

Dimond, M., Lund, D. A., & Caserta, M. S. (1987). The role of social support in the first two years of bereavement in an elderly sample. *Gerontologist*, *27*(5), 599–604. doi:10.1093/geront/27.5.599

Doka, K. J. (Ed.) (2002). *Disenfranchised grief: New directions, challenges, and strategies for practice*. Champaign, IL: Research Press.

Doka, K. J. (2015). Spirituality: Quo vadis. In J. M. Stillion & T. Attig (Eds.), *Death, dying, and bereavement: Contemporary perspectives, institutions, and practices* (pp. 233–244). New York, NY: Springer.

Doka, K. J., & Martin, T. L. (2010). *Grieving beyond gender: Understanding the ways men and women mourn* (2nd ed.). New York, NY: Routledge.

Dominick, S. A., Irvine, A. B., Beauchamp, N., Seeley, J. R., Nolen-Hoeksema, S., Doka, K. J., & Bonanno, G. A. (2009–2010). An Internet tool to normalize grief. *Omega: Journal of Death and Dying, 60*(1), 71–87. doi:10.2190/OM.60.1.d

Doran, G., & Hansen, N. D. (2007). Constructions of Mexican American family grief after the death of a child: An exploratory study. *Cultural Diversity and Ethnic Minority Psychology, 12*(2), 199–211. doi:10.1037/1099-9809.12.2.199

Döveling, K. (2015). "Help me. I am so alone." Online emotional self-disclosure in shared coping-processes of children and adolescents on social networking platforms. *Communications, 40*(4), 403–423. doi:10.1515/commun-2015-0018

Duff, N. J. (2015). Remembering World War II. *Theology Today, 72*(1), 5–10.

Durkheim, E. (1982). *The rules of sociological method* [Trans. of *Les règles de la method sociologique* by S. Lukes]. New York, NY: Free Press. Originally published 1895.

Elder, J., & Burke, L. A. (2015). Parental grief expression in online cancer support groups. *Illness, Crisis, & Loss, 23*(2), 175–190.

Elwert, F., & Christakis, N. A. (2008). The effect of widowhood on mortality by the causes of death of both spouses. *American Journal of Public Health, 98*(11), 2092–2098. doi:10.2105/AJPH.2007.114348

Eppel, A. B. (2009). *Sweet sorrow: Love, loss, and attachment in human life.* London, UK: Karnac.

Esposito, J. C. (2005). *Fire in the Grove: The Cocoanut Grove tragedy and its aftermath.* Cambridge, MA: De Capo Press.

Farnsworth, J., & Boon, B. (2010). Analysing group dynamics within the focus group. *Qualitative Research, 10*(5), 605–624. doi:10.1177/1468794110375223

Faschingbauer, T. R. (1981). *Texas revised inventory of grief manual.* Houston: Honeycomb.

Faschingbauer, T. R., Devaul, R. D., & Zisook, S. (1977). Development of the Texas inventory of grief. *American Journal of Psychiatry, 134*, 696–698.

Feigelman, W., Gorman, B. S., Chastain Beal, K., & Jordan, J. R. (2008). Internet support groups for suicide survivors: A new mode for gaining bereavement assistance. *Omega, 57*(3), 217–243.

Feigelman, W., Jordan, J. R., & Gorman, B. S. (2008–2009). How they died, time since loss, and bereavement outcomes. *Omega: Journal of Death & Dying, 58*(4), 251–273. doi:10.2190/OM.58.4.a

Ferguson, N. (2006). *The war of the world: Twentieth century conflict and the descent of the West.* New York, NY: Penguin.

Finucane, N., & McGuinness, B. (2011). Evaluating a creative arts bereavement support intervention: Innovation and rigour. *Bereavement Care, 30*(1), 37–42. doi:10.1080/02682621.2011.555244

Fors, S., & Lennartsson, C. (2008). Social mobility, geographical proximity and intergenerational family contact in Sweden. *Ageing & Society, 28*(2), 253–270. doi:10.1017/S0144686X07006617

Fortner, B. V. (1999). *The effectiveness of grief counseling and therapy: A quantitative review.* ProQuest Dissertations & Theses Full Text 304577812. Retrieved from http://www.proquest.com

Fortner, B. V. (2008). Stemming the TIDE: A correction of Fortner (1999) and a clarification of Larson and Hoyt (2007). *Professional Psychology: Research and Practice, 39*(3), 379–380. doi:10.1037/0735-7028.39.3.379

Frances, A. (2013). *Saving normal: An insider's revolt against out-of-control psychiatric diagnosis, DSM-5, big pharma, and the medicalization of ordinary life.* New York, NY: William Morrow.

Freud, S. (1957). Mourning and melancholia. In J. Strachey (Ed. and trans.), *The complete psychological works of Sigmund Freud, Volume 14* (pp. 243–258). London, UK: Hogarth Press. Originally published 1917.

Fussell, H. E., Lewy, C. S., & McFarland, B. H. (2009). Evaluating and training substance abuse counselors: A pilot study assessing standardized patients as authentic clients. *Substance Abuse, 30*(1), 47–60. doi:10.1080/08897070802606360

Futterman, A., Brown, P. J., Holland, J. M., Thompason, L. W., & Gallagher-Thompson, D. (2010). Factorial validity of the Texas revised inventory of grief—Present scale among bereaved older adults. *Psychological Assessment*, 22(3), 675–687.

Gamino, L. A., & Ritter, R. H. (2009). *Ethical practice in grief counseling*. New York, NY: Springer.

Ghesquiere, A. (2013). "I was just trying to stick it out until I realized that I couldn't": A phenomenological investigation of support seeking among older adults with complicated grief. *Omega: Journal of Death & Dying, 68*(1), 1–22.

Gillies, J., & Neimeyer, R. A. (2006). Loss, grief, and the search for significance: Toward a model of meaning reconstruction in bereavement. *Journal of Constructivist Psychology, 19*, 31–65. doi:10.1080/10720530500311182

Glaser, B. G. (1998). *Doing grounded theory*. Mill Valley, CA: Sociology Press.

Glaser, B. G., & Strauss, A. L. (1965). *Awareness of dying*. Chicago, IL: Aldine.

Glaser, B. G., & Strauss, A. L. (1967). *The discovery of grounded theory: Strategies for qualitative research*. New York, NY: Aldine.

Golden, T. R. (2000). *Swallowed by a snake: The gift of the masculine side of grieving*. Gaithersburg, MD: Golden Healing Publishing.

Goldman, L. (2014). *Life and loss: A guide to help grieving children* (3rd ed.). New York, NY: Taylor & Francis.

Goleman, D. (1987, February 6). Carl R. Rogers, 85, leader in psychotherapy, dies. *New York Times*. Retrieved from http://www.nytimes.com

Grafstrom, M., Winblad, B., & Almberg, B. E. (2000). Caregivers of relatives with dementia: Experiences encompassing social support and bereavement. *Aging & Mental Health*, 4(1), 82–89. doi:10.1080/13607860056026

Graves, D. (2012). *Setting up and facilitating bereavement support groups: A practical guide*. London, UK: Jessica Kingsley.

Greene, P. A., Kane, D., Christ, G., Lynch, S., & Corrigan, M. (2006). *FDNY crisis counseling: Innovative responses to 9/11 firefighters, families, and communities*. Hoboken, NJ: John Wiley & Sons.

GriefNet. (n.d.). *Guidelines*. Retrieved from http://www.GriefNet.org

Group Two Productions. (1987). *A family in grief: The Ameche story*. [VHS video]. Champaign, IL: Research Press.

Guldin, M.-B., O'Connor, M., Sokolowsi, I., Jensen, A. B., & Vedsted, P. (2011). Identifying bereaved subjects at risk of complicated grief: Predictive value of questionnaire items in a cohort study. *BMC Palliative Care, 10, 9*. Retrieved from http://www.biomedcentral.com/1472–684X/10/9

Guldin, M.-B., Vedsted, P., Jensen, A. B., Olesen, F., & Zachariae, R. (2013). Bereavement care in general practice: A cluster-randomized clinical trial. *Family Practice, 30*, 134–141.

Gutierrez, I. A., & Mattis, J. S. (2014). Factors predicting volunteer engagement among urban-residing African American women. *Journal of Black Studies, 45*(7), 599–619. doi:10.1177/0021934714543189

Hager, M. A., & Brudney, J. L. (2011). Problems recruiting volunteers: Nature versus nurture. *Nonprofit Management & Leadership*, 22(2), 137–157. doi:10.1002/nml.20046

Hall, C. (2014). Bereavement theory: Recent developments in our understanding of grief and bereavement. *Bereavement Care, 33*(1), 7–12. doi:10.1080/02682621.2014.902610

Hall, C.C.I. (1997). Cultural malpractice: The growing obsolescence of psychology with the changing U.S. population. *American Psychologist, 52*(6), 642.

Harrington, C., & Sprowl, B. (2011–2012). Family members' experiences with viewing in the wake of sudden death. *Omega: Journal of Death & Dying, 64*(1), 65–82. doi:10.2190/OM.64.1.e

Heidrich, K. W. (1990). Volunteers' life-styles: Market segmentation based on volunteers' role choices. *Nonprofit and Voluntary Sector Quarterly, 19*(1), 21–31.

Herman Miller. (n.d.). *Rethinking the classroom: Spaces designed for active and engaged learning and teaching*. Retrieved from http://www.hermanmiller.com/research/solution-essays/rethinking-the-classroom.html

Hodges, B., Regehr, G., Hanson, M., & McNaughton, N. (1997). An objective structured clinical examination for evaluating psychiatric clinical clerks. *Academic Medicine, 72*, 715–721.

Hoffman, C. (2014, May 16). *Definitely deleted: How to guarantee your data is truly gone before recycling old PCs and drives*. PC World. Retrieved from http://www.pcworld.com/article/2155347/

Hogan, N. S., Morse, J. M., & Tasón, M. C. (1996). Toward an experiential theory of bereavement. *Omega: Journal of Death & Dying, 33*(1), 43–65. doi:10.2190/GU3X-JWV0-AG6G-21FX

Horowitz, M., Wilner, N., & Alvarez, W. (1979). Impact of event scale: A measure of subjective stress. *Psychosomatic Medicine, 41*(3), 209–218. doi:10.1097/00006842-197905000-00004

Horowitz, M. J., Bonanno, G. A., & Holen, A. (1993). Pathological grief: Diagnosis and explanation. *Psychosomatic Medicine, 55*(3), 260–273. doi:10.1097/00006842-199305000-00004

Horowitz, M. J., Siegel, B., Holen, A., Bonanno, G. A., Milbrath, C., & Stinson, C. H. (1997). Diagnostic criteria for complicated grief disorder. *American Journal of Psychiatry, 154*(7), 904–910. doi:10.1176/ajp.154.7.904

Horwitz, A. V., & Wakefield, J. C. (2007). *The loss of sadness: How psychiatry transformed normal sorrow into depressive disorder*. New York: Oxford University Press.

Houston, T. K., Cooper, L. A., & Ford, D. E. (2002). Internet support groups for depression: A 1-year prospective cohort study. *American Journal of Psychiatry, 159*(12), 2062–2068. doi:10.1176/appi.ajp.159.12.2062

Hoy, W. G. (1996). *Finding direction in your grief: Charting a course for personal growth through loss*. Long Beach, CA: Pathways Volunteer Hospice.

Hoy, W. G. (2007). *Guiding people through grief: How to start and lead bereavement support groups*. Dallas, TX: Compass.

Hoy, W. G. (2008). *Road to Emmaus: Pastoral care with the dying and bereaved*. Dallas, TX: Compass.

Hoy, W. G. (2013). *Do funerals matter? The purposes and practices of death rituals in global perspective*. New York, NY: Routledge.

Hoy, W. G. (2014/2000). *When you face holidays in grief: Helping yourself grow through the loss. Grief Outlooks*. New Ulm, MN: Madsen Ink. Originally published 2000.

Hoy, W. G. (2015). Death, dying and bereavement: Multicultural competence in psychotherapy—A report on Melba Vasquez' address. *The Forum, 41*(3), 7.

Hoy, W. G., & Na, Y. (2015). *Examining video to clarify African-American funeral experiences*. Paper presentation, Association for Death Education & Counseling, San Antonio, TX, 11 April 2015.

Hughes, M. (1995). *Bereavement and support: Healing in a group environment*. Washington, DC: Taylor & Francis.

Hughes, V. (2009). Markers of dispute. *Nature Medicine, 15*(12), 1339–1343.

Jacobs, S., Mazure, C., & Prigerson, H. (2000). Diagnostic criteria of complicated grief. *Death Studies, 24*, 185–199.

Jacobs, S., & Prigerson, H. (2000). Psychotherapy of traumatic grief: A review of evidence for psychotherapeutic treatments. *Death Studies, 24*, 470–495.

Jakoby, N. R. (2012). Grief as a social emotion: Theoretical perspectives. *Death Studies, 36*(8), 679–711. doi:10.1080/07481187.2011.584013

James, P., & Steger, M. B. (2014). A genealogy of "globalization": The career of a concept. Globalizations, *11*(4), 417–434. doi:10.1080/14747731.2014.951186

Janoff-Bulman, R. (1992). *Shattered assumptions: Towards a new psychology of trauma*. New York, NY: Free Press.

Jarman, K. H. (2015). *Beyond basic statistics: Tips, tricks, and techniques every data analyst should know*. Hoboken, NJ: John Wiley & Sons.

Jones, A. M., Deane, C., & Keegan, O. (2015). The development of a framework to support bereaved children and young people: The Irish Childhood Bereavement care pyramid. *Bereavement Care, 34*(2), 43–51. doi:10.1080/02682621.2015.1063857

Jordan, J. R., & Neimeyer, R. A. (2003). Does grief counseling work? *Death Studies*, *27*(9), 765–786.

Kaiser, J. (2015, June 26). The cancer test: A nonprofit's effort to replicate 50 top cancer papers is shaking up labs. *Science*, *348*(6242), 1411–1413. doi:10.1126/science.348.6242.1411

Kellehear, A. (2007). *A social history of dying*. New York, NY: Cambridge University Press.

Kelly, C. G., Cudney, S., & Weinert, C. (2012). Use of creative arts as a complementary therapy by rural women coping with chronic illness. *Journal of Holistic Nursing*, *30*(1), 48–54. doi:10.1177/0898010111423418

Kessler, D., & Kübler-Ross, E. (2005). *On grief and grieving: Finding the meaning of grief through the five stages of loss*. New York, NY: Scribner's.

Keyes, K. M., Pratt, C., Galea, S., McLaughlin, K. A., Koenen, K. C., & Shear, M. K. (2014). The burden of loss: Unexpected death of a loved one and psychiatric disorders across the life course in a national study. *American Journal of Psychiatry*, *171*(8), 864–871. doi:10.1176/appi.ajp.2014.13081132

Klass, D. (1997). The deceased child in the psychic and social worlds of bereaved parents during the resolution of grief. *Death Studies*, *21*(2), 147–175. doi:10.1080/074811897202056

Klass, D. (1999). *The spiritual lives of bereaved parents*. Philadelphia, PA: Brunner/Mazel.

Klass, D., Silverman, P. R., & Nickman, S. L. (Eds.). (1996). *Continuing bonds: New understandings of grief*. New York, NY: Routledge.

Klass, D., & Walter, T. (2001). Processes of grieving: How bonds are continued. In M. S. Stroebe, R. O. Hansson, W. Stroebe, & H. Schut (Eds.), *Handbook of bereavement research* (pp. 431–438). Washington, DC: American Psychological Association.

Klimecki, O. M., Leiberg, S., Lamm, C., & Singer, T. (2013). Functional neural plasticity and associated changes in positive affect after compassion training. *Cerebral Cortex*, *23*(7), 1552–1561. doi:10.1093/cercor/bhs142

Koenig, H. G. (2013). *Spirituality in patient care: Why, how, when, and what?* (3rd ed.): Philadelphia, PA: Templeton Press.

Konigsberg, R. D. (2011). *The truth about grief: The myth of the five stages of grief and the new science of loss*. New York, NY: Simon & Schuster.

Kosminsky, P. S., & Jordan, J. R. (2016). *Attachment-informed grief therapy: The clinician's guide to foundations and applications*. New York, NY: Routledge.

Kottler, J. A., & Carlson, J. (2005). *The client who changed me: Stories of therapist personal transformation*. New York, NY: Routledge.

Krishnamurti, J. (1954). *On education: A talk to students*. Retrieved from http://www.jiddu-krishnamurti.net/en/krishnamurti-on-education

Kübler-Ross, E. (1969). *On death and dying: What the dying have to teach doctors, nurses, clergy and their own families*. New York, NY: Macmillan.

Langner, R., & Maercker, A. (2005). Complicated grief as a stress response disorder: Evaluating diagnostic criteria in a German sample. *Journal of Psychosomatic Research*, *58*(3), 235–242. doi:10.1016/j.jpsychores.2004.09.012

Larson, D. G., & Hoyt, W. T. (2007). What has become of grief counseling? An evaluation of the empirical foundations of the new pessimism. *Professional Psychology: Research and Practice*, *38*(4), 347–355. doi:10.1037/0735-7028.38.4.347

Lehman, D. R., Ellard, J. H., & Wortman, C. B. (1986). Social support for the bereaved: Recipients' and providers' perspectives on what is helpful. *Journal of Consulting and Clinical Psychology*, *54*(4), 438–446. doi:10.1037//0022-006X.54.4.438

Lewis, L., & Hoy, W. G. (2011). Bereavement rituals and the creation of legacy. In R. A. Neimeyer, G. B. Thornton, D. Harris, & H. G. Winokuer (Eds.), *Grief and bereavement in contemporary society: Bridging research and practice* (pp. 315–323). New York, NY: Routledge.

Li, J., Olsen, J., Vestergaard, M., Obel, C., Baker, J. L., & Sørensen, T. I. (2012). Bereavement in early life and later childhood overweight. *Obesity Facts*, *5*(6), 881–889. doi:10.1159/000345933

Li, Y., Ahlstrom, D., & Ashkanasy, N. M. (2010). A multilevel model of affect and organizational commitment. *Asia Pacific Journal of Management*, *27*(2): 193–213.

Li, Y., Chun, H., Ashkanasy, N. M., & Ahlstrom, D. (2012). A multi-level study of emergent group leadership: Effects of emotional stability and group conflict. *Asia Pacific Journal of Management*, *29*(2), 351–366. doi:10.1007/s10490-012-9298-4

Lindemann, E. (1944). Symptomatology and management of acute grief. *American Journal of Psychiatry*, *101*(2), 141–148.

Loder, W. (2010). *The Compassionate Friends: Four decades of caring and sharing*. Retrieved from https://www.compassionatefriends.org/Libraries/PDF/Story_of_TCF_2010.sflb.ashx

Lofland, L. H. (1985). The social shaping of emotion: The case of grief. *Symbolic Interaction*, *8*(2), 171–190. doi:10.1525/si.1985.8.2.171

Luoma, J. B., & Pearson, J. L. (2002). Suicide and marital status in the United States, 1991–1996: Is widowhood a risk factor? *American Journal of Public Health*, *92*(9), 1518–1522. doi:10.2105/AJPH.92.9.1518

Lynn, C., & Rath, A. (2012). GriefNet: Creating and maintaining an Internet bereavement community. In C. J. Sofka, I. N. Cupit, & K. R. Gilbert (Eds.), *Dying, death, and grief in an online universe* (pp. 87–102). New York, NY: Springer.

Lyu, H., Wick, E. C., Housman, M., Freischlag, J. A., & Makary, M. A. (2013). Patient satisfaction as a possible indicator of quality surgical care. *JAMA Surgery*, *148*(4), 362–367.

Machi, L. A., & McElvoy, B. T. (2012). *The literature review: Six steps to success* (2nd ed.). Thousand Oaks, CA: Corwin/Sage.

Mahgoub, N., & Lantz, M. (2006). When older adults suffer the loss of a child. *Psychiatric Annals*, *36*(12), 877–880.

May, W., Park, J. H., & Lee, J. P. (2009). A ten-year review of the literature on the use of standardized patients in teaching and learning: 1996–2005. *Medical Teacher*, *31*(6), 487–492. doi:10.1080/01421590802530898

McClatchey, I. S., Vonk, M. E., & Palardy, G. (2009). Efficacy of a camp-based intervention for childhood traumatic grief. *Research on Social Work Practice*, *19*(1), 19–30. doi:10.1177/1049731508314276

McClatchey, I. S., & Wimmer, J. S. (2014). Coping with parental death as seen from the perspective of children who attended a grief camp. *Qualitative Social Work*, *13*(2), 221–236.

McClimans, L. M., & Browne, J. (2011). Choosing a patient-reported outcome measure. *Theoretical Medicine and Bioethics*, *32*(1), 47–60. doi:10.1007/s11017-010-9163-8

Mencken, F. C., & Fitz, B. (2013). Image of God and community volunteering among religious adherents in the United States. *Review of Religious Research*, *55*(3), 491–508. doi:10.1007/s13644-013-0115-4

Middleton, W., Moylan, A., Raphael, B., Burnett, P., & Martinek, N. (1993). An international perspective on bereavement related concepts. *Australian and New Zealand Journal of Psychiatry*, *27*(3), 457–463.

Miller, K. L. (2010). *The nonprofit marketing guide*. San Francisco, CA: Jossey-Bass.

Miller, W. F. (2014). Interactive journaling as a clinical tool. *Journal of Mental Health Counseling*, *36*(1), 31–42.

Mills, J., Bonner, A., & Francis, K. (2006). The development of constructivist grounded theory. *International Journal of Qualitative Methods*, *5*(1), Article 3. Retrieved from http://www.ualberta.ca/~iiqm/backissues/5_1/pdf/mills.pdf

Mitchell, S. (2004). *Gilgamesh: A new English version*. New York, NY: Atria.

Morin, K. H. (2014). Nutritional considerations during bereavement. *MCN, the American Journal of Maternal/Child Nursing*, *39*(3), 205–205.

Mullen, M., Lynn, W., & Knell, G. (2010). Sneak preview of Sesame Street's newest outreach initiative: When families grieve. The Pentagon, Arlington, Virginia. *Congressional Hearing Transcript Database* 14 April 2010. (Gale Reference A224177421). Retrieved from http://go.galegroup.com

Murphy, S. N. (2013). Attending to countertransference. *Counseling Today*, *56*(3), 46–50.

Nadeau, J. W. (1998). *Families making sense of death*. Thousand Oaks, CA: Sage.

Nadeau, J. W. (2001). Meaning making in family bereavement: A family systems approach. In M. S. Stroebe, R. O. Hansson, W. Stroebe, & H. Schut (Eds.), *Handbook of bereavement research: Consequences, coping, and care* (pp. 329–347). Washington, DC: American Psychological Association.

Nainis, N., Paice, J. A., Ratner, J., Wirth, J. H., Lai, J., & Shott, S. (2006). Relieving symptoms in cancer: Innovative use of art therapy. *Journal of Pain and Symptom Management, 31*(2), 162–169. doi:10.1016/j.jpainsymman.2005.07.006

Nam, I., & Eack, S. M. (2012). Confirmatory factor analysis and cross-cultural examination of the Texas revised inventory of grief (TRIG). *Families in Society: The Journal of Contemporary Social Services, 93*(1), 65–73. doi:10.1606/1044-3894.4177

Neimeyer, R. A. (2000). Searching for the meaning of meaning: Grief therapy and the process of reconstruction. *Death Studies, 24*(6), 541–558.

Neimeyer, R. A. (2010). Grief counselling and therapy: The case for hope. *Bereavement Care, 29*(2), 13–16.

Neimeyer, R. A. (Ed.). (2012). *Techniques of grief therapy: Creative practices for counseling the bereaved.* New York, NY: Routledge.

Neimeyer, R. A. (Ed.). (2015). *Techniques of grief therapy: Assessment and intervention.* New York, NY: Routledge.

Neimeyer, R. A., & Hogan, N. S. (2001). Quantitative or qualitative? Measurement issues in the study of grief. In M. S. Stroebe, R. O. Hansson, W. Stroebe, & H. Schut (Eds.), *Handbook of bereavement research: Consequences, coping, and care* (pp. 89–118). Washington, DC: American Psychological Association.

Neimeyer, R. A., Keesee, N. J., & Fortner, B. V. (2000). Loss and meaning reconstruction: Propositions and procedures. In R. Malkinson, S. Rubin & Wiztum, E. (Ed.), *Traumatic and non-traumatic loss and bereavement* (pp. 197–230). Madison, CT: Psychosocial Press.

Neimeyer, R. A., & Sands, D. C. (2011). Meaning reconstruction in bereavement: From principles to practice. In R. A. Neimeyer, D. L. Harris, H. R. Winokuer, & G. F. Thornton (Eds.), *Grief and bereavement in contemporary society: Bridging research and practice* (pp. 9–22). New York, NY: Routledge.

Nesse, R. M., Wortman, C., House, J., Kessler, R., & Lepkowski, J. (2003). *Changing Lives of Older Couples (CLOC): A study of spousal bereavement in the Detroit area, 1987–1993.* ICPSR 03370-v1. Ann Arbor, MI: Inter-University Consortium for Political and Social Research. Retrieved from http://doi.org/10.3886/ICPSR03370.v1

Nieves, R. A. (2014). *Bereavement support groups: A study on the effectiveness of Branford, CT Hospice support groups.* [Thesis]. Southern Connecticut State University, ProQuest Dissertations Publishing, 1525370.

Nuttal, M. (2000). Choosing kin: Sharing and subsistence in a Greenland hunting community. In P. P. Schweitzer (Ed.), *Dividends of kinship: Meanings and uses of social relatedness* (pp. 33–60). London, UK: Routledge.

Ober, A. M., Granello, D. H., & Wheaton, J. E. (2012). Grief counseling: An investigation of counselors' training, experience, and competencies. *Journal of Counseling & Development, 90*(4), 150–159.

O'Connor, M.-F. (2005). Bereavement and the brain: Invitation to a conversation between bereavement researchers and neuroscientists. *Death Studies, 29*(10), 905–922. doi:10.1080/07481180500299063

O'Connor, M.-F. (2013). Physiological mechanisms and the neurobiology of complicated grief. In M. Stroebe, H. Schut, & J. van den Bout (Eds.), *Complicated grief: Scientific foundations for health care professionals* (pp. 204–218). New York, NY: Routledge.

O'Connor, M.-F., & Sussman, T. J. (2014). Developing the yearning in situations of loss scale: Convergent and discriminant validity for bereavement, romantic breakup, and homesickness. *Death Studies, 38*(7), 450–458. doi:10.1080/07481187.2013.782928

O'Connor, M.-F., Irwin, M. R., & Wellisch, D. K. (2009). When grief heats up: Pro-inflammatory cytokines predict regional brain activation. *NeuroImage, 47*(3), 891–896. doi:10.1016/j.neuroimage.2009.05.049

O'Connor, M.-F., Lasgaard, M., Shevlin, M., & Guldin, M.-B. (2010). A confirmatory factor analysis of combined models of the Harvard Trauma Questionnaire and the Inventory of

Complicated Grief-Revised: Are we measuring complicated grief or posttraumatic stress? *Journal of Anxiety Disorders*, *24*(4), 672–679. doi:10.1016/j.janxdis.2010.04.009

O'Connor, M.-F., Wellisch, D. K., Stanton, A. L., Eisenberger, N. I., Irwin, M. R., & Lieberman, M. D. (2008). Craving love? Enduring grief activates brain's reward center. *NeuroImage*, *42*, 969–972.

Ogrodniczuk, J. S., Joyce, A. S., & Piper, W. E. (2003). Changes in perceived social support after group therapy for complicated grief. *Journal of Nervous and Mental Disease*, *191*(8), 524–530.

Ogrodniczuk, J. S., Piper, W. E., Joyce, A. S., McCallum, M., & Rosie, J. S. (2002). Social support as a predictor of response to group therapy for complicated grief. *Psychiatry*, *65*, 346–357.

Okabayashi, H., Sugisawa, H., Yatomi, N., Nakatani, Y., Takanashi, K., Fukaya, T., & Shibata, H. (1997). The impact of conjugal bereavement and the buffering effect of social support on the health of elderly people. *Japanese Journal of Psychology*, *68*(3), 147–154. doi:10.4992/jjpsy.68.147

Olivier, C. (2009). Enhancing confidentiality within small groups: The experiences of AIDS service organizations. *Social Work With Groups*, *32*(4), 274–287. doi:10.1080/01609510902874586

Oransky, I. (2014, May 27). *Oncology researcher Getzenberg notches seventh retraction.* [Blog post]. Retraction Watch. Retrieved from http://retractionwatch.com/2014/05/27/oncology-researcher-getzenberg-notches-seventh-retraction/

Outward Bound. (2015). *Oregon rafting for grieving teens.* Retrieved from http://www.outwardbound.org

Pangrazzi, A. (n.d.). *Coming together.* Retrieved from http://www.spsamerica.org/#!sos-history/c5d2

Pargament, K., Koenig, H., & Perez, L. (2000). The many methods of religious coping: Development and initial validation of the RCOPE. *Journal of Clinical Psychology*, *56*, 519–543.

Pargament, K., Smith, B., Koenig, H., & Perez, L. (1998). Patterns of positive and negative religious coping with major life stressors. *Journal for the Scientific Study of Religion*, *37*(4), 710–724. doi:10.2307/1388152

Parker, G. B. (2013). Opening Pandora's box: How DSM-5 is coming to grief. *Acta Psychiatrica Scandinavica*, *128*(1), 88–91. doi:10.1111/acps.12110

Parkes, C. M. (1964, August 1). Effects of bereavement on physical and mental health: A study of the medical records of widows. *British Medical Journal*, 2(5404), 274–279.

Parkes, C. M. (1972). *Bereavement: Studies of grief in adult life.* New York, NY: International Universities Press.

Parris, R. J. (2011). Initial management of bereaved relatives following trauma. *Trauma*, *14*(2), 139–155. doi:10.1177/1460408611420352

Pastor, D. K., Cunningham, R. P., & Kuiper, R. (2015). Gray matters: Teaching geriatric assessment for family nurse practitioners using standardized patients. *Clinical Simulation in Nursing*, *11*(2), 120–125. doi:10.1016/j.ecns.2014.09.002

Perschy, M. K. (2004). *Helping teens work through grief* (2nd ed.). New York, NY: Routledge.

Peters, S. (2010). Qualitative research methods in mental health. *Evidence-Based Mental Health*, *13*(2), 35–40.

Pine, V. R. (2015). Death and funeral service. In J. M. Stillion & T. Attig (Eds.), *Death, dying, and bereavement: Contemporary perspectives, institutions, and practices* (pp. 193–206). New York, NY: Springer.

Pluye, P., Gagnon, M., Griffiths, F., & Johnson-Lafleur, J. (2009). A scoring system for appraising mixed methods research, and concomitantly appraising qualitative, quantitative, and mixed methods primary studies in mixed studies reviews. *International Journal of Nursing Studies*, *46*(4), 529–546. doi:10.1016/j.ijnurstu.2009.01.009

Pratt, L. A., Brody, D. J., & Gu, Q. (2011, October). *Antidepressant use in persons aged 12 and over: United States, 2005–2008.* NCHS Data Brief, 76. Hyattsville, MD: National Center for Health Statistics. Retrieved from http://www.cdc.gov/nchs/data/databriefs/db76.pdf

Prigerson, H. G., Bierhals, A. J., Kasl, S. V., Reynolds, C. F., Shear, M. K., Day, N., . . . Jacobs, S. C. (1997). Traumatic grief as a risk factor for mental and physical morbidity. *American Journal of Psychiatry*, *154*, 616–623.

Prigerson, H. G., Horowitz, M. J., Jacobs, S. C., Parkes, C. M., Aslan, M., Goodkin, K., Maciejewski, P. K. (2009). Prolonged grief disorder: Psychometric validation of criteria proposed for DSM-V and ICD-11. *PLoS Medicine*, *6*(8), e1000121. doi:10.1371/journal.pmed.1000121

Prigerson, H. G., & Jacobs, S. C. (2001). Traumatic grief as a distinct disorder: A rationale, consensus criteria, and preliminary empirical test. In M. S. Stroebe, R. O. Hansson, W. Stroebe, & H. Schut (Eds.), *Handbook of bereavement research: Consequences, coping, and care* (pp. 627–645). Washington, DC: American Psychological Association.

Prigerson, H. G., Maciejewski, P. K., Reynolds, C. F., Bierhals, A. J., Newsom, J. T., Fasiczka, A., . . . Miller, M. (1995). Inventory of complicated grief: A scale to measure maladaptive symptoms of loss. *Psychiatry Research*, *59*, 65–79.

Proctor, S. L., Hoffman, N. G., & Allison, S. (2012). The effectiveness of interactive journaling in reducing recidivism among substance-dependent jail inmates. *International Journal of Offender Therapy and Comparative Criminology*, *56*, 317–332. doi:10.1177/0306624X11399274

Quotah, E. (2008). Personal approach is key to seeking Hispanic volunteers. *Chronicle of Philanthropy*, *20*(23). Retrieved from http://www.philanthropy.com

Rando, T. A. (1984). *Grief, dying, and death: Clinical interventions for caregivers*. Champaign, IL: Research Press.

Rando, T. A. (1993). *Treatment of complicated mourning*. Champaign, IL: Research Press.

Rando, T. A. (2013). On achieving clarity regarding complicated grief: Lessons from clinical practice. In M. Stroebe, H. Schut, & J. van den Bout (Eds.), *Complicated grief: Scientific foundations for health care professionals* (pp. 40–54). New York, NY: Routledge.

Raphael, B., & Wilson, J. (2000). *Psychological debriefing: Theory, practice and evidence*. Cambridge, MA: Cambridge University Press.

Ridley, D. (2012). *The literature review: A step-by-step guide for students* (2nd ed.). London: Sage Publications.

Roberts, P. (2004). The living and the dead: Community in the virtual cemetery. *Omega: Journal of Death and Dying*, *49*(1), 57–76. doi:10.2190/D41T-YFNN-109K-WR4C

Robertson, J., & Bowlby, J. (1952). Responses of young children to separation from their mothers. *Courier of the International Children's Centre, Paris*, II, 131–140.

Rochlen, A. B., Zack, J. S., & Speyer, C. (2004). Online therapy: Review of relevant definitions, debates, and current empirical support. *Journal of Clinical Psychology*, *60*(3), 269–283.

Rogers, C. R. (1970). *Carl Rogers on encounter groups*. New York, NY: Harper & Row.

Rosales, R. (2013). Survival, economic mobility and community among Los Angeles fruit vendors. *Journal of Ethnic & Migration Studies*, *39*(5), 697–717. doi:10.1080/1369183X.2013.756659

Rosenblatt, P. C. (2013). The concept of complicated grief: Lessons from other cultures. In M. Stroebe, H. Schut, & J. van den Bout (Eds.), *Complicated grief: Scientific foundations for health care professionals* (pp. 27–39). New York, NY: Routledge.

Rubin, S. S., & Shechory-Stahl, M. (2012–2013). The continuing bonds of bereaved parents: A ten-year follow-up study with the two-track model of bereavement. *Omega: Journal of Death and Dying*, *66*(4), 365–384. doi:10.2190/OM.66.4.f

Rubin, S. S. (1981). A two-track model of bereavement: Theory and application in research. The American Journal of Orthopsychiatry, *51*(1), 101–109. doi:10.1111/j.1939-0025.1981.tb01352.x

Rubin, S. S. (1989–1990). Death of the future?: An outcome study of bereaved parents in Israel. *Omega: Journal of Death & Dying*, *20*(4), 323–339.

Rubin, S. S. (1999). The two-track model of bereavement: Overview, retrospect, and prospect. *Death Studies*, *23*(8), 681–714. doi:10.1080/074811899200731

Rummel, R. J. (1994). *Death by government*. New Brunswick, NJ: Transaction.

Sanders, C. M. (1999). *Grief—The mourning after: Dealing with adult bereavement* (2nd ed.). New York, NY: Wiley.

Sanders, C. M., Mauger, P. A., & Strong, P. N. (1985). *A manual for the grief experience inventory*. Palo Alto, CA: Consulting Psychologists Press.

Sandler, I. N., Ayers, T. S., Tein, J.-Y., Wolchik, S., Millsap, R., Khoo, S. T., . . . Coxe, S. (2010). Six-year follow-up of a preventive intervention for parentally bereaved youths: A randomized controlled trial. *Archives of Pediatrics & Adolescent Medicine*, *164*(10), 907–914.

Sandler, I. N., Ma, Y., Tein, J.-Y., Ayers, T. S., Wochik, S., Kennedy, C., & Millsap, R. (2010). Long-term effects of the family bereavement program on multiple indicators of grief in parentally bereaved children and adolescents. *Journal of Counseling and Clinical Psychology*, *78*(2), 131–143.

Satel, S. (1999, April 23). An overabundance of counseling? *New York Times*. Retrieved from http://www.nytimes.com

Sauvy, A. (1952, August 14). Trois mondes, une planète (Three worlds, one planet). *The Observer*, *118*, p. 14. Retrieved from http://www.homme-moderne.org/societe/demo/sauvy/3mondes.html

Scheper-Hughes, N. (2008). A talent for life: Reflections on human vulnerability and resilience. *Ethnos*, *73*(1), 25–56. doi:10.1080/00141840801927525

Scheper-Hughes, N. (2013, June). No more angel babies on the Alto do Cruzeiro: A dispatch from Brazil's revolution in child survival. *Natural History*, *121*(5), 28–38. Retrieved from http://www.naturalhistorymag.com/features/282558/no-more-angel-babies-on-the-alto-do-cruzeiro

Schoenfelder, E. N., Tein, J.-Y., Wolchk, S., & Sandler, I. N. (2015). Effects of the family bereavement program on academic outcomes, educational expectations and job aspirations six years later: The mediating role of parenting and youth mental health problems. *Journal of Abnormal Child Psychology*, *43*(2), 229–241. doi:10.1007/s10802-014-9905-6

Schut, H. (2010). Grief counselling efficacy: Have we learned enough? *Bereavement Care*, *29*(1), 8–9. doi:10.1080/02682620903560817

Seale, C. (1999). Quality in qualitative research. *Qualitative Inquiry*, *5*(4), 465–478.

Servaty-Seib, H. L., & Pistole, M. C. (2007). Adolescent grief: Relationship category and emotional closeness. *Omega: Journal of Death and Dying*, *54*(2), 147–167. doi:10.2190/M002-1541-JP28-4673

Shapiro, E. R. (1994). *Grief as a family process: A developmental approach to clinical practice*. New York, NY: Guilford.

Shapiro, E. R. (2001). Grief in interpersonal perspective: Theories and their implications. In M. S. Stroebe, R. O. Hansson, W. Stroebe, & H. Schut (Eds.), *Handbook of bereavement research: Consequences, coping, and care* (pp. 301–327). Washington, DC: American Psychological Association.

Shear, M. K., Frank, E., Houck, P. R., & Reynolds, C. F. (2005). Treatment of complicated grief: A randomized controlled trial. *Journal of the American Medical Association*, *293*(21), 2601–2608.

Shear, M. K., Ghesquiere, A., & Glickman, K. (2013). Bereavement and complicated grief. *Current Psychiatry Reports*, *15*(11), 1–7. doi:10.1007/s11920-013-0406-z

Shear, M. K., Simon, N., Wall, M., Zisook, S., Neimeyer, R. A., Duan, N., . . . Keshaviah, A. (2011). Complicated grief and related issues for *DSM5*. *Depression & Anxiety*, *28*, 103–117. doi:10.1002/da.20780

Shear, M. K., Wang, Y., Skritskaya, N., Duan, N., Mauro, C., & Ghesquiere, A. (2014). Treatment of complicated grief in elderly persons: A randomized clinical trial. *JAMA Psychiatry*, *71*(11), 1287–1295. doi:10.1001/jamapsychiatry.2014.1242

Shevellar, L., Sherwin, J., & Barringham, N. (2014). The human search for belonging. *Journal of Spirituality in Mental Health*, *16*(1), 2–18. doi:10.1080/19349637.2014.864541

Shih, S., Turale, S., Shih, F., & Tsai, J. (2010). Religiosity influences on bereavement adjustments of older widows in Taiwan. *Journal of Clinical Nursing*, *19*(5–6), 856–866. doi:10.1111/j.1365-2702.2009.02947.x

Silver, R. C., & Wortman, C. B. (1980). Coping with undesirable life events. In J. Garber & M. E. P. Seligman (Eds.), *Human helplessness: Theory and applications* (pp. 279–340). New York, NY: Academic Press.

Silverman, P. R. (1967). Services to the widowed: First steps in a program of preventive intervention. *Community Mental Health Journal*, *3*, 37–44.

Silverman, P. R. (1969). The widow-to-widow program: An experiment in preventive intervention. *Mental Hygiene*, *53*, 333–337.
Silverman, P. R. (2004). *Widow to widow: How the bereaved help each other* (2nd ed.). New York, NY: Brunner-Routledge.
Silverman, P. R., & Klass, D. (1996). Introduction: What's the problem? In D. Klass, P. R. Silverman, & S. L. Nickman (Eds.), *Continuing bonds: New understandings of grief* (pp. 1–9). New York, NY: Routledge.
Silverman, P. R., & Worden, J. W. (1992). Children's reactions in the early months after the death of a parent. *American Journal of Orthopsychiatry*, *62*(1), 93–104.
Simon-Thomas, E. R. (2012, September 7). *Three insights from the cutting edge of compassion research*. [Blog post]. Retrieved from http://www.greatergood.berkeley.edu
Singh, B., & Raphael, B. (1981). Postdisaster morbidity of the bereaved: A possible role for psychiatry? *Nervous & Mental Disease*, *169*(4), 203–212.
Smith, H. I. (2012). *Borrowed narratives: Using biographical and historical grief narratives with the bereaving*. New York: Routledge.
Smith, S. C. (1999). *The forgotten mourners: Working with bereaved children*. London, UK: Jessica Kingsley.
Smith, S. H. (2002). "Fret no more my child . . . for I'm all over heaven all day": Religious beliefs in the bereavement of African American, middle-aged daughters coping with the death of an elderly mother. *Death Studies*, *26*(4), 309–323. doi:10.1080/07481180275359469l
Sofka, C. J. (1997). Social support "internetworks," caskets for sale, and more: Thanatology and the information superhighway. *Death Studies*, *21*(6), 553–574.
Sommers, C. H., & Satel, S. (2005). *One nation under therapy*. New York, NY: St. Martin's Press.
Sprang, G., Clark, J. J., & Whitt-Woosley, A. (2007). Compassion fatigue, compassion satisfaction, and burnout: Factors impacting a professional's quality of life. *Journal of Loss and Trauma*, *12*, 259–280.
Spreadbury, J. H. (2011). *The role of religious and spiritual belief and practice in coping and adjusting to spousal bereavement in later life*. [Dissertation]. University of Southampton (United Kingdom), ProQuest Dissertations Publishing, U612439.
Speece, M. W., & Brent, S. W. (1996). The development of children's concept of death. In C. A. Corr & D. E. Balk (Eds.), *Handbook of adolescent death and bereavement* (pp. 29–40). New York, NY: Springer.
Stahl, S. T., & Schulz, R. (2014). Changes in routine health behaviors following late-life bereavement: A systematic review. *Journal of Behavioral Medicine*, *37*(4), 736–755. doi:10.1007/s10865-013-9524-7
Staudacher, C. (1991). *Men and grief*. Oakland, CA: New Harbinger.
Stroebe, M. S., & Schut, H. (1999). The dual process model of coping with bereavement: Rationale and description. *Death Studies*, *23*, 197–224.
Stroebe, M. S., & Schut, H. (2010). The dual process model of coping with bereavement: A decade on. *Omega*, *61*(4), 273–289.
Stroebe, M. S., Schut, H., & Stroebe, W. (2007). Health outcomes of bereavement. *Lancet*, *370*, 1960–1973.
Stroebe, M. S., Schut, H., & van den Bout, J. (2013). Introduction. In M. Stroebe, H. Schut, & J. van den Bout (Eds.), *Complicated grief: Scientific foundations for health care professionals* (pp. 4–9). New York, NY: Routledge.
Stroebe, M. S., Hansson, R. O., Stroebe, W., & Schut, H. (2001). Introduction: Concepts and issues in contemporary research on bereavement. In M. S. Stroebe, R. O. Hansson, W. Stroebe, & H. Schut (Eds.), *Handbook of bereavement research* (pp. 2–23).Washington, DC: American Psychological Association.
Stroebe, M. S., van den Bout, J., & Schut, H. (1994). Myths and misconceptions about bereavement: The opening of a debate. *Omega: Journal of Death & Dying*, *29*(3), 187–203.
Stroebe, W., Zech, E., Stroebe, M. S., & Abakoumkin, G. (2005). Does social support help in bereavement? *Journal of Social and Clinical Psychology*, *24*, 1030–1050. doi:10.2190/WMDD-EHKM-375W-MBGC

Sue, D. W., Bingham, R. P., Porché-Burke, L., & Vasquez, M. (1999). The diversification of psychology: A multicultural revolution. *American Psychologist, 54*(12), 1061–1069. doi:10.1037/0003-066X.54.12.1061

Suicide Prevention Services of America. (2012). *Thirty years of SOS*. [video file]. Retrieved from https://www.youtube.com/watch?v=zS-Qge-82bI

Sumpter, D.J.T. (2010). *Collective animal behavior*. Princeton, NJ: Princeton University Press.

Supiano, K. P., & Luptak, M. (2014). Complicated grief in older adults: A randomized controlled trial of complicated grief group therapy. *The Gerontologist, 54*(5), 840. doi:10.1093/geront/gnt076

Tedeschi, R. G. (1996). Support groups for bereaved adolescents. In C. A. Corr & D. E. Balk (Eds.), *Handbook of adolescent death and bereavement* (pp. 293–311). New York, NY: Springer.

Tedeschi, R. G., & Calhoun, L. G. (2008). Beyond the concept of recovery: Growth and the experience of loss. *Death Studies, 32*, 27–39.

Toller, P. (2008). Bereaved parents' negotiation of identity following the death of a child. *Communication Studies, 59*(4), 306–321. doi:10.1080/10510970802467379

Townsend, T. (2009). Ethics conflicts in rural communities: Privacy and confidentiality. In W. A. Nelson (Ed.), *Handbook for rural health care ethics: A practical guide for professionals* (pp. 129–141). New Lebanon, NH: Dartmouth College Press.

Turner, B. S., Halse, C., & Sriprakash, A. (2014). Cosmopolitanism: Religion and kinship among young people in south-western Sydney. *Journal of Sociology, 50*(2), 83–98. doi:10.1177/1440783311419052

U.S. Centers for Disease Control. (2014). Deaths: Final data for 2011. *National Vital Statistics Report, 63*(3). Retrieved from http://www.cdc.gov/mortality

U.S. Department of Health and Human Services. (n.d.) *Health information privacy*. Retrieved from http://www.hhs.gov/ocr/privacy/hipaa/understanding/index.html

U.S. National Library of Medicine. (2003, December 23). *MEDLINE data changes—2004 changes to MeSH headings*. NLM Technical Bulletin, 335. Retrieved from http://www.nlm.nih.gov/pubs/techbull/nd03/nd03_med_data_changes.html#updated_2

U.S. Substance Abuse and Mental Health Services Administration. (2014). *Results from the 2013 national Survey on Drug Use and Health: Mental Health Findings, NSDUH Series H-49, HHS Publication No. (SMA) 14-4887*. Retrieved from http://www.samhsa.gov/data/sites/default/files/NSDUHmhfr2013/NSDUHmhfr2013.pdf

van der Houwen, K., Stroebe, W., Stroebe, M., Schut, H., & van den Bout, J. (2010). Online mutual support in bereavement: An empirical examination. *Computers in Human Behavior, 26*(6), 1519–1525. doi:10.1016/j.chb.2010.05.019

van der Kolk, B. A., McFarlane, A. C., & Weisaeth, L. (Eds.). (1996). *Traumatic stress: The effects of overwhelming experiences on mind, body, and society*. New York, NY: Guilford.

Vanderwerker, L. C., & Prigerson, H. G. (2004). Social support and technological connectedness as protective factors in bereavement. *Journal of Loss and Trauma, 9*, 43–57.

Vasquez, M.J.T. (2015). *Death, dying, and bereavement: Multicultural competency in psychotherapy*. [video recording]. Association for Death Education and Counseling, 39th Annual Conference (San Antonio, Texas). Retrieved from http://www.adec.org/adec/ADEC_Main/Continuing-Education/Conference_Recordings/Conference_Recordings_2015.aspx#Vasquez

Wagner, B., Knaevelsrud, C., & Maercker, A. (2006). Internet-based cognitive-behavioral therapy for complicated grief: A randomized controlled trial. *Death Studies, 30*(5), 429–453. doi:10.1080/07481180600614385

Wagner, B., Knaevelsrud, C., & Maercker, A. (2007). Post-traumatic growth and optimism as outcomes of an Internet-based intervention for complicated grief. *Cognitive Behaviour Therapy, 36*(3), 156–161.

Wakefield, J. C. (2011). Should uncomplicated bereavement-related depression be reclassified as a disorder in the *DSM-5*?: Response to Kenneth S. Kendler's statement defending the proposal to eliminate the bereavement exclusion. *Journal of Nervous and Mental Disease, 199*(3), 203–208. doi:10.1097/NMD.0b013e31820cd155

Wakefield, J. C. (2012). Should prolonged grief be reclassified as a mental disorder in DSM-5?: Reconsidering the empirical and conceptual arguments for complicated grief disorder. *The Journal of Nervous and Mental Disease, 200*(6), 499–511. doi:10.1097/NMD.0b013e3182482155

Wakefield, J. C. (2013). The DSM-5 debate over the bereavement exclusion: Psychiatric diagnosis and the future of empirically supported treatment. *Clinical Psychology Review*, *33*(7), 825–845.
Wakefield, J. C., & First, M. B. (2012). Validity of the bereavement exclusion to major depression: Does the empirical evidence support the proposal to eliminate the exclusion in DSM-5? *World Psychiatry*, *11*(1), 3–10.
Wakefield, J. C., & Schmitz, M. F. (2014). Uncomplicated depression, suicide attempt, and the DSM-5 bereavement exclusion debate: An empirical evaluation. *Research on Social Work Practice*, *24*(1), 37–49. doi:10.1177/1049731513495092
Walsh, F., & McGoldrick, M. (Eds.). (2004). *Living beyond loss: Death in the family* (2nd ed.). New York, NY: W. W. Norton.
Walter, T., Hourizi, R., Moncur, W., & Pitsillides, S. (2011–2012). Does the Internet change how we die and mourn? Overview and analysis. *Omega: Journal of Death & Dying*, *64*(4), 275–302.
Weil, F. (2013). *Family trees: A history of genealogy in America*. Cambridge, MA: Harvard University Press.
Weinberg, R. J., Dietz, L. J., Stoyak, S., Melhem, N. M., Porta, G., Payne, M. W., & Brent, D. A. (2013). A prospective study of parentally bereaved youth, caregiver depression, and body mass index. *Journal of Clinical Psychiatry*, *74*(8), 834–840. doi:10.4088/JCP.12m08284
Weldring, T., & Smith, S.M.S. (2013). Patient-reported outcomes (PROs) and patient-reported outcome measures (PROMs). *Health Services Insights*, *6*, 61–68. doi:10.4137/HSI.S11093
Wilson, S. (2007). The validation of the Texas revised inventory of grief on an older Latino sample. *Journal of Social Work in End-of-Life and Palliative Care*, *2*(4), 33–60.
Wittkowski, J., Doka, K. J., Neimeyer, R. A., & Vallerga, M. (2015). Publication trends in thanatology: An analysis of leading journals. *Death Studies*, *39*(8), 453–462. doi:10.1080/07481187.2014.1000054
Wolfelt, A. D. (2004). *The understanding your grief support group guide: Starting and leading a bereavement support group*. Ft. Collins, CO: Companion Press.
Worden, J. W. (1982). *Grief counseling and grief therapy: A handbook for the mental health practitioner*. New York, NY: Springer.
Worden, J. W. (1996). *Children and grief: When a parent dies*. New York, NY: Guilford.
Worden, J. W. (2009). *Grief counseling and grief therapy: A handbook for the mental health practitioner* (4th ed.). New York, NY: Springer.
Worden, J. W. (2015). Theoretical perspectives on loss and grief. In J. M. Stillion & T. Attig (Eds.), *Death, dying, and bereavement: Contemporary perspectives, institutions, and practices* (pp. 91–103). New York, NY: Springer.
World Health Organization. (2013). *Depression: A global public health concern*. Retrieved from http://www.who.int/mental_health/management/depression/who_paper_depression_wfmh_2012.pdf
World Health Organization. (2015). *The top ten causes of death*. Retrieved from http://www.who.int/mediacentre/factsheets/fs310/en/index2.html
Wortman, C. B., & Silver, R. C. (1989). The myths of coping with loss. *Journal of Consulting and Clinical Psychology*, *57*, 349–357.
Wortman, C. B., & Silver, R. C. (2001). The myths of coping with loss revisited. In M. S. Stroebe, R. O. Hansson, W. Stroebe, & H. Schut (Eds.), *Handbook of bereavement research: Consequences, coping, and care* (pp. 405–429). Washington, DC: American Psychological Association.
Yalom, I. D. (1995). *The theory and practice of group psychotherapy* (4th ed.). New York, NY: Basic Books.
Yalom, I. D., & Leszcz, M. (2005). *The theory and practice of group psychotherapy* (5th ed.). New York, NY: Basic Books.
Zedeck, S. (Ed.). (2014). *APA dictionary of statistics and research methods*. Washington, DC: American Psychological Association.
Zhang, Z., Guo, C., & Cai, D. (2011). Governing Chinese nonprofit organizations: The promise and limits of the "third way." *International Review of Public Administration*, *16*(1), 11–30. doi:10.1080/12264431.2011.10805183x

APPENDIX

Leading Guided Discussions[1]

I like starting group meetings with a key question, usually with some introductory remarks about why I have chosen it. A key question is often all that is needed to start a rich discussion. These can be used at the beginning of the group after participants have introduced themselves or when the discussion stalls during the meeting time.

Sometimes, the discussion will wander far afield of these questions. A facilitator must always remain alert to the participants' needs and decide whether to bring the discussion back to the topic. As a rule of thumb, I try once during the time to "return home," but if the conversation reverts to the other topic, that is where we stay.

The group belongs to the participants rather than the leader. Group members stand to benefit the most from their participation and are in the best position to know what topics need discussing. Nevertheless, group leaders must protect the group from a vocal participant who always seems to have an agenda for the meetings.

Frequently, I set up the question with two or three sentences about why the topic is important. For instance, after all participants have introduced themselves and offered a brief introduction about their loss, I might say:

> Many people find anger to be one of the most troubling emotions in grief. Some of us were taught as children that anger is okay, while others of us learned that it is inappropriate. Yet anger is a gigantic piece of the bereavement puzzle for many people. What and when do you find yourself feeling the most anger, and how do you find yourself expressing it?

Asking poignant, open-ended questions is an important skill for bereavement support group leaders. Engaging questions invite group participants to share elements of their story and recount important parts of their experiences with bereavement. Asking questions that begin with who, what, when, where, and how are particularly useful for the group because they beg for details in the response, thereby making it possible for leaders to do less talking and more listening. Leaders need not fear silence. Good questions require some pondering rather than quick, easy answers. However, one way to remedy lots of "dead time" in the group is for leaders to be prepared with two or three key questions.

Even though asking a question like, "How was your week?" is an open-ended question that begs more than a yes-or-no answer, the question is vague, making it hard for grieving people to respond. The following questions invite specific details and encourage the bereaved individual to share the experiences of grief. These questions work equally well as "meeting openers" and as discussion questions when the conversation stalls.

- Where and when did you meet? Did someone introduce you or did you just find each other?
- What were your favorite holidays? What did you do together? Which special days do you expect to be/are you finding to be the hardest in your grief?
- Where were your favorite places to go? What did you most enjoy about those places?
- What was the best gift ever given to you by this person? What was the best gift you ever gave him/her?
- What did you find most meaningful/least meaningful about the funeral? Where was it held? What would you do differently?
- How do you find yourself dealing with anger in your grief and when do you find it causes you the most trouble?
- What has been the biggest adjustment for you so far?
- What are the two or three fondest memories you have of your loved one?
- What scares you the most about this experience?
- In what ways do you hope you have left a heritage for your children/community/etc.? In what ways did your loved one leave his/her mark on the world?
- If grief were no longer an issue for you, what do you think would be most different in your life?
- Who has been most supportive to you so far? What have they done to show that support?
- In what ways do you wish your friends or family members would act differently toward you right now?

- What has been the most challenging to you in your faith/belief system (your faith, your philosophy, your perspective on God, etc.)? How do you think your beliefs have been strengthened by this?
- What is the dumbest thing anyone has said to you, and how would you now respond to the same comment?
- What are the loneliest times for you, and what are you doing with them?
- What is the part of life with your loved one you are now missing most?
- How is it for you when someone says something like, "His/her death must be a relief for you?" Are there ways that is true for you? How?
- What are you doing about your loved one's personal things like clothes, jewelry, and toiletries? Have you started the process of finding new homes for those things or deciding what to keep and what to discard?
- Of all the personal items that belonged to him/her, what is the most special item for you? What do you not have that you wish you did?
- Where in your grief do you most often confront guilt and regrets? What have you found most helpful to get through those times?
- How would people around you know you are sad? Is that a true picture of the "real you"?
- What expectations do you have of yourself in your grief? Are you thinking your expectations for life are realistic right now? Why or why not?
- What are the changes you've most noticed in your eating, sleeping, and exercising habits since your loved one died? How are you managing the physical challenges of grief like sleeplessness, fatigue, and loss of appetite?

The following eight "group ideas" provide direction for the beginning bereavement support group leader who wants a proven plan for beginning a new group. These ideas should not be seen as "absolutes," but they are ideas that have been developed and refined in the crucible of bereavement group leadership experience. Leaders will want to adapt these ideas to their own interests, passions, and skill level as well as to the specific needs and personality of the group.

GROUP IDEA 1: FIRST MEETING

Building a bereavement support group is a commitment to develop a caring community. As such, individuals need an opportunity to get to know other participants and their stories of grief. Leaders will want to begin this group with an opportunity for people to get to know each other and each other's stories. The following will give you an idea of how to begin the group in an effective way. Remembering the following principles will help the group begin well and the group leader to have a good experience.

- Arrive early (by at least 15 minutes) and welcome people as they arrive.
- Begin on time and end on time (don't punish on-timers by waiting for late-comers).
- Encourage people to tell their own stories and discourage discussion of the experiences of people who are not in the group.
- Remind people often of the need for keeping confidences.
- Encourage everyone to share, but force no one.

At the time for the group to begin, the leader welcomes those who have come and congratulates them on making the choice to attend, which required much courage on the part of some. Then, the leader "models" the introduction by making his or her own introduction, remembering that the group participants will likely follow the leader's example in brevity. The leader's self-introduction can include either a sentence about a significant loss or about the reason for leading this group. In more groups that I could count, I began with words like these:

> Good afternoon and welcome. I am so glad you have come, and I congratulate you on the courage it took to get here, to walk into a strange room and meet new people to talk about a topic that is really intimate. I am so glad you made the choice to come. As we begin, I would like for us to go around the table and each person to introduce himself or herself and tell a word or two about the loss that brought you.
>
> My name is Bill and I lead this group on behalf of Pathways Volunteer Hospice. What made grief real to me, however, was the death of my father x years ago and the loss of a baby before birth in 1991.

At the first and second meetings, as well as any other group meetings where there are new people present, it helps to briefly explain the format. This explanation helps reduce the anxiety of new participants and reminds "veterans" about how the group works. Ground rules can be reviewed regularly or as needed, though a reminder about confidentiality is warranted at every meeting. One way this could work is to say the following:

> We'll begin by introducing ourselves and reacquainting ourselves with each other's stories, much like we've done tonight. Then, I'll offer a brief explanation of what we're going to talk about or an activity we will use, ask a key question to help us focus our discussion, and then provide some summary ideas at the end.
>
> Tonight, I would like to ask you to consider and then briefly share about this question: "What do you find so far has been the most difficult part of grief or the part of grief that most troubles you?"

During the meeting, the leader can encourage participation by asking follow-up and clarifying questions such as:

- How does Mary's experience compare with the rest of you?
- Could you tell us a bit more about what you mean by that?
- Do we understand you to say . . . ?
- In what ways do you sense that getting better or worse as you continue your grief journey?

Ten minutes or so before the scheduled ending time of the meeting, I take a minute or two to offer two or three sentences to summarize the meeting's topic. If participants have already discussed my "talking points," I simply summarize a few of those. A summary of the first meeting might include ideas such as,

- Grief is not well understood in our society.
- Grief includes all of life: emotional, physical, social, mental, and spiritual.
- Resolving grief is a long-term process. We do not really ever "recover from" or "get over" our losses, but we do learn to live in this new set of circumstances. Life can be good again, but after a significant loss, we must learn to live in a new world that does not include the person who died.

GROUP IDEA 2: DEALING WITH ANGER IN GRIEF

At the second meeting and at any meeting where new participants are present, I explain the group's format with words like, "We'll begin by introducing ourselves and reacquainting ourselves with each other's stories. Then, I'll offer a brief explanation of what we're going to talk about tonight, ask a key question to help us focus our discussion, and then provide some summary ideas at the end." At group meetings where we participate in a creative arts activity, I also include that explanation in this introduction.

> In a few moments, I'm going to ask you to consider and then briefly share about this question: How do you find yourself dealing with anger in your grief and when do you find it causes you the most trouble? Many people find anger to be one of the most troubling emotions in grief. Some of us were taught as children that anger is okay, while others of us learned that it is inappropriate. Yet anger is a gigantic piece of the bereavement puzzle for many people. So, the question to get us going is this: How do you find yourself dealing with anger in your grief and when do you find it causes you the most trouble?

Group leaders are wise to prepare to ask questions using different words or with slight changes to the question in order to help participants think about the topic more broadly. Examples of these kinds of "nuanced" questions are:

- What tactics do you use to manage the anger in your grief?
- What are the parts of your loss experience that seem to provoke the most anger in you?
- How do you think your anger affects how you relate to other people in your life?

Like with many of the topics discussed in bereavement support groups, leaders must be ready to correct misinformation or address unhealthy behaviors suggested by participants. Generally, I have led the group to provide other options with questions such as, "Would someone else tell us what you do that is different from John's idea?" but I have frequently said something like, "I bet that idea doesn't sit right with everybody. Some of the rest of you—what do you think about that?" If necessary, group leaders may need to address an unhealthy behavior, perhaps as follows:

> I know it seems like a great idea in the short term to drink enough so I don't feel the pain. That is a choice that has to have a lot of consideration, though. When your emotional reserves are maxed out, drinking too much makes matters worse. I think that might be one reason that folks who did not formerly have a problem with drinking too much sometimes find themselves becoming alcoholic in grief.

GROUP IDEA 3: GRIEF AND PHYSICAL WELL-BEING

If new participants are in the group at the third session, leaders will want to provide an opportunity for every participant to provide a brief self-introduction. Then, in a session focused on the relationship of grief to physical well-being, I say something like:

> While most of us know some of the emotions of grief like sadness, loneliness, anger, fear, and guilt, we also experience grief physically. Often, bereaved people express great concern about loss of appetite, sleeplessness, and the lack of energy to participate in any activities or exercise. Tonight, I want us to talk about some of these challenges and learn from each other about how to manage these issues.
>
> - What have been some of your biggest challenges with eating? What are you doing about these challenges?
> - How have you been sleeping, and how does this differ from how you slept before your loved one's death?
> - How have your exercise habits changed since your loved one's death? Are there some things you think you would like to try?

Leaders will want to be certain to address the relationship of these factors to full-blown clinical depression. Only a qualified professional should suggest that a bereaved person is depressed, but leaders need to always keep in mind that changes in physical well-being can be symptomatic of depression. Leaders can work with group members individually to assess for depression if qualified to assess and diagnosed; otherwise, leaders need to always have access to a mental health professional "consultant" to whom the leader can refer the group participant for evaluation.

In the context of this discussion topic, leaders will want to remind bereaved individuals to get a complete physical examination. Unless there is a pressing problem necessitating an earlier appointment, I recommend that bereaved people get a check-up two or three months after a loved one's death, since this allows the "dust to settle."

GROUP IDEA 4: WHEN GUILT CONSUMES US

For bereaved people, guilt usually comes from a false sense that the bereaved person *should* have been able to affect a different outcome (*should* and *ought* are always big components of this). Guilt is usually an unreasonable emotion, in that the one who feels guilty most often could have done nothing different to change the circumstances or to have made a better decision with the information that was known. To get the discussion started, ask: "When in your grief do you find yourself most consumed by guilt and regret, a sense that you should have or could have done something different?"

For follow-up questions, leaders can ask:

- In what ways has your guilt gotten better or worse since your loved one's death?
- What are the strategies you find most help with your guilt?
- How have your family and friends supported you as you grapple with guilt? Have they tried to talk you out of it, or have they allowed you to experience this part of grief's emotion?

Before the meeting ends, leaders will want to give participants an opportunity to discuss some of their own coping strategies.

GROUP IDEA 5: DEALING WITH ADVICE AND EXPECTATIONS

One of the hardest experiences for people in grief is to deal with the unrealistic expectations and the unsolicited advice offered by well-meaning friends and family members. Here are some questions to get your group talking about the advice and expectations of others:

- What is the worst advice anyone has given you so far in your grief? What is the best advice you've been given?
- How are your closest friends and family members supporting you in your grief? What do you wish they would do differently?
- What expectations do you have of yourself in grief or feel that other people have of you (i.e., get over this more quickly, get back to being your old self, etc.)

Group members will likely have some very good ideas for dealing with the expectations and unwanted advice from others. Giving participants an opportunity to discuss their ideas often leads to humor, a good coping strategy in itself: "Thank you for all the money you are saving me by not having to visit a therapist!" Others will simply ignore the advice of others, even though they may be gracious when the advice is offered.

Leaders may want to provide pens and paper or thank-you cards and invite group members to choose the person they feel has been most supportive to them in their grief. Encourage participants to write a simple note of gratitude, expressing one or two positive ways this person has been supportive and thanking them for their helpfulness. Encourage group members to be specific, and then invite two or three group participants to share their letters with the rest of the group. Group members can either mail the letters to the addressee or find other ways to communicate their gratitude.

GROUP IDEA 6: DEALING WITH FEAR

Fear is most certainly one of the most common emotions expressed by people in grief. The leading models of the bereavement process suggest that the source of the fear is most often either a sense of helplessness regarding how to get along now that the loved one has died or from a heightened sense of the bereaved person's own mortality and anxiety surrounding his or her own death.

Leaders can be most helpful by normalizing the fear, acknowledging that fear is a common experience in grief. When bereaved individuals hear the support group leader acknowledge that fear is commonly experienced by people in grief, many of the effects of fear are mitigated. Because fear is so common among the grieving, leaders can safely assume its presence in the asking of a question such as: "Of all the things that scare you about this experience, what do you suppose you fear the most?" Frequently, assuming the presence of fear helps the grieving person feel positive about expressing those emotions.

Bereaved individuals can be reminded that their fears often relate to the important work of learning to live in a radically changed world. One widow expressed this well when she reported, "I don't know how I will ever get by without him; he did everything for me." As the discussion progresses, leaders and other group members can talk about how to discover what participants do well already. If group members want help, helping the bereaved discover the things that he/she does well and helping with "problem solving" can be useful techniques. For example, for a person who has never balanced a checkbook, help him create a plan with small steps such as: 1) get your checkbook and statement; 2) ask at your bank if someone could help you the first time; 3) get familiar with the statement, etc.

It is also important to recognize that many bereavement-related fears are really fear of the unknown. If a bereaved person is afraid to be alone in the house, encourage a thorough security check. Many police departments have volunteer corps that will make a home security assessment at no cost.

Bereavement also raises concerns about one's own mortality. In her book, *Grief: The Mourning After*, Catherine M. Sanders (1999) writes that death anxiety is higher during bereavement than at other times of life, causing the bereaved to sometimes feel closer to that inevitable experience because of what he/she has seen. A thorough physical examination a few months after a loved one's death is good to discover how the grieving person's body is responding to the stress of grief. The thorough physical exam also benefits the bereaved person by helping to alleviate fears about physical health and concerns about getting the same disease that killed the deceased.

Bereaved people may fear that they "are not doing this right." A sense of hopelessness often grows out of the fear that "I'll never live through this." Participation in a support group of people who are learning to manage their grief-related fear is a valuable experience. Here, the bereaved often learn coping strategies and encounter others with similar experiences, thereby normalizing their own fears and minimizing the fear of "losing one's mind."

Anxiety disorders that existed before the loved one's death will most often be magnified by bereavement, so consultation with or referral to the mental health professional who is supervising the person's care is imperative. While not likely, bereavement can give way to new clinical anxiety disorders for which a combination of counseling and medication proves useful.

Significant experiences with fear after a loved one's death are common for people in bereavement. The support and encouragement of professionals and volunteers are important aids to healing during this period.

GROUP IDEA 7: GRIEF ON SPECIAL DAYS

Note: This is an especially good topic for consideration when a major holiday approaches while the bereavement support group is meeting. For example, if a time-limited group begins the first week of November, addressing the topic of holidays at the second or third meeting is prudent. Leaders can help alleviate inevitable dread of approaching holidays by announcing at the first meeting, "Since Thanksgiving, Christmas, Hanukkah, and New Year's Day are just around the corner, we'll be talking about dealing with holidays in grief at our meeting on November ___. I hope you will plan to join us that night."

Leaders can introduce the topic with words such as:

> Holidays and other important occasions are some of the most difficult days in grief, especially during the first year or two. Tonight we're going to be talking about ways to manage the hard times these special days bring to our lives. Holidays in grief are hard for a couple of reasons. First, holidays are filled with sentiment. The sights, sounds, and smells of the holiday bombard us. These clues tell us in unmistakable terms: "The holidays are here."
>
> In the second place, holidays remind us of relationships. Whether the relationship with our loved one was good, bad, or some mixture of both, we collide with the reality that we are now alone. While

families gather for celebration, we realize that our family now feels very incomplete. Some bereaved people have not celebrated their own birthday in many years without this person. Anniversaries are especially painful after our mate dies. Holidays are all about relationships, and we have said goodbye to a very important person.

Here are some questions that will help your group talk about holiday plans and ways to manage grief on special days:

- Which holidays/special days do you most dread since your loved one died?
- What were your favorite activities for holidays/special days? How are those altered now with his/her death?
- If you have already lived through a holiday or special day in your grief, what was it like and how did you get through it?

Take a few minutes near the end of your meeting time to offer these ideas about handling the holidays:

- Acknowledge that grieving on special days and holidays is painful. Pretending that this holiday will be like those in the past is not realistic.
- Take care of your physical well-being. Good nutrition, rest, and exercise are important in all parts of grief but especially during the extra stresses of special days.
- Make a plan. The special day is often as bad in the "dreading" as in the living. Having a plan for where to go and what to do will lessen your anxiety about the day.
- Find someone to help during the season of special days. Consider volunteering to feed homeless people at Thanksgiving. At Easter, try volunteering to usher at church or provide some other ministry of service. Offering to become a "buddy" at a nursing home is always welcome.

GROUP IDEA 8: SAYING GOODBYE TO THE GROUP

Saying goodbye is never easy, and for the group members who have become a community of supportive friends, the last meeting comes as a bittersweet experience. The following ideas will help as the "formal" group comes to a close:

- The end of the group does not have to mean we will never see each other; encourage group members to maintain contact with those they have become especially close to during the group.

- A balloon launch can be an especially powerful way to close the group time. Secure helium and balloons at a party store or florist, and make sure to get a few extra balloons since some always pop when inflated or when written on. Have group members write a special memory or goodbye message on the balloon with permanent felt-tip markers. Then, join in a circle, invite group members to share something special they are taking from the group, and release the balloons together. You will be amazed at the silence as participants—adults and children alike—quietly watch the balloons float upward until out of sight.
- While some program leaders like to mail a survey or evaluation to participants a few days after a group concludes, others find it useful to take 10 or 15 minutes in the final group to get participants' written evaluation. Chapter Five provides specific ideas about group evaluations.
- If the group participants want, let them plan a potluck for the final meeting. If your group meets in borrowed facilities, make sure you learn what requirements must be met to serve food that is not professionally prepared and what arrangements must be made for clean-up.
- Close the meeting with a unison reading like the "Farewell Blessing." Standing in a circle while reading the words creates a very meaningful ceremony. Before the reading, invite group participants to share how they have been most touched by the group.

A Farewell Blessing

Our lives have been turned upside down by this loss. We were not sure we could get through it—and sometimes, we still wonder if we will. But together we have learned that expressing emotion is okay, that making new friends is essential, that wondering about faith is normal. We have grown.

Now, as we leave this place and this group, we acknowledge that we are different people. We still have far to go on this journey through grief. But, overall, we are changed people with new tools and resources for the road ahead. We could never forget the ways our lives have been touched and changed by these people through whose deaths we have been thrust into the dark night of grief. Their memories provide joy and comfort even though they often bring us to tears.

It will not always be easy, but with God's guidance and the patient compassion of family and friends, we are confident we will grow through our grief. After the harsh cold and dark of winter, we will feel the warm glow of love in our lives, and we will burst forth in full bloom again, welcoming the spring of new life. From this place, we go forth on the grief journey, confident that even though sorrowing, we are not without hope.

The future is filled with new people and experiences to cherish. Like a tiny plant poking its head through the remnants of the last winter snow, we will stretch into the warm sunshine of spring, burst forth in radiant color, and live fully again.

NOTE

1. With very slight adaptations, the contents of this appendix were first published in William G. Hoy's *Guiding people through grief: How to start and lead bereavement support groups* (Dallas, TX: Compass Press, 2007). Over the years the book was in print, the author received feedback from many bereavement support group leaders about the value of that section. This section is reprinted here with permission of the author and Compass Press.

INDEX